Since the turn of the century, performance studies has emerged as an increasingly vibrant discipline. Its concerns – embodiment, ethical research, and social change – are held in common with many other fields, but a unique combination of methods and applications is used in exploration of this field. Bridging live art practices – theatre, performance art, and dance – with technological media, and social sciences with humanities, it is truly hybrid and experimental in its techniques. This *Companion* brings together specially commissioned essays from leading scholars who reflect on their own trajectory into performance studies and the possibilities this offers to representations of identity, self-and-other, and communities. Theories that have been absorbed into the field are applied to compelling topics in current academic, artistic, and community settings. The collection is designed to reflect the diversity of outlooks and provide a guide for students as well as scholars seeking a perspective on research trends.

TRACY C. DAVIS specializes in performance theory, theatre historiography, and research methodology. Her most recent books are *Stages of Emergency: Cold War Nuclear Civil Defense* (2007), *The Performing Society: Nineteenth-Century Theatre's History* (with Peter Holland, 2007), and *Considering Calamity: Methods for Performance Research* (with Linda Ben-Zvi, 2007). She is currently Director of the Interdisciplinary PhD in Theatre and Drama at Northwestern University and President of the American Society for Theatre Research.

A complete list of books in the series is at the back of this book.

WITHDRAWN

THE CAMBRIDGE
COMPANION TO

PERFORMANCE
STUDIES

EDITED BY
TRACY C. DAVIS

CAMBRIDGE
UNIVERSITY PRESS

CAMBRIDGE UNIVERSITY PRESS
Cambridge, New York, Melbourne, Madrid, Cape Town, Singapore, São Paulo, Delhi

Cambridge University Press
The Edinburgh Building, Cambridge CB2 8RU, UK

Published in the United States of America by Cambridge University Press, New York

www.cambridge.org
Information on this title: www.cambridge.org/9780521696265

First published 2008

Printed in the United Kingdom at the University Press, Cambridge

A catalogue record for this publication is available from the British Library

Library of Congress Cataloguing in Publication data
The Cambridge companion to performance studies / edited by Tracy C. Davis.
p.   cm.
Includes bibliographical references (p. 182) and index.
ISBN 978-0-521-87401-4 (hardback)
1. Performance.   I. Davis, Tracy C., 1960–   II. Title: Companion to performance studies.
BF481.C34   2008
790.2 – dc22   2008026913

ISBN 978-0-521-87401-4 hardback
ISBN 978-0-521-69626-5 paperback

CONTENTS

CONTENTS

ILLUSTRATIONS

NOTES ON CONTRIBUTORS

PHILIP AUSLANDER teaches Performance Studies in the School of Literature, Communication, and Culture of the Georgia Institute of Technology and the Department of Theatre and Film Studies of the University of Georgia. He contributed the essay on "Postmodernism and Performance" to the *Cambridge Companion to Postmodernism* edited by Steven Connor (2004). He is the author, most recently, of *Performing Glam Rock: Gender and Theatricality in Popular Music* (2006) and *Theory for Performance Studies: A Student's Guide* (2008). In addition to his work on performance theory, performance and technology, and popular music, Auslander writes regularly on the visual arts and contributes reviews to *ArtForum International*.

SUSAN BENNETT is University Professor in the Department of English and the Graduate Program in Performance Studies at the University of Calgary, Canada. She is the author of *Theatre Audiences* (1990; rev. edn 1997) and *Performing Nostalgia* (1996), as well as very many essays on a wide variety of theatre and performance topics. She has also completed numerous editing projects including a term as editor of *Theatre Journal*, the first collection of essays on feminist theatre and performance in Canada (published by Playwrights Canada Press in 2006), and a special issue of *Western Humanities Review* (co-edited with Wayne McCready) on the question "What is a City?" (Fall 2007). Her most recent work has been concentrated on theatre and tourism, especially in urban settings. She is also a member of a multidisciplinary research team investigating an anonymous seventeenth-century play manuscript held in the University of Calgary's collection and plans to edit a volume of essays on performances of country house drama of the early seventeenth century in conjunction with this endeavor.

TRACY C. DAVIS specializes in performance theory, theatre historiography, and research methodology. Her most recent books are *Stages of Emergency: Cold War Nuclear Civil Defense* (2007), *The Performing Society: Nineteenth-Century Theatre's History* (with Peter Holland, 2007), and *Considering Calamity: Methods for Performance Research* (with Linda Ben-Zvi, 2007). She has also authored *Actresses as Working Women: Their Society Identity in Victorian Culture* (1991),

George Bernard Shaw and the Socialist Theatre (1994), *The Economics of the British Stage 1800–1914* (2000), and co-edited *Women and Playwrighting in Nineteenth-Century Britain* (with Ellen Donkin, 1999) and *Theatricality* (with Thomas Postlewait, 2004). She is currently Director of the Interdisciplinary PhD in Theatre and Drama at Northwestern University and President of the American Society for Theatre Research.

JOHN EMIGH is a Professor in the Theatre, Speech, and Dance and English Departments at Brown University. He has studied Balinese Topeng with I Nyoman Kakul and written extensively on the masked drama of New Guinea, Bali, and India. He has published *Masked Performance: The Play of Self and Other in Ritual and Theatre* (1996) and made a film on the life of Hajari Bhand, a Rajasthani street performer. His performance work includes one-man shows based on Balinese mask techniques; these have been performed at schools, hospitals, universities, and theatres (including The Performing Garage in New York City, The New Theatre Festival of Baltimore, the Indian National School for Drama, the Tibetan School of Drama, and the Balinese Academy for the Arts). He is founding chairperson of the Association for Asian Performance.

SUSAN LEIGH FOSTER, choreographer and scholar, is the author of *Reading Dancing, Choreography and Narrative* (1996), and *Dances that Describe Themselves* (2002). She is also the editor of two anthologies, *Choreographing History* (1995) and *Corporealities* (1996) and co-editor of the journal *Discourses in Dance*. She is currently working on a genealogy of the terms "choreography," "kinesthesia," and "empathy."

SHANNON JACKSON is Professor of Rhetoric and Professor and Chair of Theatre, Dance, and Performance Studies at the University of California, Berkeley. Her publications include essays in *The Drama Review, Theatre Journal, Cultural Studies, Performance Research*, and *The Journal of Visual Culture Studies* as well as her books, *Lines of Activity* (2000) and *Professing Performance* (2004). She is currently at work on a manuscript tentatively entitled *Social Works: The Infrastructural Politics of Performance*.

E. PATRICK JOHNSON is Chair, Director of Graduate Studies and Professor in the Department of Performance Studies and Professor in African American Studies at Northwestern University. He is the author of *Appropriating Blackness: Performance and the Politics of Authenticity* (2003), and co-editor of *Black Queer Studies: A Critical Anthology* (with Mae G. Henderson, 2005). His next book, *Sweet Tea: An Oral History of Black Gay Men of the South*, is forthcoming with the University of North Carolina Press.

AMELIA JONES is Professor and Pilkington Chair in Art History and Visual Studies at the University of Manchester. She has organized exhibitions on feminism and contemporary art, has co-edited the anthology *Performing the Body/Performing the Text* (1999), and edited the volumes *Feminism and Visual Culture Reader* (2003) and *A Companion to Contemporary Art Since 1945* (2006). Following on from her *Body Art/Performing the Subject* (1998), Jones's recent books include *Irrational Modernism: A Neurasthenic History of New York Dada* (2004) and *Self Image: Technology, Representation, and the Contemporary Subject* (2006). Her current projects are a co-edited volume, *Perform, Repeat, Record: Live Art in History*, and a book provisionally entitled *Identity and the Visual*.

BAZ KERSHAW (Professor of Performance, University of Warwick) trained and practiced as a design engineer before studying English and Philosophy at the University of Manchester, then performance at Hawaii and Exeter. His writings include *Engineers of the Imagination: The Welfare State Handbook* (with Tony Coult, 1982/1990), *The Politics of Performance: Radical Theatre as Cultural Intervention* (1992), *The Radical in Performance: Between Brecht and Baudrillard* (1999), *Theatre Ecology: Environments and Performance Events* (2007), and many articles in international journals. He edited *The Cambridge History of British Theatre: Volume III, Since 1895* (2004), which was nominated for the Theatre Book Prize. He has extensive experience as a director and writer in research-oriented radical and community-based performance, including recent performance research projects sited at Bristol Docks and Bristol Zoological Gardens. From 2000 to 2006 he led the major research project PARIP (Practice as Research in Performance) at Bristol University.

DELLA POLLOCK is Professor in the Department of Communication Studies at the University of North Carolina at Chapel Hill, specializing in the areas of Performance and Cultural Studies. She is the author of *Telling Bodies Performing Birth: Everyday Narratives of Childbirth* (1999), and the editor of *Exceptional Spaces: Essays in Performance and History* (1998) and *Remembering: Oral History Performance* (2005). She is co-editor of the journal *Cultural Studies*.

NICHOLAS RIDOUT teaches in the Department of Drama at Queen Mary, University of London. He is the author of *Stage Fright, Animals and Other Theatrical Problems* (2006), co-author of *The Theatre of Sòcietas Raffaello Sanzio* (with Claudia Castellucci, Romeo Castellucci, Chiara Guidi, and Joe Kelleher, 2007), and co-editor of *Contemporary Theatres in Europe* (with Joe Kelleher, 2006).

DIANA TAYLOR is Professor of Performance Studies and Spanish at New York University. She is the author of *Theatre of Crisis: Drama and Politics in Latin America* (1991), *Disappearing Acts: Spectacles of Gender and Nationalism in Argentina's "Dirty War"* (1997), and most recently *The Archive and the Repertoire: Performing Cultural Memory in the Americas* (2003), which won the Outstanding Book award from the Association of Theatre in Higher Education, and the Katherine Singer Kovacs Prize from the Modern Language Association. She is the founding director of the Hemispheric Institute of Performance and Politics, funded by the Ford Foundation and the Rockefeller Foundation.

ACKNOWLEDGMENTS

At its best, teaching is a mutual process. Teaching about performance almost invariably draws attention to the reciprocity of communication and mutuality of expression that show how teaching and learning are two related kinds of performance among a myriad of performative circumstances. When performance is the topic, practice cannot help but show theories in action, and even performative malfunctions, mishaps, and misfires produce more grist for the mill. It is humbling to experience how the feedback loop is social as well as internal; through this process selves are made, and communities reified, in the act of performing. I have found this to be as true of locally organized further education classes as of scholarly conferences. In the latter case I have been enthralled by insights offered by all the contributors to this volume. Bringing their perspectives together allows me to highlight what I currently find most compelling about performance studies, both as a scholarly field and as insight into lived practice. These essays indicate what I believe will be our collective directions for many years to come.

Not so much a culmination as a record of work in progress, this book also represents the collective exchange between myself, colleagues, and a generation of students at Northwestern University, where I have had the pleasure, and privilege, of advising in the Interdisciplinary PhD in Theatre and Drama and the Department of Performance Studies since 1991. For many of those years, our lodestar was Dwight Conquergood. This book is testament to his ongoing legacy: may our efforts always be epitomized by Dwight's deep investments in ethical reciprocity, social justice, and the transformative power of imagination expressed through performance.

Special thanks to Victoria Cooper, who inspired this project, and so many others at Cambridge University Press.

TRACY C. DAVIS

Introduction: the pirouette, detour, revolution, deflection, deviation, tack, and yaw of the performative turn

Since the 1970s, we have marked the "linguistic turn" (emphasizing language's role in constructing perception), the "cultural turn" (tracking the everyday meanings of culture, and culture's formative effect on identities), and more recently the "performative turn" (acknowledging how individual behavior derives from collective, even unconscious, influences and is manifest as observable behavior, both overt and quotidian, individual and collective). Each "turn" has its principal philosophical inspirations, holding in common an oppositional stance toward more "orthodox" approaches. The "turns" were executed not strictly successively but certainly interrelationally. In league with widely influential social movements – notably feminism and antihomophobia – and the related activist-academic fields of gender studies, queer studies, and cultural studies, the "turns" have had a momentous impact on the arts, humanities, and humanistic social sciences in the West and Western-influenced universities.

As important as the performative turn has been to fields as diverse as anthropology and English – and other erstwhile improbable pairings, including neuropsychology and dance, ecological science and theatre – not everyone acknowledges that performance studies is a discipline in its own right. Is it constituent of all disciplines, an emergent discipline, or an already established discipline undergoing change? One common refrain is the lack of two-way interaction between adherents of performance studies and academics in other disciplines who claim performative territory, making use of the power of "performance" as an explanatory metaphor without regard for the implications of such claims, especially any "limits" to the performative. Yet there is plenty of evidence to the contrary: performance scholars can be found under the mantle of philosophy, ethnography, art history, political theory, media studies, music, rhetoric, theatre, and literary studies, though this is by no means an exhaustive list. Wherever the performance *scholars* are, at this point in time, is of less consequence than what they recognize in common: performance studies has its own pantheon of theorists, describes the world in its own image, and increasingly trains students under its own auspices. Thus it is a discipline, though rarely a university department. Practitioners of the discipline are theoretically eclectic, catholic in subject interests, and highly reflexive about methodologies. As the essays in this book show, performance scholars are acutely conscious of who contributes knowledge, and how, both in the history of ideas culminating in what has become recognizable as performance studies and the practices of co-constitutive knowledge derivation, definition, preservation, and interpretation between the ostensible researcher and the de facto subject, audience, informant, art-maker, or a myriad of other terms invoking co-investigative dynamics. These essays challenge reigning concepts while accepting others: sometimes the challenges in one chapter go to the very core of the concepts or thinkers embraced elsewhere in the book. These are the building blocks of disciplinary change, and understanding, upon a well-settled foundation.

The invocation of the "turns" suggests that linguistics, culture, and performance "make heads turn," or "turn around ways of thinking." When turning occurs en masse but not universally, it becomes sharply noticeable to anyone still looking straight ahead. But "turn" also denotes opportunity. For those interested in performance per se, our attention has been reoriented, our orbit broadened, and we are newly attentive to the implications of bodies and embodiedness. The greatest effects, however, were upon the *means* to study performance in a truly heteronomous fashion, and the *rationales* for connecting performance to culture. We accepted that performance matters – we saw it, felt it, and knew it – so concentrated on how to describe, document, and account for it.

The performative turn is not accomplished simply by swiveling on one's heels and facing a new cardinal direction. As goes the body, so goes the gaze, but new conceptions of textuality and the legibility of culture send many people *moving*, functionally and rhetorically, in whole new ways and directions. What I call the pirouette, detour, revolution, deflection, deviation, tack, and yaw of the performative turn are rhetorical devices, to be sure, but beyond metaphor they convey how performance itself is a tool for innovative exploration, flexing under many circumstances, transforming when necessary, and apt to flow from one instantiation to another. It is both the *subject* of study and often the *means*. The performative turn is variously, fluidly, and playfully a turn, yes, but a turn that is alternately a technique of dance (pirouette), leads to an unconventional routing (detour), champions social change (revolution, social or otherwise), bends for new use (deflection), proudly questions the culturally normative (deviation), like a sail propels us forward yet is obliquely positioned to the wind (tack), and though unsteady is wide open (yaw), depending upon what is apt.

As Richard Biernacki wrote of the cultural turn, "these three emerging visions – culture as the corporeal knowhow of practice, as the organizing ethos of practice, and as the experienced import of practice – can easily overlap in any particular study."[1] So, too, in performance studies. For example, Baz Kershaw describes how the SS *Great Britain*, an early Victorian steamship built at Bristol and recently retired there in dry dock, reverberated as drummers repeatedly struck its engine during a promenade performance in 2000. Everywhere on the nearly 2,000-tonne vessel the effect registered as a simulacrum for motion, redolent of ocean journeys long past, even for audience members who had never been to sea. This visceral information, made percussively and absorbed corporeally, turned experience into knowledge – or a kind of knowledge enabled by aesthetic effect. Here theatre is the institutionalized term for the performance. As a knowledge regime in its own right, theatre "makes sense" of the reverberation along with the other staged elements in the performance and the "given circumstances" of the historic artifact on which the event occurred.

Diana Taylor explains how UNESCO's concept of intangible cultural heritage acknowledges performances' role in preserving and conveying social memory and identity, but falls short – institutionally – in fulfilling the promise inherent in this concept. In this sense knowledge formerly the prerogative of books is recognized *in* bodies. But now that this is a sanctioned viewpoint, how can such knowledge best be protected? The rapid disappearance of indigenous and minority languages and folkways in the path of nationalist, pan-nationalist, and globalizing forces – performative regimes in their own right – underline the urgency of UNESCO's task.

Susan Leigh Foster explains how neurological perception of action results in an "inner mimicry" of what is seen. Thus movement is contagious – through the conduit of sight – because spectators' brains mirror the actions in their bodies, which in turn rehearse what is seen even if muscles are immobile. Seeing, in effect, is doing. This concept of the neurological basis of the duet between Foster's dancer and viewer is a microcosm of the "practical knowing" that Kershaw reveals on the SS *Great Britain*. Not merely the traces of events but events per se are knowledge. Performance, in the aestheticized contexts that Kershaw and Foster describe, is a means to both express knowing and acquire knowledge. Its artifact, if any, is neurochemical, for performance registers in the cerebral cortex and is processed in kind. Foster suggests, by implication, that sensory perception works in tandem with Kershaw's homology of reflexive circuits; Kershaw extends his investigation to digital media as a way for performance to "survive" the moment of its doing, but Taylor argues that safeguarding intangible performances is neither unambiguous legal ground nor clearly a matter of assigning responsibility to "archive" practices.

Philip Auslander is also concerned with the co-presence of performers and audience members in the phenomenology of reception and the mutuality of making meaning. Because of technological innovations of webcasting, looping, and other delayed-action, remote-broadcast techniques, mediation has become an ever more important question in performance studies. Auslander works primarily within the interpretive arts to show how the "liveness" of performance is a question of degree, not an either/or, and that presence is no longer a limiting condition for performers any more than for witnesses to a performance. This accounts for an expanded range of cultural objects and effects within the fold of performance studies – into media studies, for example – while allowing for the relationality of liveness to mediation, presence to absence, embodiedness to technology, and willed "spontaneous" action to programmed effects.

Nicholas Ridout considers how performance studies is deemed a "democratic" discipline because of its attentiveness to participatory involvement as a means to acquire knowledge. What is this knowledge, anyway, and how is its acquisition democratic? For Ridout, the maintenance of a guise in public – not the private or true self but a projected self – enables participation in open debate without the danger of incurring psychic injury. By occupying the space between one's self and one's role, "politics" is made apparent to the individual. Thus a technique readily recognizable from theatre is revealed in the arena of performance and made indispensable in social relations.

For most of the contributors to this book, the role of performance in enabling immanent critique is of keen interest. Invariably, this is conditionally described in relation to historical circumstances, not an *a priori* condition of all times, places, and cultures. To Shannon Jackson, for example, "heteronomy," or externally imposed order, accounts for how performance art (including installations and durational art) transcends its material conditions in order to aspire to social effects (as a result of aesthetic effects but not limited to them). Practice and theory are mutually constitutive, equally traceable through the social work of early twentieth-century settlement houses and the art world of trained practitioners. For Amelia Jones, the twentieth-century history of reluctantly accrediting value in subjectivity, notably in the body's inevitability in art-making, once again implicates the importance of space and time in the social practices of making and being witnesses to art. In happenings, body art, and performance art, viewers identify bodily with the work, and this is critical to debunking deeply held convictions about the necessity for "universality" in art, apportioned by elites and appreciated only by specialists.

Experiential knowledge, therefore, is a cornerstone of performance studies. E. Patrick Johnson's overview of the contested terms "queer" and
"LGBT" (lesbian, gay, bisexual, and transsexual) rests upon antiessentialist arguments about gender, race, and class geared to disrupt power relationships. Personal claims are validated, even beyond collectively identified categories, to *count* as knowledge. Thus "engaged critical praxis" is
not reducible to citationality, but consistently questions "authentic" versus
"performative" identities; or, as Johnson writes, this keeps the performance
in performativity. For Della Pollock, too, "liminal truths" revealed through
oral histories negotiate past and present, and differences between the teller
and listener make witnessing an act of co-performing. Private issues are transcended by "critique, poesis, intervention, and translation," to come forward
as public concerns, without spectacle or histrionic excess, in a "representational real" of memory. In making memory public, performance transforms,
even in cases of inconceivable trauma, making experience legible to others.

John Emigh writes about one such case. Decades after the mass killings
that accompanied General Suharto's transition to power in Indonesia in
1965–6, Balinese informants (colleagues and fellow artists) told Emigh about
the events of those grim months. For Emigh, this is the basis for critiquing
Clifford Geertz's rendering of Bali as a "theatre state" in which the Balinese
people blend dreamlike perception with pragmatic reality: this account of
a place where performance "matters" deeply is an ahistorical misapprehen-
sion of Bali. Because the time span in which Geertz did his fieldwork in Bali
and then wrote *The Interpretation of Cultures* (1973) brackets this period,
his ahistoricism is highly significant. For Geertz, Bali's legibility rests in its
timelessness, evacuated of acts-in-history. For Emigh's informants, however,
the unique cultural patterns, stories, and mythic figures of Bali come through
precisely in response to the historical events of the killings. Place, time, and
circumstance reveal how myths, characters, and performance genres are
strategically utilized for immanent critique. Sometimes overt resistance is
legibly coded for non-Balinese or opposing factions, but more often it is an
intracultural communication, recognizing common religious beliefs through
practices – even fratricide – of indigenous significance. These examples illustrate how a culture processes itself through performance, but without knowledge of both the history of referenced performance and contemporaneous
circumstances, performance is insufficiently understood as chosen expressions or politics-as-culture constantly undergoing negotiation.

Individuals and the cultures to which they belong are mutually constitutive. While this is expressed in interpersonal encounters, it is also manifest
in the built environments that we occupy, interact with, shape, and are
shaped by. Susan Bennett's chief example of how this works is London's

South Bank, recently revitalized as a tourist destination along the stretch of the River Thames from the former London County Council building to the recreated Globe Theatre. A "stage" set for tourists, it maps identities for individuals and groups: identities that are as likely to be authentic as assumed. Gender shapes these interactions, revealing the unlikelihood of a "universal" experience, however adamantly it is claimed.

Inventive reading practices, which Roger Chartier calls "effects of meaning targeted by the texts through the devices of their writing," constraints caused by the mode of transmission, and "the competencies or reading conventions proper to each community of interpretation" have had an impact on many fields. But as Emigh and Bennett show, the content produced by "deep reading" is only as sensitive as the interpreter is attuned to the sensibility of the culture they study.[2] This connects what Chartier calls "three areas of reality":

> first, the collective representations that embody, within individuals, the divisions of the social world and that organize the schemes of perception and appreciation by which individuals classify, judge, and act; second, the forms in which social identity or political power is exhibited, as seen in signs and such symbolic "performances" as images, rites, or what Max Weber called the "stylization of life"; third, the "presentification" within a representative (individual or collective, concrete or abstract) of an identity or a power, a process that endows that identity or power with continuity and stability.[3]

This is as good definition as any of the abiding concerns of cultural studies. What does performance studies add? Emphatically, in performance studies "bodies" are corporeal not merely textual, and "speech" emanates from people with corporeality as well as identities. As Caroline Bynum notes,

> despite the enthusiasm for the topic, discussions of the body are almost completely incommensurate – and often mutually incomprehensible – across the disciplines. ... Sometimes *body, my body*, or *embodiedness* seems to refer to limit or placement, whether biological or social. That is, it refers to natural, physical structures (such as organ systems or chromosomes), to environment or locatedness, boundary or definition, or to role (such as gender, race, class) as constraint. Sometimes – on the other hand – it seems to refer precisely to lack of limits, that is, to desire, potentiality, fertility, or sensuality/sexuality (whether "polymorphously perverse," as Norman O. Brown puts it, or genital), or to person or identity as malleable representation or construct. Thus *body* can refer to the organs on which a physician operates or to the

assumptions about race and gender implicit in a medical textbook, to the particular trajectory of one person's desire or to inheritance patterns and family structures.[4]

Performance studies embraces this heterogeneity as the means to understand living in bodies. Sometimes the experience of a body is sensory, sometimes highly abstracted by medicalization or otherwise. Our bodies both form and are formed by our identities; our identities, in turn, citationally reflect our surroundings and circumstances. As we negotiate life as social beings – sometimes but not always consciously, sometimes but not always overtly – we perform. *As we perform, we are also historical.* This can be codified and held in common, as ritual, or not; coordinated and aestheticized, as theatre, or not; quotidian and mundane, the lived experience of the everyday, or not.

Performance can be radically transformative, either through extraordinarily masterful technique or through the strength of the performer's conviction and the power of the message. Unlike theatre, artistic technique is not a precondition of performative efficacy. Indeed, J. L. Austin's concept of the performative as an utterance that calls something into being would seem to democratize access to such acts.[5] If so, then performance potentially becomes ubiquitous, no longer subject to heteronomous epistemologies. But, as Stanley Cavell argues, a performative utterance – such as a phrase accompanied by a gesture in the christening of a ship – is governed by a set of conditions:

> According to these rules, for me, for example, successfully or happily to christen a ship I must (1) participate in a culture in which christening exits, (2) be the one authorized in the relevant subculture to do the naming, and in the presence of the appropriate authorities, celebrities, and onlookers, (3) at the appropriate place and time and with the appropriate implement in hand (here a bottle of champagne), say the required words (including I suppose 'I christen this ship the So-and-so') and break the bottle on the ship's edge, and (4) speak audibly, visibly, and without abbreviation.[6]

Austin famously precluded the theatre from his explication of the performative precisely because of its insincerity: theatre merely *plays at* something, so how can something come from mere pretence? Performatives have to meet cultural conditions, including sincerity. Cavell states, "Performatives may fail to fit the facts in the way statements do; and ... statements may fail to fit the facts the way performatives do."[7] This is just as important a brake on the ubiquity of performance as a reminder of the pirouetting, detouring, revolutionizing, deflecting, deviating, tacking, and yawing of performance.

Notes

1. Richard Biernacki, "Method and Metaphor after the New Cultural History," in Victoria E. Bonnell and Lynn Hunt, eds., *Beyond the Cultural Turn: New Directions in the Study of Society and Culture* (Berkeley: University of California Press, 1999), 77.
2. Roger Chartier, *On the Edge of the Cliff: History, Language, and Practices*, trans. Lydia G. Cochrane (Baltimore: Johns Hopkins University Press, 1997), 22.
3. *Ibid.*, 23.
4. Caroline Bynum, "Why All the Fuss about the Body? A Medievalist's Perspective," in Bonnell and Hunt, eds., *Beyond the Cultural Turn*, 243.
5. J. L. Austin, *How to Do Things with Words* (Cambridge, MA: Harvard University Press, 1962), 14–15.
6. Stanley Cavell, *Philosophy the Day After Tomorrow* (Cambridge, MA: Belknap Press, 2005), 165.
7. *Ibid.*, 168.

I

Social polities:
history in individuals

I

NICHOLAS RIDOUT

Performance and democracy

What is democracy?

It is no doubt a coincidence that the internet user eager to know what democracy might be who types the question "What is democracy?" into Google should be directed first to a page on the website of the US Department of State. That the second-ranked hit leads to a lecture given by Larry Diamond at Hilla University in Iraq in January 2004 is similarly fortuitous, since Diamond, an academic expert in democracy who served as an advisor to the Coalition Provisional Authority in Iraq in 2004, went on to write a widely praised book that offered a sharply critical account of American efforts to promote democracy in the wake of the invasion of 2003.[1] Despite Diamond's later criticism of the implementation of democracy in Iraq, he is broadly in agreement with the State Department in his answer to the initial question. The State Department's website offers this:

> Freedom and democracy are often used interchangeably, but the two are not synonymous. Democracy is indeed a set of ideas and principles about freedom, but it also consists of a set of practices and procedures that have been molded through a long, often tortuous history. In short, democracy is the institutionalization of freedom. For this reason, it is possible to identify the time-tested fundamentals of constitutional government, human rights, and equality before the law that any society must possess to be properly called democratic.[2]

Diamond, addressing his audience in Hilla, offers an almost identical definition, entirely in keeping with the idea that democracy is "the institutionalization of freedom":

> I want to begin with an overview of what democracy is. We can think of democracy as a system of government with four key elements: 1) A political system for choosing and replacing the government through free and fair elections. 2) The active participation of the people, as citizens, in politics and civic

life. 3) Protection of the human rights of all citizens. 4) A rule of law, in which the laws and procedures apply equally to all citizens.[3]

Neither the State Department nor Diamond can articulate the idea that democracy might involve conflict. Diamond, of course, is speaking to an audience in a mosque in an occupied country already suffering an incipient civil war. To speak of democracy in the terms in which it is articulated in the recent political philosophy of Jacques Rancière, for example, would be very dangerous. For Rancière, democracy "is not a set of institutions or one kind of regime among others."[4] It is, rather, "a way for politics to be,"[5] in which the people appear in such a way as to disrupt the categories by which political power seeks to manage or contain them or determine who among them may take part in politics, which is inherently constituted by dispute. Thus, in democracy, the very terms of the dispute are in dispute, and a radically egalitarian principle prevails in which the only qualification to govern is that you possess no such qualification. A key question here will always be: who appears? It is not difficult to see how such a democracy might become synonymous with "insurgency" if we start to consider the insurgency in Iraq as simply the appearance of the wrong (unqualified) people in the wrong places.

In this chapter I suggest some of the ways in which it might be useful to think about the relations between performance and democracy between the two poles of "institutionalization" and "insurgency." I propose such thinking primarily as a way of identifying what, if any, political value there might be in performance studies itself or in one of its primary objects of study, theatrical performance. My focus on theatrical performance arises not out of any supposition that theatrical performance is the only proper object of performance studies, but because, in discourses about democracy, issues of both participation and representation are often addressed in terms that point toward a "special relationship" between democracy and theatre. A secondary aim of this chapter is therefore to explore and contest this relationship. The US State Department is fully aware of the historical origins of this relationship when it informs visitors to its website that "Ancient Athens, the world's first democracy, managed to practice direct democracy with an assembly that may have numbered as many as 5,000 to 6,000 persons – perhaps the maximum number that can physically gather in one place and practice direct democracy."[6] This looks very much like a subject to which performance studies might have something to contribute, if only to ask the simple question: what happens when people "gather in one place" to "practice" something?

Tragedy in New York

The action involves four women in resolutely everyday clothes – sweaters, hooded tops, trainers, track-pants – and a young man in what looks like a thrift-store jacket and a yellow sports headband. They inhabit a civic space, but not one of neoclassical grandeur. This is no Capitol. It is a modest functional place – a community center, school or church hall. It has a wooden floor, partly marked up for sport (basketball or badminton, perhaps) and red curtains separating it from the space behind, presumably a stage. It is the kind of stage on which a school play or amateur dramatic society production might be presented, with the red curtains a loving gesture toward more luxurious theatre occasions. There is a projection screen set up on a stand in front of the curtain, and the space is decorated by flower arrangements which seem to assert a claim of particularity over a space which speaks most insistently the language of homogenized and official community in all its worthiest, most mundane and unglamorous accents. This is the basic theatrical set-up for a theatre production devised from Euripides' tragedy *The Suppliant Women*, presented at the Ohio Theater in New York by Target Margin Theater under the title *As Yet Thou Art Young and Rash*.[7]

In an online announcement of the production, and the season of work derived from classical Greek sources of which it formed part, the company's artistic director, David Herskovits, posed the following rhetorical questions – "So what body of theatrical work expresses energetic civic-mindedness? What literature speaks with fire to a community of citizens about their role as citizens? What culture debated with itself ferociously about how to build a successful polity?" – and answered them thus: "The Greeks!"[8] That such questions can be asked rhetorically testifies to the persistence and pervasiveness of what I am going to characterize here as a myth of simultaneous origin, in which performance (and theatre in particular) and democracy are imagined as sharing a more than coincidental birth in Athens. In sustaining this myth we imagine that "the Greeks" speak to us through an almost uninterrupted line of performative reenactments of their political practices and theatrical productions. Critical responses to Target Margin's production suggest that this imaginary connection is very much alive. Garrett Eisler, writing in *Time Out New York*, is typical in his analysis of the production's effect:

> Contemporary resonances are not difficult to locate in this 2,000-year-old tale of Athens, a hubristic democracy led by a boy-king, coming to the aid of a decimated people wronged by a tyrant. Euripides' eulogies to the fallen soldiers are movingly translated into a slide show of everyday faces, accompanied by

the kind of quotidian personal details we read in *New York Times* spreads about the Iraq War dead. In bringing classical tragedy down to earth without losing its forceful poetry, this idiosyncratic version gives our current polis a surprisingly faithful – and satisfying – dose of healing tragic vision.[9]

That the production, which was highly experimental in form, is here commended for being "surprisingly faithful" is perhaps evidence of a widespread conviction that fidelity, in the particular case of Greek tragedy, is the surest means of securing "contemporary resonances." This assumption involves a conviction that the line of inheritance has, indeed, been unbroken, and that when we speak of theatre and democracy we speak of the same things as did our forebears in fourth- and fifth-century Athens. What often disappears, where myths of this kind are in play, is history. To construct an argument, as I seek to do here, about the nature of the connections between performance and democracy encoded in this myth is thus to run the risk of a radical ahistoricity.

It is precisely such an approach which Simon Goldhill warns against in the introduction to his and Robin Osborne's collection of essays, *Performance Culture and Athenian Democracy*. Goldhill makes a persuasive opening argument in favor of performance – a word without Greek root, and which it is hard to claim as "an ancient Greek category" – as "a useful heuristic category" for consideration of a range of activities undertaken as "an integral part of the exercise of citizenship": theatre, symposia, games, assemblies and law courts. He suggests that "the persuasiveness of the connection depends upon a set of barely concealed, if rarely articulated, assumptions about the subject and the subject's relations to social norms and agendas,"[10] which operates in analysis of both contemporary and ancient Greek practices. Later, though, in a summary of the contributions of the discipline of performance studies, Goldhill is briefly critical of "muddled approaches to universality" in some works of performance studies in which an "admirable pursuit of interdisciplinarity has a far from adequate historical frame."[11] He suggests that these offer largely formalist analyses of social process, identifying homology rather than causality and risking an erasure of historical specificity and material difference. Goldhill warns, therefore, that such works might encourage us to believe in a narrative of direct inheritance, in the inevitable contemporaneity of antiquity.

An alternative snapshot might reveal something very different, including a very persistent determination, on the part of scholars and historians of performance, to tarry with the particular, to emphasize alterity and unpick ideological accounts of historical causality. In both views, however, performance studies seems to position itself as a self-consciously "democratic" discipline: either by affirming formal continuities in ritual practices and the persistence of theatre as a drama of social participation, or, as Dwight Conquergood has suggested, by unsettling epistemological hierarchies by proposing new modes of knowing "grounded in active, intimate, hands-on participation."[12]

In its revised form, then, the myth may be stated as follows. Theatre and democracy were born together; both represent a sociality and a mode of appearing in public which is beneficial to the construction of community; performance itself, as an embodied practice, embeds the abstractions of democratic representation in a participatory constellation of activities (theatregoing, sports); and finally, performance studies reasserts these connections by giving voice to the underrepresented, advocating for an antielitist culture, and restoring the body's performance to its place alongside the text in academic practice.

The melancholic turn

A key element in this myth, at least from a European perspective, is that it constitutes a narrative of loss. The European civilization that liked to proclaim – in its architecture, its universities, its literature and its theatre – its foundations in Athenian democratic culture is now irremediably tarnished by twentieth-century genocide and totalitarianism. This is a key argument of Theodor Adorno and Max Horkheimer's *The Dialectic of Enlightenment*, in which European Enlightenment rationality turns out to have been inextricably enmeshed in a project of violent domination, culminating in the Nazi genocide.[13] After Adorno and Horkheimer, much European philosophical consideration of the legacy of Athenian culture in modern politics works in melancholic mode, grieving the loss but unable to let go of a conception of a political community, which is variously imagined as "inoperable," "unavowable," or, in a slightly messianic vein, departed but "coming."[14] Hannah Arendt's well-known account, in *The Human Condition*, of the Athenian "polis" as a model for political action and relations is less obviously melancholy.[15] But it refrains so totally from a consideration of the material conditions of Athenian democracy (including, of course, slavery) – so wide is the gulf between the ideal and any possibility of its historical manifestation – that its idealization of Athens achieves an inadvertent melancholy. Arendt is perhaps the useful limit case which illustrates most vividly the mythic nature of our contemporary uses of antiquity as utopia.

It is the Trinidadian Marxist C. L. R. James, however, who offers perhaps the most compelling articulation of this myth, and who does so in the fullest form: performance, rather than just theatre, appears as the enabling condition or representative practice of the democratic polity. It is in the practice of sport, from Athenian athletics to twentieth-century cricket, that James finds his richest example of how a culture might represent itself to itself. James also embodies the ambivalence in the myth itself, poised between European melancholy and American optimism. He writes as a revolutionary opponent of European colonialism who also embraced the political and cultural mythology with which the colonial powers sought to identify themselves. He shares with Adorno and Horkheimer a conviction that the genocide and enslavement perpetrated by modern European nations have decisively disqualified any claim their culture might make on behalf of human freedom. But, unlike Adorno and Horkheimer, who viewed American popular culture with gloomy despair, James saw democratic potential in the development of a mass public culture. As David Scott notes, in *Conscripts of Modernity*, James's view of "the potential of the United States" derived from his "appreciation" of "its relaxed untheoretical relation to popular culture, meaning by this, Hollywood, comic strips, radio drama, baseball."[16] For James, mass production in the United States has created an entirely new historical situation: "No such social force has existed in any society with such ideas and aspirations since the citizens of Athens and the farmers around trooped into the city to see the plays of Euripides, Sophocles and Aeschylus and decide on the prize-winners by their votes."[17] For James, the connection between Greek democracy and tragic drama was immediate: "when Athens won the great victory over the Persians and after years of struggle had established the new democracy, suddenly overnight as it were, Aeschylus created practically single-handed the Athenian drama."[18]

Alongside the drama, James sees athletic competition as equally important in the Athenian conception of human capability. Like the tragic drama, athletic competition involved the individual in public, in representative or ideal form: "Lucian's Solon tells us what the Olympic Games meant to the Greeks. The human drama, the literature, was as important to them as to us. No less so was the line, the curve, the movement of the athletes which inspired one of the greatest artistic creations we have ever known – Greek sculpture."[19] The connection between this drama, as representative enactment of a democratic culture, and the sport of cricket is equally obvious and direct for James: "The batsman facing the ball does not merely represent his side. For that moment, to all intents and purposes, he is his side. The fundamental relation of the One and the Many, Individual and Social, Individual and Universal, leader and followers, representative and ranks, the part and the whole, is structurally imposed on the players of cricket."[20] In his account of cricket as sociopolitical drama, James seems to prefigure the insights of Clifford Geertz, who famously analyzed the Balinese cockfight as a cultural performance through which one might understand how a society imagined itself.[21] Like Geertz, James offers an account of performance, rather than merely theatre, or drama, as a way of understanding a social or cultural imaginary. Like the cockfight, cricket and tragic drama both enact and represent competitive relations among formally equal participants, in ways which appear to reveal something of the nature of these relations within the society of which they form part.

This is the crucial innovation of such analysis: that it enables us to think of performance – whether it is theatre or sport – as something that forms part of the entire ensemble of social relations rather than as an autonomous viewpoint from which the culture of the society in question may be interpreted. That is to say that performance – including theatre – enjoys no privileged knowledge about itself or its world, no position which might allow it to stand apart from the myths or ideologies which shape and sustain the society of which it is part. Its knowledge can only be immanent critique, making partially visible, in the very act of ideological transmission, the nature of the ideological form. The task of performance studies might be to draw out and extend this immanent critique in ways which would help us identify whatever kernel of the real there might be within the mythology of simultaneous origin. One might begin by examining in more detail the nature of the "loss" around which the myth forms: not simply in terms of an idealized Golden Age, but in terms of specific social and historical developments within our own capitalist modernity.

Theatricality and the public sphere

For Richard Sennett, one of the defining and lamentable characteristics of capitalist modernity is the way in which it precludes a certain kind of public theatricality in favor of a sense of selfhood founded in values associated with the individual, interiorizing, and supposedly authentic self. In *The Fall of Public Man*, he locates in the public sociality of eighteenth-century London a viable and healthy model of social and political appearing, which he describes as theatrical, in which individuals were able to represent themselves in public on the basis that their identity resided in who they appeared to be through their speech and their action in public.[22] Sennett suggests that the change in the relationship between public and private realms that occurs in the transition from *ancien régime* to European modernity brings about a decisive shift in which this sense of an identity defined in public interaction starts to give way to a new conception of identity, increasingly founded on the individual as private person rather than public appearance. One element of this is what he calls intimacy in public: the development of social codes that require that public behavior be governed by norms dictated by the standards of intimate relations. One might say, to put this very simply, that as the private sphere of family and sexuality is increasingly identified as the source for personal self-validation and authenticity, it becomes essential to convince others of one's integrity as a human self by displaying those qualities that make you a good, authentic person in that place that now matters most, that place where you come face to face with the truth of the other, in the intimate personal encounter.

Sennett also argues that the modern city produces the characteristic and debilitating experience of "isolation in the midst of visibility to others,"[23] in which the preservation of one's own individuality, founded in the values of intimacy and the private sphere, becomes one's main priority in social interaction. A defensive posture, which the sociologist Georg Simmel has memorably characterized as "the blasé attitude,"[24] becomes the tactic by means of which the individual manages increasingly difficult social relations in public, and by which individuals are therefore, to some extent at least, themselves constituted. The paradoxical effect of this historical shift is that the increasing emphasis on the individual constituted in terms of their own authentic interiority goes hand in hand with an increasing anonymity. When individuals go out in public, they have to hide who they are behind a mask of uniform disinterest.

In the premodern public sphere in which Sennett's version of public theatricality still obtains, the individual appears, speaks and acts on the basis that their appearance, speech, and action will be taken at face value and will constitute their public identity, at least for the duration of the appearance in question. No one will be inquiring into who they are, where they come from, what they really feel, think, or believe. In a posttheatrical modernity, by contrast, the individual imagines himself or herself as containing an internal, privately constituted identity, which must be protected against intrusion, exposure, and surveillance. In order to preserve this sense of individual identity, they make sure that when they are in public no one knows what they are really thinking, or who, in the end, they really are. For Sennett, this is central to a narrative of social and cultural decline. Theatrical appearing emerges in Sennett's work as a means to preserve certain distances, certain spaces between people that permit, even facilitate, vital socialities, socialities upon which senses of community, interdependence, and political agency ultimately depend. Such spaces might allow people to articulate political dissensus, and to debate issues without, as it were, "getting involved" in ways that threaten their sense of individual self. On the other hand, social relations modeled upon the intimate relationship rather than public appearances tend to encourage a politics of consensus. If our sense of authentic self is always at stake in public interactions, then we will tend to behave in ways that minimize, negotiate, or manage conflict. To do otherwise would be to risk not surviving the conflict (self-annihilation).

What the bourgeoisie created, Sennett implies, the bourgeoisie have since destroyed. Sennett's account of the "fall" of public man is echoed in a wide range of other theoretical writings, which offer a vision of "postmodernity" in which a three-dimensional "public sphere" has collapsed into the two dimensions of the screen, rendering meaningful political appearance, speech, and action impossible. Echoes of this are audible in the work of such melancholics as Jean Baudrillard (there is nowhere "real" for action to "take place"), Marc Augé (place itself is being superseded by "nonplace"), and Jean-François Lyotard (politics is governed by performance indicators rather than ideology); as well as among all the advocates of a nonconflictual, postideological politics (from Francis Fukuyama to Tony Blair). Indeed, it is this state of affairs, in which a supposed consensus threatens to abolish the political, for which Rancière uses the term "postdemocracy."[25] For Rancière, postdemocracy names the strange state of affairs in which "democracy," legitimized by its "victory" over totalitarian regimes, abolishes in advance any future political conflict in the name of a utopian consensus, in which dispute, disagreement, conflict – in short, the very people (the *demos*) after whom democracy is named – are made to disappear. "It is, in a word, the disappearance of politics."[26]

This is one of the problems facing a political theatre practice at the beginning of the twenty-first century: how to make politics appear. In my closing example of recent performance practice, I will try to show how the event of theatre might constitute a temporary space of public appearance, representation, and participation which, while failing to restore the mythic community of the Athenian *polis*, might articulate some measure of democratic resistance to the threat of a postdemocratic future. Here politics is made to reappear, not by means of a "political theatre" that proposes agendas or even critiques specific injustices, but by means of a politics *of* theatre, in which the form's entanglement with the constitution of political relations is exposed.[27]

Tino Sehgal: *This Progress*

My friend and I are invited to step into the downstairs gallery at the Institute of Contemporary Arts in London. We are greeted by a boy who seems to be about nine years old, who introduces himself and then asks us both what we think "progress" is. We are caught. As left-wing academics fully aware of the Marxist critique of capitalism as creative destruction and of environmental objections to economic and technological development, we naturally have more or less ready-made "thoughtful" responses to such a question. Something about the situation, encumbered as it is with all our acculturated ideas about the adult's relation with the child, seems to be forcing us to offer something more "authentic." But to do so would be mere condescension. So, here in the white space of the gallery, we offer our "ready-mades," with which, of course, our guide is already more than familiar. Spoken out loud, they sound as stale to him, we guess, as they do to us. This is very embarrassing indeed. Our conversation continues, teetering anxiously between poles of formality and false authenticity, until we are met at the far end of the gallery by a girl, a little older than the boy. The boy introduces us to her, adding to our names his gloss on what we have said we think progress is. His transmission of our "ready-made" opinions is flawless yet also, in their further repetition, makes them sound intolerably trite. He entrusts the idiots to their new guide, who picks up the conversation with some observations about environmental ethics, which, she says, she has been studying at school. After leading us upstairs to a further gallery, this guide hands us over in turn to a woman about our own age, with whom the conversation continues as she leads us through the "backstage" spaces of the ICA, disappearing suddenly, mid-conversation and inexplicably, to leave us in the company of the last of the four guides, a man who offers himself, as the oldest of the four, as the one who might have some answers to the question through which we have been "progressed." Such was my experience of Tino Sehgal's *This Progress*.[28]

It is the political meaning of the embarrassment of the initial encounter that shapes my subsequent understanding of this theatrical event. A gap opens up between who I feel myself to be and who I appear to be in this public encounter. I am other to my own political opinions, however sincerely held. In offering them up in this situation, I make myself other, not only to a child, who is a stranger, but also to my friend, and to myself. I find a distance opening up within myself. This distance is what Rancière argues is essential to the continuation of politics, and thus democracy. As Peter Hallward comments in a recent essay on the place of theatre in Rancière's writing:

A theatrocratic conception of equality can only proceed, in short, if its actors remain other, but not absolutely other, than themselves. They must adopt the artifice of an "unnatural role", but not identify with it. The only place they occupy is the one between themselves and their role – between Rousseau's sincerity and Diderot's technique. Politics is extinguished when the distance between actor and role collapses into a paranoid and definitive immediacy.[29]

To become other than oneself, then, is a precondition of democratic politics, which suggests why there might, after all, be some political purpose to the otherwise mysterious action involved in staging a play by Euripides in New York in 2007. The *mise en scène* of *As Yet Thou Art Young and Rash* further suggests that this staging (recall the community center aesthetic with its glance at competitive sports) – or even staging as such – might still be a mode of participation in civic life, a means by which to articulate not political truths, as such, but something truthful about politics as democratic practice, however modest such action might be compared to something as democratic as an insurgency.

Notes

1. Larry Diamond, *Squandered Victory: The American Occupation and the Bungled Effort to Bring Democracy to Iraq* (New York: Times Books, 2005).
2. "What is Democracy?," United States Department of State, http://usinfo.state. gov/products/pubs/whatsdem/whatdm2.htm. Accessed April 1, 2007.
3. Larry Diamond, "What is Democracy?," lecture given at Hilla University for Humanistic Studies, Iraq, January 21, 2004, http://www.stanford.edu/~ ldiamond/iraq/WhaIsDemocracy012004.htm.
4. Jacques Rancière, *Disagreement: Politics and Philosophy*, trans. Julie Rose (Minneapolis: University of Minnesota Press, 1999), 99.
5. *Ibid.*, 99.
6. "What is Democracy?," United States Department of State.
7. *As Yet Thou Art Young and Rash*, directed by David Herskovits for Target Margin Theater at the Ohio Theater, Wooster St., New York City, January 9 – February 3, 2007. The company devised the production by working from seven different English translations of the Euripides play. The title I give here, *The Suppliant Women*, is that used in the University of Chicago Press edition, *The Complete Greek Tragedies, Volume VI: Euripides*, ed. and trans. David Grene and Richmond Lattimore (Chicago: University of Chicago Press, 1958).
8. David Herskovits, "Fellow Marginites: A Letter from Artistic Director David Herskovits," *Target Margin Tatler* 16.1 (September 2002), http://www. targetmargin.org/tatler.html (accessed March 24, 2007). In the light of Herskovits's articulation of the ideal of a space of civic speech, the choice of the term "Tatler" to designate the company's newsletter seems particularly appropriate, recalling as it does the moment in the development of what Jürgen Habermas was to call the "public sphere" in the coffee houses of eighteenth-century London, by borrowing from Richard Steel's publication of the same name.
9. Garrett Eisler, "*As Yet Thou Art Young and Rash*," review, *Time Out New York*, 590 (January 18–24, 2007).
10. Simon Goldhill, "Programme notes," in Simon Goldhill and Robin Osborne, *Performance Culture and Athenian Democracy* (Cambridge: Cambridge University Press, 1999), 1.
11. *Ibid.*, 10, fn. 20.

12. Dwight Conquergood, "Performance Studies: Interventions and Radical Research," *TDR: The Drama Review* 46.2 (Summer 2002), 145.

13. Theodor Adorno and Max Horkheimer, *The Dialectic of Enlightenment*, ed. and trans. John Cumming (London and New York: Verso, 1997).

14. See Jean-Luc Nancy, *The Inoperative Community*, ed. and trans. Peter Connor *et al.* (Minneapolis and London: University of Minnesota Press, 1991); Maurice Blanchot, *The Unavowable Community*, trans. P. Joris (Barrytown: Station Hill Press, 2006); and Giorgio Agamben, *The Coming Community*, trans. Michael Hardt (Minneapolis: University of Minnesota Press, 1993).

15. Hannah Arendt, *The Human Condition* (Chicago: University of Chicago Press, 1999).

16. David Scott, *Conscripts of Modernity: The Tragedy of Colonial Enlightenment* (Durham and London: Duke University Press, 2004), 140. Thanks to my colleague Bill Schwarz for recommending this book.

17. C. L. R. James, *American Civilization* (Oxford: Blackwell, 1993), 36.

18. *Ibid.*, 153.

19. C. L. R. James, *Beyond a Boundary* (London: Hutchinson, 1966), 205.

20. *Ibid.*, 205.

21. Clifford Geertz, "Deep Play: Notes on the Balinese Cockfight," in Geertz, *The Interpretation of Cultures* (New York: Basic Books, 1973).

22. Richard Sennett, *The Fall of Public Man* (New York and London: W. W. Norton, 1992).

23. *Ibid.*, 27.

24. Georg Simmel, "The Metropolis and Mental Life," in Charles Harrison and Paul Wood, eds., *Art in Theory 1900–1990: An Anthology of Changing Ideas* (Oxford: Blackwell, 1992), 130–5.

25. Rancière, *Disagreement, passim*.

26. *Ibid.*, 102.

27. In addition to the work of Tino Sehgal discussed here, one might consider recent performances by Kinkaleri (*I Cenci: Spettacolo*, 2004), Via Negativa (*More*, 2003) and Socìetas Raffaello Sanzio (*Tragedia Endogonidia*, 2002–4).

28. Tino Sehgal, *This Progress*, Institute of Contemporary Arts, London, 2006.

29. Peter Hallward, "Staging Equality: On Rancière's Theatrocracy," *New Left Review* 37 (January–February 2006), 122.

2

BAZ KERSHAW

Performance as research: live events and documents

Introduction: three object lessons in performance as research – Dr. Johnson kicks a stone

The English eighteenth-century diarist James Boswell tells a well-known story about Samuel Johnson that has particular resonance for contemporary notions of performance as research. Boswell writes:

> We stood talking for some time together of Bishop Berkeley's ingenious sophistry to prove the non-existence of matter, and that everything in the universe is merely ideal. I observed that, although we were satisfied his doctrine is not true, it is impossible to refute it. I never shall forget the alacrity with which Johnson answered, striking his foot with mighty force against a large stone, till he rebounded from it, "I refute it *thus*!"[1]

That instant of low drama as the foot makes contact with the stone is the moment of performance as research. Let us call it, just half-seriously, a dictionary-maker's creative practical experiment in energy exchange between his foot and a stone. One kind of knowledge – theory, philosophy, books, libraries, archives – is challenged profoundly by another. As such, twenty-first-century artist-scholars might consider this a quintessential practice-as-research experiment.

But where were its results located? Were they in the stone, in Johnson's body, in the story told by Boswell, in this reflection on its significance, or in some relationship between all four and more? The point of knowledge is always open to refinement. So maybe the sharpest tactic here is to read Berkeley's challenging treatise and try out for oneself Johnson's paradigmatic kick, thus gaining some toe-tingling, body-reverberating insights into practical knowing.[2]

Two Americans bat the binaries

Toward the end of the first decade of the third millennium, performance as research (PaR) – creative practices considered as a research methodology in their own right – was a well-established or emergent part of the performing arts in universities in the UK, Australia, Canada, Scandinavia, South Africa, and elsewhere. Some measure of its radical potential is provided by how a related discipline – performance studies – typically describes its challenges. For example, in his popular introductory textbook the American practitioner-scholar Richard Schechner claims, "Artistic practice is a big part of the performance studies project. A number of performance studies scholars are also practising artists working in the avantgarde, in community-based performance . . . The relationship between studying performance and doing performance is integral."[3] He also quotes a more polemical view from Dwight Conquergood, himself an eminent practitioner-scholar in ethnographies of performance:

> The ongoing challenge . . . [of performance studies] is to refuse and supersede the deeply entrenched division of labor, apartheid of knowledges, that plays out inside the academy as the difference between thinking and doing, interpreting and making, conceptualization and creativity. The division of labour between theory and practice, abstraction and embodiment, is an arbitrary and rigged choice, and like all binarisms it is booby-trapped.[4]

This full-frontal assault on the modernist traditions of knowledge-making, coupled with Schechner's invocation of the scholar-artist, indicates how much may be at stake through PaR. Its creative investigations reach beyond university performing arts departments, coinciding with innovation by experimental artists in the wider culture. Its protocols have equivalents to "hands on" research procedures in nonarts disciplines, potentially eroding traditional demarcations between science, technology, and the arts. Such combinations of radical method and disciplinary iconoclasm can revisit formative components in performance studies itself, including its common aversion to binary-based knowledge-making. Hence in this chapter I approach binary analysis – either/or thinking – as a welcome familiar, important to positioning PaR as a *collaborative* challenger to established paradigms of knowledge.

A queasy project director

PARIP (Practice as Research in Performance) was a large-scale research project that I led between 2000 and 2006. It involved, investigated, and championed research creativity in the performing and screen-media arts by many UK university practitioner-scholars. Reaching back to at least the 1980s, their projects addressed Conquergood's call and exemplified Schechner's claim long before they were made. The Arts and Humanities Research Council (AHRC – formerly, Board/AHRB) was PARIP's main source of funding, and its rules required the project to produce "outputs." These included a symposium (2001) and two conferences (2003, 2005), a website, and many presentations by its core researchers.[5] A book and DVD will include documentation from many of its 400-plus participating researchers.[6] The project also produced four interactive DVDs. These present creative investigations into studio experimentation, site-specific spectacle, historical theatre reconstruction, and improvisatory choreography.[7] But without such "evidence" the creative events made by PARIP researchers did not (and still do not) officially count as "knowledge."[8] Marking this policy, the AHRC's preferred terms were "practice-based research" or "practice-led research," implying that practical creativity must have add-ons to join in the business of knowledge-making.

The policy reflects the fact that live performance events are conventionally regarded as disappearing acts, because they are ephemeral.[9] But for many UK performance-as-researchers, the official discounting of events-as-knowledge was both illogical and deeply conservative. The issue was debated intensely as the millennium turned, with radical artist-scholars arguing that the AHRC policy marginalized PaR in universities and transformed their creativity into commodities. As PARIP lead investigator, I was queasy about the officially produced paradox that the traces of a creative performance event had more value than the event itself. Is an empty plate always the best part of a meal? But I was also intrigued, as the paradox suggested a lacuna (or aporia) at the heart of PaR, and of performance studies as well. Back in the 1950s, the Absurdist playwright Eugène Ionesco pinpointed this more positively when he wrote that "only the ephemeral is of lasting value."[10]

Ionesco's paradox haunted my choice of the Bristol nineteenth-century heritage ship the SS *Great Britain* as a site for PaR productions. I staged the first of three there in 2000, when the dry-docked iron hull of the first steam-powered luxury ocean liner was being eaten away by sixteen types of rust. This world-record corrosive mix would turn the 1,961-tonne vessel into rotted fragments within twenty years. For me, the lacuna of that future richly reflected the key issues of performance studies: the instability of its "objects" of investigation, its hotch-potch of research problems/methods, its lack of definable limits. It also inspired the scenes I value most from my onboard productions, which ironically celebrated the great ship's precarious future, such as when, perched beneath its huge screw propeller, the last mermaid alive sang a lament for all her sisters poisoned by its waste.

A paradoxology of performance

Paradox is crucial to my arguments about PaR because it is a chief characteristic of performance itself, as well as of performance studies. The latter conventionally claims performance as boundless – "there is no cultural or historical limit to what is or is not 'performance,'" writes Schechner[11] – yet it is always embodied or embedded at particular places in specific times. This paradox of boundless specificity is encapsulated in a saying of Buddha that nicely complements the impact of Dr. Johnson's boot: the foot feels the foot when it feels the ground. Such conundrums, I think, are the elusive generators of the "performance paradigm" – performance as a new paradigm of knowledge – promoted by the "field" of performance studies in the twenty-first century, including its championing of "performance art" as a global icon of creative freedom opposed to all forms of oppression.[12] Not surprisingly, PaR also participates in this paradoxical choreography of knowledge-making, being a collection of specific research methods able to elucidate all types of performance.

These factors in performance research create complex ontological and epistemological issues – questions of being and the nature of knowledge – that are hard to keep in perspective because, by definition, neither the "field" nor the "methodology" can encompass themselves. This produces the chief lacunae of research through performance, which tend always to be paradoxical. To sharpen *this* point by example I will extend a saw coined by the philosopher Ralph Waldo Emerson: the field cannot well be seen from within the field, nor can the wood for the trees.[13] So is this where performance knowledge always gets stumped? Excuse that unecological pun, but it signposts a shortcut to this chapter's main destination, which aims to deal *paradoxically* with the constitutional *paradoxes* of PaR and performance studies. My main stratagem here is a question that is quite simply complex: how might the chief lacunae of performance research as a scholarly and creative endeavor become its greatest strengths?

I approach this question through two major problems of PaR. Firstly, how *can* the ephemeral be of lasting value; that is, how might valid knowledge claims emerge through the ephemerality of performance events? Secondly, how *can* the "live" of the past be revived through its remains; that is, how might knowledge created by the liveness of performance be transmitted in its documentary traces? In this quest my main tactic is to juxtapose one of my modest SS *Great Britain* projects with a performance art piece that is justifiably famous internationally: Coco Fusco and Guillermo Gómez-Peña's *Two Undiscovered Amerindians Visit...*[14] Both shows dealt with the effects of global colonialist histories, the complexities of which made them especially paradoxical. So their contrasting qualities will help advance a method of analytical inquiry based on an emergent theory that I call a "paradoxology of performance."[15] This paradoxology does not deny the power of binary thinking to produce knowledge, even "truths." But it recognizes the limitations of such knowledge by testing it against the kinds of "encompassing truths" (or insights) that paradox produces. Likewise, just as paradoxes yoke together contradictory "universes" to create such "truths," so my method brings to bear multiple perspectives of interpretation on particular performances. Together, theory and method work to ensure that enhanced *reflexivity* – a process that reveals the assumptions of knowledge claims – is basic to the validity of its results.

Have no doubt that we are heading for quite complicated territory here. It features terrain that Bishop Berkeley ironically predicted as usually appearing when speculation goes in pursuit of reason:

> Prejudices and errors of sense do from all parts discover themselves to our view; and, endeavouring to correct these by reason, we are insensibly drawn into uncouth paradoxes, difficulties and inconsistencies, which multiply and grow upon us as we advance in speculation, till at length, having wandered through many intricate mazes, we find ourselves where we were, or, which is worse, sit down in a forlorn Scepticism.[16]

But this chapter aims beyond skepticism, prospecting for pathologies of hope in a deeply troubled world. The main "compass" for this task will be the *homologies* that my method discovers between, as well as within, itself and the "objects" that it studies. In biology homologies occur when diverse species share similar structural factors, such as the five digits of a human hand and a bat's wing. I search for homologies that link performance effects and spectator responses in and between live events and their traces. To discover these I use methods of paradoxical analysis – for example, considering weaknesses as strengths, absence as presence – that are homologous to the paradoxes of the performances they investigate.

These homologies are founded on other, more obvious, similarities between my two examples. As *live performances* they were both *site-specific spectacles* by being placed in highly determined public spaces, and both aimed to *deconstruct* global colonial histories.[17] I am interested in whether through such commonalities they share similar *performance ecologies*. By this I mean performances being ecosystems that work to established ecological principles – for example, all components interacting together holistically to create a *diversity* of species/results – enabling them to "survive and thrive" in various particular environments. So my arguments, as the good bishop warned, may involve "intricate mazes" and we could end up back where we started. But in a paradoxology of performance, that is not necessarily a bad thing. Such a destination might just be a defect of the journey's best qualities.[18]

Part 1: Performance as research live

The Iron Ship – drumming engines

The Iron Ship was a site-specific spectacular staged on the SS *Great Britain* in 2000. Launched in 1846 at Bristol Docks, the vessel is an icon of the age of industrial revolution and empire. The first iron hulled ship, first steam-driven screw propeller, first to keep to tight global timetables, it was the Concorde of its day. In May 2000, back in the dry dock where it was built, this vessel was a moderately successful heritage attraction that told a story of engineering innovation and maritime conquest.[19] Possibly 25 percent of Australia's population of 20 million are descendants of the 13,000 European migrants who traveled on its 32 voyages to Melbourne between 1852 and 1875. But its part in colonial exploitation and the kickstart of industrially driven climate change did not figure on its many visitor display boards. As heritage industry analysts have often noted, such sites are memorials to forgetting even in the moment of remembrance.[20]

The show involved fifty student performers and twenty professional support staff, and treated its 180-a-night spectators as global citizens in an ecocolonial morality play. From a conventional theatre set-up built in a large dockside shed, they promenaded down into the dry dock (meeting the last mermaid alive), then in subgroups through four simultaneous scenes on different decks, to a dinner party hosted by the ghost of Isambard Kingdom Brunel (the ship's famous designer), then a grand finale on the forward deck. The whole spectacle appealed to the gaze, but my paradoxical method of analysis will focus on a scene that was also very visceral.

The ship's engine room is an amidships atrium that rises over 10 meters from the keel to above the level of the top deck, where originally the massive main gearwheel protruded into a skylight. In 2000 a partly reconstructed replica engine filled this space and, amazingly, the ship's curators agreed that our show's six "smutty stokers" and six "aerial engineers" could use it as a huge drum. For about forty-five minutes, as the audience moved in groups between this and three other simultaneous scenes, the stokers' pounding of the engine's metal made the whole 107-meter-long iron hull vibrate. A low rumbling and gentle shuddering was heard and felt even at the ship's prow, producing an impression that the ship was afloat and still steaming on.

1. The engine-room scene from above: white-shirted "smutty stokers" drumming and "aerial engineers" dancing in the replica machinery. Note the audience members on the elevated walkway. *The Iron Ship*, SS *Great Britain*, Bristol, 2000.

2. The engine-room scene from below: a "smutty stoker," two "aerial engineers" rising and falling, and audience members looking down. Foreground performer: Tom Wainwright. *The Iron Ship*, SS *Great Britain*, Bristol, 2000.

A curious effect, because obviously the aging vessel could not be cruising. It was stuck in its dry dock, full of rust holes. But everywhere onboard people were somatically experiencing the tremors, *participating* in this visceral-aural spectacle. Moreover, that sensation was surely echoing a historical "truth": that the SS *Great Britain* had indeed once trembled with such living energy as it sailed the oceans. Yet the effect also was obviously just a fairground trick, a "falsehood," eons away from historical truth. In other words, any "knowledge" that this scene may have produced was profoundly contradictory, both a truth and a travesty, created by incompatible binaries that disallow any claim to historical validity. From this perspective the AHRC is correct to deny any enduring "truth" produced *in* staged live performance. There can be no guarantee that any truth in a performance will *not* be ontologically compromised, simply a sham, because besides being ephemeral its deepest nature is to be ambivalent and indeterminate. Thus PaR is a case of having the excessive cake of live creativity and eating it!

Is there any way through this epistemological impasse? Under what conditions could *The Iron Ship* become more productive? I have some "insider knowledge" that might be relevant here. Even as one of the production's directors, the effects of the drumming surprised me. Our rehearsals focused on bringing the aerial "ballet" of circus performers and the pounding of the "stokers" into sync with each other. So the hull's vibrations were a happy "side effect." This made them a *supplement* in both senses of the word as used by Jacques Derrida, because they (a) completed a manifest insufficiency – a ship that *certainly* could not sail – *and* (b) added to its completeness – *becoming* the tactile impression of it sailing.[21] The effect exceeded the performers' actions to produce an immersive experience for spectators, potentially transforming them into participants. As spectator-participants they *embodied* these supplementary qualities, potentially enjoying excesses that paradoxically contradicted the contradictions that characterized the scene. So if the sense of phantom sailing touched other spectators than myself, maybe that was because it generated some key paradoxes of performance. From this perspective, the ambivalences of the scenic effect – the hull moving/not moving, "historical truth"/"fairground trick" – were transformed into paradoxes, so that its excesses could produce some "quality" of "encompassing knowledge." A kind of metamimesis: a transport of illusion sublimely beyond the production of "reality effects." The defects of its qualities became creative, perhaps proving Picasso's dictum: art is a lie that makes us realize the truth.[22]

However, from conventional perspectives on knowledge-making, this conclusion will still be suspect as defective simply because I am discussing my "own" work. It is based too much on subjective reflection. The *argument* might add an epistemological justification for thinking, paradoxically, that the *flawed method* of subjective reflection is potentially a *procedural strength* (as Berkeley thought). But its *theoretical* status will be judged inadequate as a basis for truth, because it rests on a position that is weakly reflexive regarding its own assumptions. From this point of view, my analysis, like a good grift, is set up for a foregone result, always already begging the questions it asks. Thus its conclusions need to be tested against more robust parameters. This would be best provided by "evidence" which is empirically free of the subjectivity of the creative practitioner.

The research design for *The Iron Ship* included a reception study that gathered audience feedback. This explored the workings of memory through performance on the SS *Great Britain* as a place of *suppressed conflicting histories*.[23] A postdoctoral researcher worked with four types of "memory group": randomly chosen audience members; local community residents invited to see the show; heritage professionals from the ship and city museums; student performers from circus school and university. The table that follows presents their main comments on the engine-room scene.

| | |

AUDIENCE	PROFESSIONALS	STUDENTS	COMMUNITY
BRYONY I thought the bit when it was the men working in the ship was very good. When they were all kind of clanging on their metal thing.	DAVE Yes. It's interesting, I mentioned earlier the treatment of the engine room, which I saw, which I read. [pause] Matthew said that he feels that that had an element of the construction of the ship involved in it as well. But it seemed to me, simply because I was looking into the engine room and watching what was going on, this is just a depiction of – of their impression of what the engine must have been like and what the conditions in the engine room must have been like for working in. You know, sweat of your brow stuff, again. Umm. And there was an interesting sense of how people perceive big engines like that as being very, very noisy, umm, and I know from having heard steam engines that they're not, they're actually very quiet …	CHLOE And I think with the engine room, I think that – I remember the first rehearsals in the department, and it was all going to be very kind of physical, lots of movement and things, and once it became a sound thing – you got into the space and realized there was so much potential – once we realized we were allowed to – I wasn't actually acting it but was involved in it.	JEAN Were there stories that made you think about the ship in a different way? To think about aspects of the ship that you hadn't considered before?
KAREN Oh yes.			CAROLINE [pause] Not particularly, except, umm, we talked at our first discussion [community focus group] about what an absolute marvel of engineering it was.
ALEC In the engine room.			
KAREN That was wonderful.		LOTTE Mmm.	JEAN Mmm.
BRYONY That was very good.			
JOYCE That's interesting because I thought that was one of the worst bits.		CHLOE But you were – you were allowed to bang on the machinery and actually use – that completely came from the space. I think it was really effective.	CAROLINE And I suppose the engine-room scene helped to bring that through.
BRYONY Oh.			JEAN Right [pause].
JOYCE Because it's noisy and you were peering down there, thinking "What is going on here – what is the meaning of		LOTTE Yeah. [pause]	*****************
			EDWARD I'm sorry I'd forgotten one of the bits that I liked best of all. And that was

MARK Yes.

DAVE . . . in operation. Umm. The sense that when you're stoking a boiler you have to spend all your time shoveling coal in, and that's all you do. And that isn't what happens at all, it's a different technique altogether. But there's just two ideas which they hadn't even thought to question or investigate, particularly if they're trying to put over a point . . .

MARK Quite.

DAVE . . . without really knowing

MARK You're right, Dave, of course. But, umm, a number of people, myself included, thought that the engine-room sequence was very exciting.

this?" And it just was bang, bang, bang, bang and it was so –

BRYONY I thought it was quite easy to kind of think about what life would have been like for them, though.

ALEC 'Cos it was noisy, wasn't it?

BRYONY All the noise and –

KAREN It was musical noise, wasn't it?

BRYONY Yeah.

KAREN I think that was – 'cos engines do make that sort of noise, it's –

ALEC It struck me that the passengers lots of them must've gone on the journey with that sort of noise as well.

JEAN I think the engine room's quite an interesting one, 'cos one of the museums professionals said, "Of course, steam engines weren't like that." Everybody else had said "Oh, it was so atmospheric, it was great and hearing the noise resonating through the ship" – . . . and he went "They weren't like that at all. Steam engines were really quiet."

LOTTE Ohh, how strange.

CHLOE Details, details. Artistic licence. [laughter]

LOTTE Yeah, we had a few people on the after deck come up and say, "Actually, you tied that on wrong" or, umm, "You don't actually wind it like that at all, that's used for something else." And it was like, right [laughter]. And I actually feel that I wish

the engine room. I thought that was very imaginative. The sort of ballet of the characters on these, umm – on the great wheels of the engine, which is a magnificent engine. And the model – the full-sized model is wonderful to look at.

JEAN Mmm.

EDWARD And the music that they made by banging on bits of tin and so on. Made a wonderfully – it really did sound like an engine room.

JEAN Right.

EDWARD In a sort of imaginative way. I thought that was fantastic. [pause]

JEAN Right. Oh, that's interesting – and they were talking as well in the engine room, weren't they?

AUDIENCE	PROFESSIONALS	STUDENTS	COMMUNITY
KAREN Yes.	DAVE Oh yes, I thought it was wonderful, very good.	we'd had more time to research that [expressions of agreement] because I didn't – I didn't want it to be fake ["No, no" from the other group members], I wanted it to be real.	EDWARD Yes, I'm not sure – I think I could hear some – it was sort of shouts of "Stoke!" you know. I can't remember.
ALEC A metal ship like that, that noise from the engines I guess would carry over, if not the whole ship, most of it. So, there must've been a constant noise.	MARK A great piece of theatre.		JEAN Right.
	SUSAN Mmm.		EDWARD It was the overall effect, umm, of this busy engine room, with sweat and so on which was created I thought by the dance and the music.
OLIVER And perhaps would've looked over in the way that we looked over. I don't know whether that was open at the time, I think it was, wasn't it, the gallery? Because the flywheel went right up into the – so people did wander along and look at the dirty little stokers down below [gentle laughter from group]. Yes, yes. I – I thought that was very well done, actually. Both – both the noise and the bodily interpretation of the mechanical movements.	MARK So, yes, divorced from any sense of creating what the engine was like in any way at all, it worked as a piece of theatre but –		JEAN Ah, right.
	DAVE Absolutely.		EDWARD Which I thought was very good.
	MARK There was a whole host of things where you could pick out sections which don't fit into the context at all.		
KAREN Mmm.			
OLIVER That – you know people were moving in that sort of manner.			

All four groups showed strong positive and negative reactions to the scene, each bringing very different perspectives to their interpretations, resulting in a wide variety of conclusions. The audience group concentrate on *aesthetic quality* (music versus noise), the heritage professionals on *historical veracity* (history versus theatre), the students on *mimetic accuracy* (fake versus authentic), the community group on *historical significance* (exceptional versus typical). All four focus on contradictory qualities and present strong signs of ambivalent responses. Overall they reinforce the conventional idea of performance/theatre reception as mainly a matter of diverse interpretations produced by unique, individual perspectives. But the binary structuring of all four discussions – music or noise, history or theatre, etc. – shapes them as *inquiries*, attempts to make common sense of the scene. Perhaps this indicates that participation and spectatorship were in tension with each other, in that a shared somatic experience (vibration) was coupled with a freedom to gaze on the scene however they wished. Even so, it seems clear that the former produced a common process of reaction as all four groups comment on the strong *effects* of the scene.

The combination of individual interpretation, binary-based inquiry, and common reaction to effect points to a paradox of "shared diversity" which is unexceptional in live performance. Visceral spectacles that trade in supplemental excess prove the rule of this contradictory pull between reception/analysis and perception/affect. In *The Iron Ship* the contradictions both in processes of response and between individual meanings were perhaps transformed into the paradox of shared diversity because they were *integral* to immersive somatic experience. The transcripts also seem to demonstrate another common cause, so to speak, as all four groups try to make various kinds of *historical sense* of the scene. The audience group discuss what sailing was like for passengers and stokers, the professionals the operation of the engine, the community members its spectacular qualities, and students the experience of getting the history "wrong." They are not interested in "suppressed contested histories," but there is a strong involvement in what one might call a collective undertaking of popular historiography, of history-making. Here is another paradox, perhaps one of "diversities shared," as very different reactions/interpretations regarding the event congregate in a common process of historicizing.

Hence *two* contrasting but complementary patterns of response seem to have been sparked by the engine-room scene, which are homological in being similarly paradoxical in their creation of possible historical "truths." Together these maybe point to an "encompassing truth" or two about the general methodology of PaR, the first being that to arrive at these conclusions required several research methods: aesthetic experimentation, reception study, and paradological analysis. This is hardly surprising: as performance is multidisciplinary, it needs multiple means to identify the knowledges it produces. The second is harder to specify, because it concerns the ecological processes and principles that all performances involve.

It is remarkable that such contrasting but compatible processes – immersive somatic experience and popular historiography – could be generated by the same scene, and this indicates another substantive methodological principle for PaR. Performance knowledge is most likely to be produced by creative processes that animate some constitutive paradoxes of performance. For example, that its *ephemeral excess can create lasting value*. So as the SS *Great Britain* moved without moving, such excess touched on historical "truths." The relevant ecological principle here is that negative feedback circuits are essential to systemic sustainability: appropriate pruning/predation promotes systems' growth/diversity. Hence the iron ship was heavily pounded to produce embodied knowledge that fostered new "history in the making." Some truths concerning the past were resuscitated in the present through knowledge created *in* performance. The feedback of excessive vibration resulted in the collective practices of popular historiography that even now may be helping keep the dead hulk "alive."

Part 2: Performance as research documented

Two Undiscovered Amerindians Visit . . . – caged freedoms

The white man wears a white shirt and his right hand, inside a white plastic glove, holds a half-peeled banana. He reaches between the golden bars of a cage, offering it to a woman whose face is "primitively" painted in three colors. Black hair falls below her shoulders and she wears a leopard-skin bikini top, a "grass" hula skirt, and a pair of ordinary white sneakers. Her skin is light brown. Opening her mouth, she bites the banana. The man laughs energetically at her, then walks across the front of the cage and repeats the routine with a bizarrely costumed, dark-skinned male, also behind the bars. All the time he laughs and laughs.

This sequence occurs twenty minutes into the half-hour video called *The Couple in the Cage*.[24] It documents *Two Undiscovered Amerindians Visit...*, which Marvin Carlson describes as "probably the best-known performance piece of the 1990s" and as touching "upon many of the central concerns of performance at the end of the century."[25] Guillermo Gómez-Peña provides a succinct account of the show:

Coco [Fusco] and I lived for three-day periods in a gilded cage, on exhibition as "undiscovered Amerindians" from the (fictional) island of Guatinau. I was dressed as a kind of Aztec wrestler from Las Vegas, and Coco as a Taina straight out of *Gilligan's Island*. We were hand-fed by fake museum docents [guides], and taken to the bathroom on leashes. Taxonomic plates describing our costumes and physical characteristics were displayed next to the cage. Besides performing "authentic rituals" we would write on a laptop computer, watch home videos of our native land, and listen to Latin American rock music on a boom box.[26]

It was performed in public spaces and museums in Madrid, London, Sydney, and other "global cities" between 1992 and 1994, attracting attention from many academics internationally.[27] It was a high-quality, carefully documented, ideologically dynamic presentation of intercultural communication that provides an excellent example of innovative artists making PaR: experimental creative practice as a contained and relatively stable source of performance knowledge.

Accounts of the show in progress belie this impression, though. Carlson describes it as a "playful reconstruction" through which "the performers gradually realized that all [its] concerns had to be freshly negotiated, often in surprising and unexpected ways, in every new encounter."[28] He bases this account on Fusco's explanation that the event focused "less on what we did than on how people interacted with us and interpreted our actions."[29] Hence think improvisation, fluidity, instability and ambiguity. But Fusco also reports a strange uniformity of spectator response: "Consistently from city to city, *more than half of our visitors believed our fiction and thought we were 'real.'*"[30] A starkly bifurcated reception, then, challenging the anti-binary theology generally embraced by performance studies. I will explore this paradoxical PaR dynamic through another common performance studies tenet – that performance does not survive its doing[31] – looking more closely at *The Couple in the Cage* to test this doctrine of ephemerality.

Fusco also writes that such trace documents are "our only means of sustaining the *life* of our performance."[32] This implies some sustainability of the effects generated in those live moments of subjection meted out by the banana-proffering spectator-participant. So I set it beside *The Iron Ship*'s drumming scene, to investigate how the processes of knowledge-making in performance reception might be resuscitated through postevent documents. This requires that I evoke the paradoxical notion of documentary traces producing "degrees of ephemerality" according to the conditions of reception they create, which naturally are affected by their environment. I also propose that, in the twenty-first century, the "distributed archives" of the digital

3. Coco Fusco performs an "authentic" Guatinauan dance for paying punters. Fusco and Gómez-Peña in *Two Undiscovered Amerindians Visit... Buenos Aires*. Patricios Fundación Banco, Buenos Aires, 1994.

4. A punter participates by paying for a photograph with the Guatinauans. Fusco and Gómez-Peña in *Two Undiscovered Amerindians Visit... Madrid*. Columbus Plaza, Madrid, 1992.

media, especially the World Wide Web, may commonly resonate with this paradox in their varied intensities of remediated immediacy.[33] But surely here we are in danger of entering an "intricate maze" of quasi-necromancy, addicts of the "live" hit by extreme archive fever,[34] mad for the slightest spectre of ephemerality in the traces of past events? This strange quest turns us Hamlet-like, by indirection finding direction out. To see what we seek means looking away.

I did not experience *Two Undiscovered Amerindians Visit . . .* as a live event. Unlike *The Iron Ship*, I have no "insider knowledge" of the piece. Given such absence in my personal history, what perspective on that lacuna might best reactivate performance knowledge from the show? My paradox-ology suggests a search for homologies to my ignorance in any *absences* that created the event's effects, a quest for how those "defects" can indi-cate its best "qualities." So what "defective absences" produced the show's most powerful results? The latter must surely include the remarkable binary reception between spectators believing that the "Guatinauans" were real or realizing they were not real. This was produced through the taxonomic plates outside the cage simply withholding information about its "true" status as an artwork. That deliberate "defect" generated the amazing "qualities" of the show's exposure of latent racism in a majority of its spectators.

Moreover, the interaction improvised between the bars *added* to that absence through another simple performative tactic. Outside the cage was a money box, and for a few cents spectators could buy a story in "Guatin-auan" from the male, watch the female dance, be photographed with the caged natives, see a display of the male's genitals (wittily held out of sight between his legs), or even feed the two unfortunates. So some golden-cage spectators became participants in the visual, aural, and tactile spectacle, and like *The Iron Ship* drumming this also generated strong contradictory reactions. Thus in *Two Undiscovered Amerindians Visit . . .* the equivalent excess to vibrating metal was the exchange of money. It became a Derridean double-supplement to the display boards, completing their insufficiency – making the "natives" natives ("not real"/real) – *and* exceeding their effects – exposing "truths" about racism. Again, supplements generated paradoxical "truths" *in* performance. For many spectator-participants, racism was set free by the golden bars. Others might simply witness this, speak up, or walk away. But all were caught up publicly in histories that officially had ended. Want it to end? Never say never!

The histories "brought to life" by the cage were constructed through pervasive binaries as between white skin/black skin, humans/animals, mas-ters/monstrosities, civilization/barbarism, culture/nature.[35] This ensured that its allusions to prisons and zoos could spark unspeakable paradoxical "truths." Colonial history is a nightmare dreamed up by an empire's victims. Genocide favored the dead with an unbeatable wholesale deal. The human – the paradoxical primate – is an animal that thinks it isn't one. Did this potential constitute the show's best "qualities"? Such paradoxes, blossoming through simple acts of withholding information and inviting participation, show the powers of the "live" in performance. The performing of the cage did this: it riotously released what it dangerously confined.

Under what conditions might a performance document turn this trick of releasing what it confines of the "liveness" in a past event? Fusco's metaphor for the paradoxical power of *Two Undiscovered Amerindians Visit . . .* is especially resonant in this regard: "The cage became a *blank screen* onto which audiences projected their fantasies of who and what we were."[36] Hence my paradoxology's final questions now become: how could a flickering video image *reactivate* the phenomenal interactivity of the "live" in this show? Are there any blanks on a screen filled by *The Couple in the Cage* homologous to the absences in the live performance?

My focus is the plastic-gloved hand reaching through the golden bars to feed the "natives" a banana. I suggest this action releases more "qualities" than can be confined by the two-dimensional screen precisely *because* of the latter's "defects," its "blanks." The ante is raised on this claim by the patent fact that the "defect" of the live racist moment, like sexually explicit scenes, can be fetishized in a mediatized image! Roland Barthes's photographic "punctum," magically firing up an image with a sense of life, might be invoked, ironically, as reversing such commodification.[37] But a more commonplace route into the paradox of degrees of ephemerality in documents would be a better bet. Barthes supplies this in the conventional notion of the photographic image as *analogon*, an "analogical perfection which, to common sense, defines the photograph."[38] The ambiguity of that "common *sense*" – as between perception/affect (sensing) and reception/analysis (making sense) – is crucial to how humans may *practice the use* of homologies shared by live events and documents. Sensing one makes sense of the other, much as intuition spots corresponding digits in bat's wing and human hand.

My hunch derives from a live encounter with *The Couple in the Cage*, which I recommend readers undertake in order to test what follows. The banana feeding lasts about thirty seconds, but the preceding twenty minutes of carefully edited film reconstruct multiple perspectives on the live performance, including how different spectators/participants interacted with it and explained their vastly varied reactions.[39] The video's viewers are thus "trained" to perceive the event as one of intersecting gazes and contradictory interpretations. Just before the feeding, the man is filmed through the sidebars, pulling on the plastic glove. Cut to cage-front view: he places the banana in Fusco's mouth, she bites, and he quickly convulses into laughter. Fusco steps back from the bars and – zoom in – her relaxed attitude is completely in contrast to earlier performance styles, as she coolly surveys the shaking man. The documentary "defect" here is generic to current visual technologies: the perspectives are inevitably partial, blanking out much of the scene, viewpoints highly selective. But the selection captures the altered gaze of the performer, creating what Fusco calls a "reversed ethnography."[40] The video viewer sees the previously watched watching the watcher.

I suggest that the video's partiality activates a viewer-reception dynamic that is homologous to the now long-gone live interaction witnessed on the screen. The scene on screen is designed to structure a performer-spectator reflexivity – reversed ethnography – that operated in the live event, so the video viewer views the viewed as formerly they had *viewed each other*. That reproduces the *formal* structuring of the live event created by the cage. Moreover, video viewers, I think, may gain a doubled perspective on the live event as they can choose to become self-conscious in watching the watchers watching each other – a reflexive viewing of reflexive viewing.[41] But that is not sufficient for the defects of the technology to resonate the unique qualities of the event. For degrees of ephemerality to be released, the viewer has commonly to sense something of the excessive tactile/embodied force of the "live" in the "original" performance. For *The Couple in the Cage*, two factors work powerfully to create an ecology of performance homologies between event and document required to trigger this effect.

Firstly, the "reversed ethnography" in the structure of both event and video taps into continuing cultural stresses which, as Fusco claims, "dramatize the colonial unconscious of American society" created by "a 'naturalised' splitting of humanity along racial lines."[42] Both event and document thus engage global performance histories in which all humans, as noted already, currently participate.[43] Hence the show generated profoundly paradoxical perspectives on those histories, which the video is made to replicate. Secondly, the banana feeding surely resonates with a wide range of primal "scenes" stretching back to the earliest days of hominids. It is a paradigmatic scene that of course is highly sensitive to contradictory interpretations – familial, sexual, gustatory, animalistic, and so on – and so potentially fabulously charged with paradoxical energy.

I propose that the homologies created between live performance and documentary trace, especially *but not only* in this moment, work to the ecological principles of plenitude and recycling: natural abundance that multiplies itself. Those structural event/document similarities conceivably activate *shared common senses* of spectator perception-reception that regenerate such powerful energies, variously replicating responses in the lacunae that link events and documents. Inevitably, there can be no guarantee of such responses. But given even the slightest chance that they might occur, degrees of ephemerality in documentary transmission may, paradoxically, have the potential to resuscitate something of the "live" in past performance events. Hence my paradoxology does not *deny* the lacuna of binary differences between ontologies of live performance and reproductive mediation as claimed by the theology of ephemerality in performance studies. But it also asserts that they can be productive of profound homologies between events and documents whose "qualities" have been generally overlooked. Performance as research, I contend, is especially well placed to investigate those qualities, as it can produce the creatively reflexive methods required to engage fully with the paradoxical natures of documents and performance events.

In summary

To summarize my argument at its simplest: the physical energies of the drumming scene in *The Iron Ship* are paralleled by the psychic energies of the banana scene in *The Couple in the Cage*. Both generate a common sense of the "live," the first *in* the event itself, the second *shared* between event and document. In both instances a paradoxical complex of ecologically inflected homological structures may be common to past performance events and their documentary traces. These partly constitute the conditions for regenerative degrees of ephemerality that may foster resuscitation of the "live" of past performances in the present. As these conditions depend crucially on the activation of a variety of paradoxical excesses that produce major lacunae in performance, perhaps Voltaire should have the penultimate word here: the superfluous, a very necessary thing.[44]

I have aimed to demonstrate how faultlines conventionally assumed between live events and documents are being redrawn by new methods of research through performance practice. PaR is the preeminent methodology here, but it also includes experiments in ecological performance, applied theatre, "intermediality," and more.[45] Inevitably, these areas of performance research open up fresh problems of knowledge production in the paradoxical ecological era of the third millennium, when humanity threatens *no less than* an end to ecology. For sure, these problems are new when compared with the earth's oldest stones. But it could be, too, that they reach back to the moment when the earliest homo sapiens first tried to kick stones into life.

Notes

Acknowledgments *The Iron Ship*: SS *Great Britain* Project staff; John Marshall, co-director; Dr. Jean Rath, researcher; Bim Mason, director of Circomedia; Bristol University Drama Department production staff; Drama Department and Circomedia students 1999–2000. Funding: Bristol University Alumni Association, Arts and Humanities Research Board.

1. James Boswell, *The Life of Samuel Johnson* (1791) (London: Folio Society, 1968), 292.
2. George Berkeley, *The Principles of Human Knowledge with Other Writings* (1710), ed. G. J. Warnock (London: Collins, 1962).
3. Richard Schechner, *Performance Studies: An Introduction* (London: Routledge, 2002), 1.
4. *Ibid.*, 18.
5. PARIP: www.bris.ac.uk/parip. Core researchers: Dr. Ludivine Allegue-Fuschini, Professor Baz Kershaw, Dr. Angela Piccini, Dr. Caroline Rye.
6. Forthcoming as *Practice as Research: In Performance and Screen Studies* published by Palgrave Macmillan.
7. Simon Jones, *Double Happiness* (2002); Baz Kershaw, *Mnemosyne Dreams* (2004); Martin White, *Chamber of Demonstrations* (2006); and Rosemary Lee, *The Suchness of Heni and Eddie* (2007).
8. Arts and Humanities Research Council: AHRC Funding Guide, Section C, 80 at www.ahrc.ac.uk/about/programmesoverview/research_programme_overview.asp. Accessed July 19, 2007.
9. Peggy Phelan, *Unmarked: The Politics of Performance* (London and New York: Routledge, 1993), 146.
10. From *Improvisation* in Eugène Ionesco, *Plays, Volume III: The Killer; Improvisation, or The Shepherd's Chameleon; Maid to Marry*, trans. Donald Watson (London: John Calder, 1960), 121.
11. Schechner, *Performance Studies*, 2.
12. Jon McKenzie, *Perform or Else: From Discipline to Performance* (London: Routledge, 2001), and Adrian Heathfield, ed., *Live: Art and Performance* (London: Tate, 2004).
13. Ralph Waldo Emerson, "Circles," in Emerson, *Essays and English Traits* (Harvard: Harvard Classics, 1909–14), 18.7, www.bartleby.com/5/109.html. Accessed July 20, 2007.
14. Available as documented by *The Couple in the Cage: A Guatinaui Odyssey*, video, directed and produced by Coco Fusco and Paula Heredia, 1993 (Chicago: Authentic Documentary Productions, 1993).
15. Baz Kershaw, "Performance Studies and Po-chang's Ox: Steps to a Paradoxology of Performance," *New Theatre Quarterly* 22.1 (February 2006), 30–53. See also Baz Kershaw, *Theatre Ecology: Environments and Performance Events* (Cambridge: Cambridge University Press, 2007), 98–130.
16. Berkeley, *The Principles of Human Knowledge*, 45.
17. Baz Kershaw, "Curiosity or Contempt: On Spectacle, the Human, and Activism," *Theatre Journal* 55.4 (December 2003), 591–611.
18. From Honoré de Balzac's paradox: they must have the defects of their qualities. Cf. "his good qualities are as negative as his defects" in "Study of

43

a Woman," *Human Comedy*, www2.hn.psu.edu/faculty/jmanis/Balzac/Study-Woman.pdf. Accessed July 20, 2007.

19. SS *Great Britain*: www.ssgreatbritain.org/. Accessed December 10, 2006.

20. For example, David Lowenthal, *The Heritage Crusade and the Spoils of History* (Cambridge: Cambridge University Press, 1997), 156–62.

21. Jacques Derrida, *Of Grammatology*, trans. Gayatri Chakravorty Spivak (Baltimore: Johns Hopkins University Press, 1976), 144.

22. Pablo Picasso, "Picasso Speaks," interview with Marius de Zayas, *The Arts* (New York, May 1923), 315–26.

23. Baz Kershaw, "Performance, Memory, Heritage, History, Spectacle: *The Iron Ship*," *Studies in Theatre and Performance* 22.3 (2002), 132–49.

24. *The Couple in the Cage: Guatinaui Odyssey*, dir. Fusco and Heredia.

25. Marvin Carlson, *Performance: A Critical Introduction* (1996), 2nd edn (London: Routledge, 2004), 202.

26. Guillermo Gómez-Peña, *The New World Border: Prophecies, Poems, Loqueras for the End of the Century* (San Francisco: City Lights, 1996), 97.

27. See, for example, Diana Taylor, *The Archive and the Repertoire: Performing Cultural Memory in the Americas* (Durham: Duke University Press, 2003), 65–75; Caroline Vercoe, "Agency and Ambivalance: A Reading of Works by Coco Fusco," in Coco Fusco, *The Bodies That Were Not Ours and Other Writings* (London and New York: Routledge/IVA, 2003), 231–46; and Loren Kruger, "Geographical Acts: Place, Performance, and Pedagogy," *American Literary History* 17.4 (Winter 2005), 781–93.

28. Carlson, *Performance*, 200.

29. Coco Fusco, *English is Broken Here: Notes on Cultural Fusion in the Americas* (New York: New Press, 1995), 40.

30. *Ibid.*, 50 (my italics).

31. Phelan, *Unmarked*, 148–9.

32. Fusco, *English is Broken*, 62 (my italics).

33. For "degrees of ephemerality" and "distributed archives," see Kershaw, *Theatre Ecology*, 41–54, 75–97; for "remediation," see Jay David Bolter and Richard Grusin, *Remediation: Understanding New Media* (Cambridge, MA: MIT Press, 1999).

34. Jacques Derrida, *Archive Fever: A Freudian Impression*, trans. Eric Prenowitz (Chicago: University of Chicago Press, 1996).

35. Fusco, *English is Broken*, 47–8.

36. *Ibid.*, 46 (my italics).

37. Roland Barthes, *Camera Lucida: Reflections on Photography*, trans. Richard Howard (New York: Hill and Wang, 1981), 27.

38. Roland Barthes, *Image, Music, Text*, trans. Stephen Heath (New York: Hill and Wang; London: Fontana, 1977), 17. Digital documents raise the ante on this conundrum as their binary technologies can offer exact reproductions that are not subject to significant decay. See Anthony Smith, *Software for the Self: Culture and Technology* (London: Faber and Faber, 1996), 96.

39. Fusco, *English is Broken*, 55–7.

40. *Ibid.*, 38.

41. Taylor denies this possibility with "the video watcher is outside the frame, the unseen see-er" (*The Archive and the Repertoire*, 75). Her discussion forecloses

on a doubled reflexivity in which seeing always implies another watcher "looking over one's shoulder," as it were.

42. Fusco, *English is Broken*, 47.

43. I write this in 2007, as commemorations of the "abolition of slavery" ignite heated arguments about the continuing worldwide practice of human trafficking. For a moderate version, see Opening the Adjournment Debate on the 200th Anniversary of the Abolition of the Slave Trade, House of Commons, UK, www.dpm.gov.uk/speeches/070320_abolition.aspx. Accessed August 21, 2007.

44. Voltaire, "Le Mondain," in *The Complete Works of Voltaire*, ed. John Dunkley *et al.*, *Volume XVI: Works of 1736* (Oxford: Voltaire Foundation, 2003), l. 21.

45. Gabriella Giannachi and Nigel Stewart, eds., *Performing Nature: Explorations in Ecology and the Arts* (Bern: Peter Lang, 2005); Helen Nicholson, *Applied Drama: The Gift of Theatre* (Basingstoke: Palgrave Macmillan, 2005); and Freda Chapple and Chiel Kattenbelt, eds., *Intermediality and Performance* (Amsterdam: Rodopi/International Federation of Theatre Research, 2006).

3

SUSAN LEIGH FOSTER

Movement's contagion: the kinesthetic impact of performance

This chapter pursues answers to a question, most urgently posed in relation to dance events, but equally central to all performance: what do you feel, physically, when you watch another body performing? How and why do you respond to the motions of another body? What do you sense? How does your physical experience of what you are seeing help you understand what you are watching? Focusing the inquiry with these questions, I seek to emphasize the sensations of our bones, muscles, ligaments, tendons, and joints. The sensory experience provided by these corporeal elements, often referred to as the kinesthetic sense, has been largely ignored in theories of performance, yet for those of us in dance studies, it remains a predominant aspect of aesthetic experience, one that must be interrogated as part of any inquiry into dance's significance.

In the 1930s the dance critic John Martin described movement's effect on viewers as contagious, a term that is defined as the rapid spread of influence or emotion from one body to another, but that also suggests pollution and disease. More recently, the neurophysiologist Vittorio Gallese has described the phenomenon of yawning when someone yawns, or laughing when they laugh, as contagious behavior.[1] What kind of interkinesthetic connectivity forms the basis for such claims? What hold does the kinesthetic have over subjectivity such that its influence would be described as contagious? In what follows I offer a brief and partial genealogy of the term kinesthesia, framed to historicize the claims to know or feel what another body is feeling. Juxtaposing neurophysiological investigations of the term and aestheticians' accounts of dance's impact, I hope to show how the influence that one body can exert over another, its propensity toward contagion, has changed radically over the past hundred years.

Kinesthesia as interiorization

The term kinesthesia, deriving from the Greek *kine* (movement) and *aesthesis* (sensation), is first implemented in physiological studies of the late nineteenth century to refer to the sense of the body's movement, yet the notion of internal bodily sensation was widely discussed in eighteenth-century philosophy and aesthetics. Often referred to as a kind of "sixth sense," this repertoire of sensations is isolated from the other senses by the Abbé de Condillac, who calls it the most fundamental feeling. In order to examine the act of perception, Condillac posits the existence of a statue whose senses are enlivened one at a time:

> Our statue, deprived of smell, of hearing, of taste, of vision, and limited to the sense of touch, now exists through the feeling which she has of the parts of her body one upon the other – above all the movements of respiration: and this is the least degree of feeling to which one may reduce her. I call it fundamental feeling, because it is with this play of the machine that the life of the animal begins; she depends on it alone. . . . This feeling and her "I" are consequently the same thing in their origin.[2]

Utterly immobile, the statue nonetheless feels parts of her body touching other areas, and also the sensation of breathing. For Condillac, both the viscera and the muscles and joints contribute to this bodily sensing.

Slowly over the nineteenth century, however, the sixth sense begins to acquire increased precision. Investigating the skeletal musculature, Thomas Brown, as early as 1820, observes that "our muscular frame is not merely a part of the living machinery of motion, but is also truly an organ of sense."[3] In the 1820s and 1830s, Sir Charles Bell identifies "muscle sense" as responsible for three groups of sensations – pain and fatigue, weight and resistance, and movement and position – all of which result from sensations arising when a muscle contracts. The Pancinian corpuscles, muscle spindles, and Golgi tendon organs that all contribute to these sensations are identified in the 1840s, 1860s, and 1880s respectively.[4] In 1880 Henry Charlton Bastian is able to synthesize investigations of these specialized receptors with his own work on their connections to the cerebral cortex in order to assert definitively the sense of movement which he names kinesthesia.[5]

Thereafter, kinesthesia is replaced by a new term, proprioception, that focuses investigation of muscular sensation on its participation in the afferent-efferent arc. Named by C. S. Sherrington in 1906, proprioceptors are those sense organs that deliver internal or afferent sensations about the status of the muscle or joint to the spinal cord and brain where they connect to motor, or efferent, responses.[6] Functioning at an unconscious level, proprioceptors participate in spinal-level reflexes that primarily assist in maintaining posture and balance, and they also contribute to the learning and remembering of physical activities such as sports. Sherrington's pioneering studies of reflex actions and the role of proprioception in guiding and refining muscular action dominate the field for several decades.

The interest in skeletal musculature evidenced in the work of Bastian and then Sherrington parallels a new fascination with physical fitness that likewise focuses on the muscles. In a period of mass migration into urban centers, where daily living offers far fewer opportunities for physical exercise, exercise is seen as an effective way of building up nervous reserves. It both interrupts the depletion of those reserves brought on by laboring in the factory, with its highly repetitive phrases of motion that frequently interface with machinery, and at the same time it provides a respite from the nervous taxation of city life.[7] For many psychologists of the period, the whole body is seen as contributing to the energy needed to maintain mental and motor activity. They also see the cultivation of the body as a manly pursuit.[8]

As part of this growing interest in the musculature, Dudley Allen Sargent is awarded a professorship at Harvard to establish physical education in 1879.[9] There he elaborates an exercise regime that implements pulley-weight machines that can be adjusted to the strength of the individual and focused around the cultivation of specific muscle groups. By 1912, Sargent boasts that 270 colleges now offer programs in physical education; 300 city school systems around the United States require it; and 500 YMCA (Young Men's Christian Association) gymnasiums with 80,000 members provide versions of his machines.[10] Sargent's regimens, along with several other similar systems of exercise that work with dumbbells, balls, and ropes, help forge an entirely new experience of the body as a muscular entity. Its newly identified muscles, contributing vitally to the health and wellbeing of the person, must be developed and maintained through regular exercise devoted specifically to them.

This elasticity and tensility of the musculature in motion provides the medium of expression for the newly emerging modern dance; its chief apologist, the *New York Times* critic John Martin, draws heavily on assumptions about kinesthesia to formulate his theory of dance expression. Martin argues that the viewer, on witnessing the dancing body, is inspired to feel equivalent kinesthetic sensations. This process, which he calls "inner mimicry," is grounded in a fundamental physical reactivity to all events: we pucker when we witness someone tasting a lemon, and when they yawn or cry we feel similar impulses.[11] Not only events but also objects elicit this kinesthetic responsiveness:

Since we respond muscularly to the strains in architectural masses and the attitudes of rocks, it is plain to be seen that we will respond even more vigorously to the action of a body exactly like our own. We shall cease to be mere spectators and become participants in the movement that is presented to us, and though to all outward appearances we shall be sitting quietly in our chairs, we shall nevertheless be dancing synthetically with all our musculature. Naturally these motor responses are registered by our movement-sense receptors, and awaken appropriate emotional associations akin to those which have animated the dancer in the first place. It is the dancer's whole function to lead us into imitating his actions with our faculty for inner mimicry in order that we may experience his feelings.[12]

Viewers' bodies, even in their seated stillness, nonetheless feel what the dancing body is feeling – the tensions or expansiveness, the floating or driving momentums that compose the dancer's motion. Then, because such muscular sensations are inextricably linked to emotions, the viewer also feels the choreographer's desires and intentions.

Martin's argument is geared to rationalize the emergence of a new genre of concert dance, the modern dance, which deploys radically new presuppositions about movement and meaning. Rather than locate the dancer within a story, as in ballet, or as part of a spectacle, as burlesque had done, the modern dance utilizes dance movement itself as the vehicle for developing narrative. The body's special proximity to both emotional and unconscious realms of the psyche endows its movement with a special charge. When properly cultivated by the choreographer, dance movement can unite both dancer and viewer in the experience of fundamental human emotion:

The modern dancer, instead of employing the cumulative resources of academic tradition, cuts through directly to the source of all dancing. He utilizes the principle that every emotional state tends to express itself in movement, and that the movements thus created spontaneously, though they are not representational, reflect accurately in each case the character of the particular emotional state. Because of the inherent contagion of bodily movement, which makes the onlooker feel sympathetically in his own musculature the exertions he sees in somebody else's musculature, the dancer is able to convey through movement the most intangible emotional experience.[13]

Emotional states, described here in the language of disease as contagious, are transmitted through movement that has been devised spontaneously. The choreographer, tapping the emotional depths of his or her psyche, is moved by the force of the feelings found there. Even as re-presented on the concert stage, the resulting dance carries this primal force.

Martin's theory relies on the increasingly individuated experience of the musculature and its particular properties of tensility, dynamism, and momentum. At the same time, he connects this musculature intimately with the unconscious depths of the psyche, assuming that the kind of impulse originating there is so rudimentary that it can never be articulated verbally. Establishing an organic opposition between movement and language, Martin argues that the peripatetic volatility of kinesthetic information as it journeys through the unconscious is what the dance so uniquely captures. The creative process of making a dance, an entirely individual rather than collective experience, does not socialize the unconscious so much as enrich the number of ways in which to witness what a human being is. Choreography, not unlike psychoanalysis, may shed light on the inner workings of the psyche, but the energy it taps within the human body undercuts civilizing mechanisms with its primal veracity about the human condition.

Kinesthesia as orientation

Although Martin's theory of meaning in dance depends on kinesthetic empathy, the term kinesthesia was rarely used, apart from an occasional dance class, for the first half of the twentieth century.[14] It came into new and more widespread use with the 1966 publication of James J. Gibson's influential study, *The Senses Considered as Perceptual Systems*. Following Sherrington, scientists working in psychology and perception studies upheld an absolute separation between perception and action. They agreed that afferent and efferent neural systems were entirely distinct and incommensurate: the afferent processed incoming stimuli and the efferent conveyed the command for bodily movements. As it had been for Condillac's statue, perception was investigated as the passive experience of receiving input from distinctive kinds of receptors, individually responsible for sight, hearing, taste, touch, and smell. Gibson, in contrast, argues that perception is the act of extracting information from the environment. A highly active project, perception requires participation from both afferent and efferent systems. In fact, any given act of perceiving depends on a complex sorting through of that which is invariant and that which is in flux. Gibson identifies proprioception as central to that process.

Kinesthetic information, identified now as a subset of proprioception, comes from muscle and joint receptors and also the vestibular organs of the inner ear. Gibson argues that these sense organs contribute a continuous sense of one's orientation with respect to gravity and one's motion through space as well as a generalized sense of bodily disposition – where one is tense or relaxed, expanded or compressed, even the precise angle of each joint. Gibson further proposes that any act of perception depends on the detection of the just-noticeable difference between sensory input and bodily disposition. The eyeball itself can tell us very little about the visual world around us, but the eyeball combined with the ocular musculature that surrounds it and the vestibular system that orients it with respect to gravity can give very precise information about our surroundings. Gibson identifies this integrative processing of external and internal stimuli as the perceptual system. He further argues that kinesthesia plays a central role in integrating all the senses.

Gibson's theory of perception is almost literally fleshed out in the dance practice known as contact improvisation that emerged just a few years after the publication of his book. Like contact improvisation, which asks participants to forge a moving point of contact between two bodies and to follow that contact wherever it leads, Gibson's theory proposes an ongoing duet between perceiver and surroundings in which both are equally active. The environment does not impinge upon a passive observer. Nor does the perceiver survey the environment, as Condillac's statue does, from a static and omniscient position. Instead, the perceiver negotiates the perpetual flux of surroundings by determining that which is constant and that which is changing. Gibson argues that vision is especially successful in determining these constancies, and as a result, we associate a sense of self with the head. I (my head) and my body (the rest of my body) exist as identifiably separate, partially because of vision's extreme precision in coordinating with locomotion to navigate the world, and partially because of our ability to see many other parts of our bodies. Recognizing this hierarchical arrangement of the senses, contact improvisation encourages participants to defuse the visual and to focus more intensively on their sense of touch. In so doing, a new experience of self is produced in which the "I" is contingent upon and a product of the ongoing contact between the two bodies.

As Cynthia Novack has observed, contact improvisation emerged during a period of prolific experimentation with altered states of consciousness, some drug-induced, that endeavor to probe the boundaries of perception and its effects on subjectivity.[15] Numerous forms of meditation, martial arts practices, and yoga, as well as social dancing, all conceptualize the body's movement as a potential conduit to new ways of perceiving and orienting oneself in the world. Rather than offer access to repressed or primal experience, as in Martin's theory, movement holds the promise of expanding consciousness. Like Gibson's understanding of the role that movement plays in extracting information from the environment, movement can be tapped to give insight into new dimensions of reality.

Gibson's theory of perception likewise aligns with a general shift in conceptions of dance meaning that occur in the 1960s and 1970s in response to choreographic initiatives of the same period. Rather than impressing itself upon viewers, the dance now presents itself to viewers, asking them to extract from the dance whatever meaning they find. As the composer John Cage observes, in outlining his collaboration with the choreographer Merce Cunningham:

> We are not, in these dances and music, saying something. We are simpleminded enough to think that if we were saying something we would use words. We are rather doing something. The meaning of what we do is determined by each one who sees and hears it ... I may add there are no stories and no psychological problems. There is simply an activity of movement, sound and light.[16]

Unlike Martin, who assumes that dance is intrinsically connected to the emotions, making its meaning felt by staging a progression of feelings, Cage asserts the primacy of physical activity as distinct from any other psychological experience. What a dance offers its viewers is the opportunity to perceive bodies in motion. As part of that process, viewers can focus on whatever parts or aspects of the dance they find interesting, and as a consequence, they will each experience the dance differently. Nonetheless, their experience of the dance will be grounded in the physical factuality of the body's articulations.

Similarly, Gibson's vocabulary for discussing the phenomenon of perception focuses on the "real" experience of sensing the world around us. Rather than immobilize the subject in order to study an isolated reflex, he devises experiments that simulate the ways we actually perceive as part of moving through our surroundings. Like Cunningham's ideal viewers, he envisions his subjects as active and willful perceivers. At the same time, he identifies the features of our surroundings using a neutral terminology – stimulation, ambient array, external invariants – that rebuffs any cultural or historical specificities.

Thus both conceptualizations of kinesthesia – as the muscular connection to our deepest feelings, and as the orientor of our senses and sense of identity – are rationalized by distinctive universalist worldviews. Kinesthesia as entwined with the emotions presumes that all humans share this same connection and that they are all equally moved by the same depictions of human predicament or struggle. Kinesthesia as baseline for evaluating the senses presumes that all humans have equal access to the same conditions for sensing the world. Although physical impairment can cause a person to perceive the world differently, social difference does not. Both conceptions of the kinesthetic cast dance as a unique medium of communication; it functions either to awaken and enliven feelings or to assert the vitality of physicality as separate from the emotions. In the first case, the dancer's body becomes a vessel for the dance's message and the viewer receives that message by being moved by it. In the second, the dancer's body emits actions to a viewing body that actively seeks out their message.

Kinesthesia as simulation

The definition of kinesthesia transforms once again in the 1990s with work done by Alain Berthoz, among others, on the brain's sense of movement and with the discovery of a new class of brain cells, called "mirror neurons." Building on Gibson's theory of perception as an active engagement with the world, Berthoz approaches the external senses as systems rather than channels and as interrelated rather than mutually exclusive.[17] And like him, he sees kinesthesia as playing a central role in orienting and organizing all the senses. He departs from Gibson, however, in two crucial ways: firstly, he argues that perception is a simulation of action; and secondly, he does not assume that observers share a common environment, instead holding that each individual may perceive the world quite differently, based on the kinds of cultural and gendered differences from which the *habitus* is formed.

Synthesizing a large number of experiments on perception and cognition, Berthoz emphasizes the anticipatory quality of attention. As one is looking at the armchair, one is already simulating the motions associated with seating oneself in it. As one sees the brake lights on the car ahead, one is already coordinating exactly when and how strongly to apply the brakes. Increasingly, neuroscientists are establishing that perception and action are embedded in each other, arguing that

> cortico-ponto-cerebello-thalamo-cortical loops exist, within which internal simulation of movement can occur completely independent of its actual execution. These loops contain . . . here I do well to hesitate, like Faust. "Representations" is too vague; "models" is modern but probably vague as well; "images" is too visual; "schema" is the term perhaps most common in the literature; "kinesthetic series" would make Husserl happy.[18]

Through these "kinesthetic series" the brain simulates various movement options in order to choose the best strategy. Thus the cat can catch a mouse, anticipating its future position, because "its neurons are sensitive to the velocity of movement: they do not calculate a velocity."[19] Rather, the cat has evolved this capacity as part of its adaptation to and survival in its environment.

Although most cats are similarly talented at catching mice, humans, Berthoz argues, undergo a far more complex perceptual process. They do not necessarily perceive all events in the same way. Where Gibson assumes that all individuals can stand in the same place at different times and be afforded an equal opportunity to explore it,[20] Berthoz emphasizes research that shows that "the oculomotor path followed to explore a face is completely different depending on what the observer is thinking: whether she thinks that the individual is rich, sad, or well-coifed, that his ears are protruding, and so on."[21] Pleasure or fear or interest all influence the tiny motions of the eye, known as saccades, through which visual perception occurs.[22] One's history of engagement with the environment profoundly affects how one sees, and consequently what one sees.[23] Berthoz references Pierre Bourdieu's notion of the *habitus* as a way to theorize these perceptual inclinations.[24] The long-standing features of our cultural as well as physical environment inform the way we perceive the world.

Strong evidence in support of Berthoz's argument that perception simulates action has been provided with the discovery of mirror neurons, located in several areas of the cortex. These neurons fire when the subject performs an action, and they also fire when the subject sees the action being performed. Thus as we watch someone moving, motor circuits in the brain are activated that do not necessarily result in visible movement but nonetheless rehearse that movement. Although the physiological mechanisms underlying this response are not entirely understood, many scientists describe the mutuality of observing and acting as a kind of resonance. As Vittorio Gallese, among others, puts it:

> A metaphor that describes well this correspondence between observed and executed biological motions is that of a physical "resonance." It is as if neurons in these motor areas start to "resonate" as soon as the appropriate visual input is presented. This "resonance" does not necessarily produce a movement or an action. It is an internal motor representation of the observed event which, subsequently, may be used for different functions, among which is imitation.[25]

This resonance is responsible for our ability to predict others' actions, and to know what will result if we move in a certain way. It also accounts for "'contagious behavior' commonly experienced in our daily life, in which the observation of particular actions displayed by others leads to our repetition of them ... including such actions as yawning and laughter."[26]

So there seems to be strong neurophysiological support for Martin's theory of why a dance moves us. The viewer, watching a dance, is literally dancing along. Yet Martin's conceptualization of inner mimicry attaches the physical feelings of the musculature to universally felt emotions, whereas the resonance hypothesis focuses simply on behavior. Although the acts of perceiving and moving may be infused with emotion, what the mirror neurons indicate is the mutuality of sensing and physical action. Whether or not we feel afraid as we watch someone walk along the edge of a precipice, we may well move our arms and legs so as to displace our body's weight to the side of safety.[27] Whether or not we are hoping for victory, we twist and incline as if to exert a magic force over the bowling ball as it rolls toward the pins. And as many scientists have determined, "the resonance phenomenon [is] present not only during the observation of goal-oriented movements, but also during the observation of meaningless art movements."[28]

In keeping with Berthoz's hypothesis that the perception of these "meaningless movements" could be culturally specific, scientists have found that viewers trained in a specific form of dance will "dance" along more intensively with that form than with a form they do not know. Studying the mirror-neuron responses of ballet and capoeira practitioners, chosen especially because the two forms manifest well-established yet distinctive vocabularies, they note that those trained in the form they are watching have a significantly greater neural activity.[29] Furthermore, their study shows that what the observers see is not muscle activation, but rather cultivated action. Many of the movements in both forms, such as jumping and turning, for example, involve the use of the same muscles, yet what viewers respond to is the organized interplay of these muscles as it constructs a specific vocabulary of movements.

Speculating on the evolutionary implications of mirror-neuron activity, Gallese argues that the ability to sense the physical actions of those around us forms the basis on which socialization and the experience of the social takes place. Although none of this neuromuscular activity registers in consciousness, according to Gallese, it does not exist in opposition to language and culture. Rather, the kinesthetic simulation of others' actions establishes an empathetic connection among all humans who recognize in those actions an equivalent intention and goal. Action thus becomes the "*a priori*" principle that enables social bonding.[30]

Gallese cites both phenomenology and American pragmatist branches of philosophy as having anticipated early in the twentieth century this shared consciousness.[31] However, the architecture of the brain's sense of movement established through the discovery of mirror neurons seems more to approximate the networked and hyperlinked world that has emerged with the advent of new digital technologies.[32] It likewise summons up the theories of performativity, such as those proposed by Judith Butler in her application of speech act theory in the 1990s.[33] The perceiver no longer performs a contact improvisation with the environment, but instead rehearses and simulates multiple roles, through his or her own actions as well as those of others. In the process of rehearsing these roles, individuals formulate a self, not as an entity that will then perform an action, but rather as performance itself.

What implications does this theorization of individual and social bodies hold for the experience of watching a dance? Extrapolating from the anticipatory function of mirror neurons, the dancer and dance scholar Ivar Hagendoorn proposes that dance's intrinsic appeal lies in its ability to excite viewers' interest in movement's trajectory.[34] Many laboratory studies show that when a person executes a simple task, such as grabbing a cup, the brain of the observer creates movement arcs that it sees itself or others fulfilling. But what if the goal of the movement arc is not obvious? What if the form of movement is exploratory rather than goal-oriented?: "meaningless" as one study terms it, rather than functional? Hagendoorn argues that the viewer completes the movement in advance and then sees the guess confirmed or refuted, leading to added engagement with the movement and increased efforts to predict the next arc correctly.

Where Martin presumes that kinesthetic engagement leads to emotional attachment, and Cage hopes that movement can be enjoyed simply for its physical factuality, Hagendoorn envisions watching a dance as a continual conjecturing of possible arcs and flows. The viewer, like the choreographer, thinks up the movement and decides how and where to move next. He or she does not simply decide where or what to watch, but instead creates versions of the dance. The process of comparing possible dances with the dance being seen can provoke many feelings and sensations in the viewer, which, according to Hagendoorn, have likely been experienced by the choreographer in the process of making the dance. In this way the choreographer's intention is communicated to the audience.

Rather than flesh out a narrative, or convey a deep psychic impulse, dance movement in Hagendoorn's conception emphasizes its physical unpredictability. Like the choreographers he discusses – William Forsythe, George Balanchine, and Cunningham, his idea of dance, based on the body's articulateness, envisions dance as opening up the viewer to new moves that one can make. Rather than a body that is beefed up and fortified through muscular exertions, or a body that serves as channel for various perceptual states, Hagendoorn focuses on the body as malleable indicator of multiple scenarios. Like the bodies in the twenty-first-century gyms that sculpt the musculature to approximate (simulate) whatever social identity the user desires, the bodies on stage revel in the many directions their moves could take.

What do we feel, kinesthetically, when we watch a performance? This chapter's trajectory suggests that our experience is contingent, in part, on the conception of the body that pervades our historical moment. The dancing body's "contagion" can impel our bodies as outward manifestations of an interiorized psyche, to mimic its movement, and, as a result, feel its feelings. Or it can prompt an active engagement with physicality, enlivening our perception of our own bodies' articulateness. Or it can beckon us to try out/on various scenarios for moving. However it moves us, it does affect our bodies, and this need not be construed as an act of contamination to which we succumb, but instead, as Gallese suggests, as the basis for creating our social existence. Perhaps with an awareness of this crucial interaction between performer and viewer we can cultivate a more conscious registering of the kinesthetic impact that movement exercises. Perhaps such an awareness, enhanced by a few dance classes, can enable us more purposefully to feel how bodies move as they do and why.

Notes

1. Vittorio Gallese, "The Shared Manifold Hypothesis," *Journal of Consciousness Studies* 8 (2001), 38–9.
2. E. B. Abbé de Condillac, *Treatise on the Sensations* (1754), trans. G. Carr (London: Favil Press, 1930), 75.
3. Quoted in E. G. Edwards, "The Development of the 'Muscular Sense' Concept during the Nineteenth Century and the Work of H. Charlton Bastian," *Journal of the History of Medicine and Allied Sciences* 27 (July 1972), 299.
4. See E. G. Boring, *Sensation and Perception in the History of Experimental Psychology* (New York: D. Appleton-Century, 1942), 523–35.
5. See Edwards, "The Development of the 'Muscular Sense' Concept," for an excellent overview of Bastian's work.
6. Proprioception is the term introduced by C. S. Sherrington in his 1906 publication *The Integrative Action of the Nervous System* (New York: Scribner, 1906).
7. See J. C. Whorton, *Crusaders for Fitness: The History of American Health Reformers* (Princeton: Princeton University Press, 1982), 287.
8. Not only did they see physical education as manly, but many also found a religious dimension in daily exercise. Described as "muscular Christianity," the impetus to develop the physique is rationalized by the educator G. Stanley Hall in these terms: "We are soldiers of Christ, strengthening our muscles not against a foreign foe, but against sin within and without us." Quoted in *ibid.*, 289–90.
9. *Ibid.*, 283.

10. J. Ross, *Moving Lessons: Margaret H'Doubler and the Beginning of Dance in American Education* (Madison: University of Wisconsin Press, 2000), 58.
11. J. Martin, *Introduction to the Dance* (New York: W. W. Norton, 1939), 47.
12. *Ibid.*, 53.
13. J. Martin, *The Dance* (New York: Tudor Publishing Company, 1946), 105.
14. The dance educator Margaret H'Doubler, who founded the first dance program in the United States at the University of Wisconsin, did invoke the term frequently. See, for example, M. H'Doubler, *The Dance* (New York: Harcourt, Brace and Company, 1925), 60. For information on H'Doubler, see Ross, *Moving Lessons.*
15. See C. Novack, *Sharing the Dance: Contact Improvisation and American Culture* (Madison: University of Wisconsin Press, 1990).
16. J. Cage, "In This Day," *Dance Observer* (January 1957), 10.
17. A. Berthoz, *The Brain's Sense of Movement*, trans. G. Weiss (Cambridge, MA: Harvard University Press, 2000), 58.
18. *Ibid.*, 164.
19. *Ibid.*, 22–3.
20. See J. J. Gibson, *The Ecological Approach to Visual Perception* (Boston: Houghton Mifflin, 1979), 43.
21. Berthoz, *The Brain's Sense of Movement*, 196.
22. *Ibid.*, 201.
23. *Ibid.*, 221.
24. *Ibid.*, 187–8.
25. See G. Rizzolatti, L. Fadiga, L. Fogassi, and V. Gallese, "From Mirror Neurons to Imitation: Facts and Speculations," in A. N. Meltzoff and W. Prinz, eds., *The Imitative Mind* (Cambridge: Cambridge University Press, 2002), 253.
26. Gallese, "The Shared Manifold Hypothesis," 39.
27. W. Prinz, "Experimental Approaches to Imitation," in Meltzoff and Prinz, eds., *The Imitative Mind*, 155–7.
28. Rizzolatti *et al.*, "From Mirror Neurons to Imitation," 256.
29. B. Calvo-Merino, D. E. Glaser, J. Grèzes, R. E. Passingham, and P. Haggard, "Action Observation and Acquired Motor Skills: An fMRI Study with Expert Dancers," *Cerebral Cortex* 15 (August 2005), 1243–9.
30. Gallese, "The Shared Manifold Hypothesis," 41–2. Gallese is not alone in speculating along these lines about human development and the foundation of social and individual identities. See also A. N. Meltzoff, "Elements of a Development Theory of Imitation," in Meltzoff and Prinz, eds., *The Imitative Mind*, 19–42.
31. Gallese cites Herbert Mead, who at the beginning of the twentieth century argued that the individual determines the boundaries of self through the use of gesture. Similarly, he looks to the work of the phenomenologists Edith Stein, Edmund Husserl, and Maurice Merleau-Ponty. See Gallese, "The Shared Manifold Hypothesis," 43–4.
32. I am indebted to Harmony Bench for her research on mirror neurons, her comments on this essay, and her insight that the metaphor of the "network," so pervasive in contemporary culture, likewise pervades neuroscientists' theorization of mirror neurons.

33. See Judith Butler, *Gender Trouble: Feminism and the Subversion of Identity* (New York: Routledge, 1990).
34. See Ivar Hagendoorn, "Some Speculative Hypothesis about the Nature and Perception of Dance and Choreography," *Journal of Consciousness Studies* 11 (2004), 79–110.

4

JOHN EMIGH

Culture, killings, and criticism in the years of living dangerously: Bali and Baliology

In the last days of 1965 and the first three months of 1966, between 80,000 and 100,000 people were killed in Bali, Indonesia.[1] Many of these were artists and teachers associated, however loosely, with the Indonesian Communist Party (PKI). Since many of the bodies were mutilated and dumped into mass graves or rivers – preventing cremation and possibly rebirth[2] – we will probably never know a more exact number. In 1965 80,000 people constituted 5 to 7 percent of Bali's population: approximately the same percentages for those lost, a few years later, in the killing fields of Cambodia. In Cambodia, though, it took four years and a deal of organizational planning for the Khmer Rouge to effect such carnage; in Bali it took under four months.[3] In all, 500,000 to a million people perished in Indonesia. The American CIA (which supplied information to the Indonesian army) stated in an intelligence report of 1968, "In terms of the numbers killed the ... massacres in Indonesia ranks as one of the worst mass murders of the 20th Century ... far more significant than many other events that have received much more attention."[4] No place had a higher percentage of dead than Bali.

Culture and criticism

The example of Bali has been so significant to the concept of "culture" in relation to performance, and symbolic anthropologist Clifford Geertz's writing so influential – and controversial – in this discourse, that it may prove useful to revisit that cultural site in precisely those years when Geertz's essays on Indonesia that yoked culture to performance were being written and distributed. These were tumultuous times for performers in Bali – quite different from what might be expected from Geertz's writings – and the differences serve as a warning and a challenge to performance studies.

A few years before these killings, Geertz had returned from Indonesia to the United States to convert his Balinese fieldnotes into books and articles. These came out in rapid succession, from 1963 to 1967. In 1972, after further fieldwork, he added "Deep Play: Notes on a Balinese Cockfight,"[5] and in 1973 he republished the essays on Bali and others in *The Interpretation of Cultures*.[6] The Bali he describes is a place outside linear time – where life is cyclically renewed by the reintroduction of the past into the present in elaborate ceremonies that provide the standards for an essentially unchanging "web" of symbolic actions that both reveals and determines "Balinese culture." Geertz's "Balinese," "de-personalized and de-temporalized," "live their social life in a vectorless now,"[7] in "a haze of ceremony,"[8] as participants in a "theatre state in which kings and princes are impresarios, the priests the directors, and the peasantry the supporting cast, stage crew, and audience."[9] In Geertz's Bali "power serves pomp, not pomp power."[10] It is "a steady state," impervious to history, and with a marked preference, in life and in art, to avoid climactic events, such as – specifically – the killing of one human being by another.[11]

Why this disparity between the Bali Geertz describes and the one that was emerging at the exact time of his writing? How could he have gotten it so wrong? Why did the tumultuous events in Bali receive so little attention from him even as the essays were revised and republished – especially when (as we now know from a parenthetical note written three decades later) thirty families were burned alive on one horrific night in the Balinese village that Geertz had made his home?[12] Decades later, with other critical models in place, what are we to learn from this disjunction?

In Geertz's semiotic approach the "web of significance" that constitutes "culture" is to be read as one reads a text, or "ensemble of texts," "over the shoulders" of the Balinese as they go about their lived lives.[13] Of course, when looking over shoulders, one cannot see faces. The makers of those webs lack individuated form; they are, always, "the Balinese." Dwight Conquergood[14] and Vincent Crapanzano[15] have already noted the limited and limiting use of this visual metaphor, and the Sri Lankan anthropologist Gannath Obeyesekere has wryly commented that, "in reading Geertz, one sees webs everywhere, but never the spider at work."[16] Problems of imagery and metaphor aside, though, if culture is viewed and comprehended "as we read a text," how did Geertz – a would-be novelist and English and Philosophy major before he took up Anthropology in graduate school – assume that texts are to be read? This matter is crucial to performance studies – so dependent upon and influenced by the critical models that inform it.

A revealing footnote in *The Interpretation of Cultures* refers readers seeking critical models to René Wellek and Austin Warren's New Critical *Theory of Literature* (1949) and to works by members of the Chicago School of neo-Aristotelean philosopher-critics.[17] In a brilliant and paradoxical move, Geertz applied the methods and assumptions of New Criticism to cultural contexts, just as those methods had lost their patina of newness and were coming under fire for their dubious pretensions to objectivity and inability to deal with diachronic changes – especially, and ironically, for their failure to factor in those social contexts that help determine and alter meaning.

New Criticism and neo-Aristotelean structuralism, deemphasizing issues of politics and power and privileging formal integrity over authorial intent, were welcomed by scholars stung by Stalinism and fascism and laboring in the shadow of McCarthyite purges. The approach thrived: a complex surface gives way, through close reading, to ultimate unity – once the text is read with sufficient care and cunning. Citing W. K. Wimsatt's "explicative holism," Mark Spilka, in his 1961 critique, summarizes this "blend of theory and practice" as "the careful analysis of specific texts considered as autonomous wholes."[18] The final words of *The Interpretation of Culture* elegantly reformulate the *a priori* foundation of New Critical interpretive strategies: "Societies, like lives, contain their own interpretations. One only has to learn how to gain access to them."[19] The Balinese culture that Geertz describes is composed of intricate webs, spun by a species that (uniformly, it seems) conceives of life in aesthetic rather than political terms. No less than T. S. Eliot's *The Waste Land* or James Joyce's *Ulysses* (both 1922), Geertz's Bali is a modernist masterpiece, balancing complexity and unity. Of course, Geertz also warns, "there is nothing so coherent as a paranoid's delusion or a swindler's story."[20]

But Geertz was neither paranoid nor a swindler. He did not simply make up the textlike Bali he described. Leaving Bali in 1958 (the year of an election hotly contested between Nationalists and Socialists, but before obvious signs of the disasters to come), he absorbed and made his own a utopian view of Balinese life often expressed by the priests, princes, and artists, who were no doubt his informants. While Carol Warren has chided Geertz for his overreliance on "elite truths" that lead to "an illusory integrity,"[21] Geertz's influence on the understanding of Balinese performance still bulks large, not just for anthropologists, but, implicitly, for "the Balinese" themselves: the notion of Balinese culture as an "autonomous whole" functions complexly in current Balinese discourses about tourism and development, sometimes (as in Geertz's writings) working to obscure operations of power and wealth.[22] More to the point, the modeling of "culture" exemplified by his essays on Balinese life has deeply influenced the field of performance studies, even though it has been countered by more politically focused (though not necessarily less reductive) models of "culture." What is to be salvaged? And what needs to be rethought?

Performance studies both draws from and challenges anthropological assumptions. Geertz's approach to "culture" as revealed in performed actions and his depiction of a "theatre state" have obvious appeal. Yet, despite all the drumbeating for "thick description," he rarely describes specific events and never the actions of specific performers. "Balinese culture" – both a product of "interpretation" and a heuristic concept used in the interpreting – assumes problematic agency. Performances have proven difficult for anthropologists trying to determine an "ethos" or "worldview." Performers play fast and loose with rules and expectations, often confronting, confounding, and slip-sliding around taboos. They tend to play between precedent and the unprecedented, the past and the present. Grounded in the familiar, performances seek out the novel, the extra-ordinary. They complicate as well as suggest structuralist dyads. Inescapably public, they insist on the primacy of the particular and the immediate.

Recent scholarship has supplanted Geertz's "theatre state" with far more dynamic, less "steady" views of Balinese history. These works include the first sustained account of Bali in the tumultuous years of the 1960s, Geoffrey Robinson's *The Dark Side of Paradise: Political Violence in Bali*.[23] Robinson, though, determined that he had to all but ignore the performance-oriented anthropological descriptions of Balinese life; they simply did not jibe with the political events.[24] Robinson's work has now been joined by the ongoing studies of Leslie Dwyer and the Balinese anthropologist Degung Santikarma.[25] While they stress how ritual patterns were appropriated and disrupted during the time of the killings, little work has been done on the overall role of performance, or on the effect of the killings on Balinese performance and performers.[26] In the discourses of performance studies, Bali is still, most often, stuck in the never-never land of the anthropological present. If Bali is a "text," however, it is a messy one, with agents and patterns of action and signification very much vulnerable to linear time. Bali's "culture," like all cultures, is always in process and deeply contested by the people whose disparate and sometimes conflicting lives constitute its being.

Performance in the years of living dangerously

I came to Bali thirty-three years ago, as a theatre director trying to learn how to use masks. In the process of seeing shadow shows and masked dances, bending my body into alien forms, and (literally as well as figuratively) "finding my feet,"[27] I began to hear stories about what it was like to be a performer in the dark days of 1965–6. Only much later, when General Suharto's New Order was gone and the world seemed somewhat less dangerous, did I pursue these stories in a more organized way. What follows are a few examples from what will be a longer work setting forth the stories entrusted to me.

As I heard these accounts, it struck me that they almost never started with the killings. Usually, the stories started with the rats. In 1961–2 there was a plague of field rats in the rice paddies. No one had seen such huge rats before, and the result of this infestation was a growing famine. This brought into focus inequalities in the distribution of wealth and power in Bali's semifeudal economic system – issues that found their way into performance, often, though not always, viewed through the lens of a growing Marxist movement.

Balinese performance practice is marked not only by highly constrained patterns of movement, music, and narrative structure, but also by a high degree of improvisation and reflexivity. Traditional forms are given theatrical life and familiar stories are retold in accordance with the appropriateness to "*desa, kala*, and *patra*": place, time, and circumstance.[28] Stories themselves rise and fall in popularity in relation to their "fit" with contemporary concerns and can be reshaped to accommodate a better "fit." During the early 1960s, one story that grew in popularity told of the arrival in Bali, during the sixteenth century, of a strange, ugly priest, known at first as "Brahmana Keling," whose initial rejection precipitated famine and disaster for the royal family of Gelgel and the Balinese people, and whose eventual incorporation into Balinese society is emblematic of the utopian principle of achieving harmony through a balancing of inclinations, interests, and powers. This is how I Gusti Ngurah Windia suggests that a Topeng *penasar* (narrator and clown for the masked theatre of Bali), performing in 1961, might have laid out the situation:

> There was no food, no rice. The harvest was not successful. First locusts were in the field, then rats. Huge rats! Thousands of them! I wanted to sacrifice an animal, but the animals all died. All but the rats! Beh! The rats were very healthy! Finally there was help from the gods. Brahmana Keling completed the ceremony and forever more will be known as Sidha Karya – he who completes the sacred work.[29]

Those familiar with Victor Turner and Richard Schechner's principle of an infinite loop between "social dramas" and "cultural performances" will recognize what seems a perfect example here as, in performance, a semi-historical tale from the sixteenth century picks up immediate referents to the events of 1961.[30] But in Bali (as elsewhere), "cultural performances" and "social dramas" are not always so neatly separable. To deal with the rats, Dewa Agung Oka Geg, Raja of Klungkung and first among equals of the princes of Bali, declared that, whatever their purpose, the rats must have been sent by the gods and so ordered cremations of "Jero Ketut" ("Most Honorable Little Brother"). All over Bali mounds of dead rats were piled high and set ablaze, while priests politely thanked these unlikely emissaries for their visit and asked them not to return.[31]

Meanwhile, grander plans were afoot to purify the island ceremonially. A celebration of Eka Dasa Rudra – a major purification rite supposed to be held every 100 Balinese "years" (each lasting 210 days) – was in the works. Endorsed by Bali's left-leaning, high-caste Governor, Anak Agung Suteja, and spurred on by the recent infestation of rats and a desire to please the half-Balinese President Sukarno, the event was to show the workability of NASAKOM – the unlikely fusion of nationalism, religion (*agama*) and communism that Sukarno espoused. Bali would be an example of the national and the local working in harmony. Pomp would serve power. While some pundits argued that the ceremony was not due until 1979, a constellation of unlikely allies pressed to advance the calendar. Advocates included I Gde Puger, an influential leftist businessman, and the Hindu Dharma Parishad, a council on Balinese religion that, in 1962, was finally winning the long battle to have Balinese Hinduism recognized as an acceptable state religion. A reluctant Dewa Agung Oka Geg agreed to officiate and elaborate plans were made to hold the event at Besakih temple, high on the slopes of Bali's most sacred mountain, Gunung Agung.[32]

The decision to go forward generated a need to prepare the island ritually. All cremations had to be completed before the great ceremony; this imposed a great financial strain on a people already reeling from infestation and famine, and incited discussions about the amount of funds expended on ritual ceremonies. Amid considerable controversy, the plans proceeded. The events of Eka Dasa Rudra were to start on March 17, 1963. On February 19 Gunung Agung, a long-dead volcano, came rumbling and sputtering to life. Nevertheless, the Raja and his advisors decided to go ahead, though cutting some corners: there would be no walking to the top of the newly active volcano.

The inaugural ceremonies were marked by disaster – or, according to some instant interpreters, spectacular success. The great mountain erupted, literally blowing its top, sending tons of debris and hot lava down its sides, and killing more than 1,500 people. Ni Made Tjandri, then a teacher in Sabuti, on the volcano, watched in horror from a nearby town as 700 of the 1,100 villagers, including most of her students, were swept away under a wave of molten lava and rock. As disaster approached, the village's *gamelan angklung* ensemble (who usually performed for cremations) set up their instruments and played, accepting their hopeless situation with *nyupat* – an offering of one's self to death. Elsewhere, music was used to defy the seeming will of nature. In the mountain village of Iseh, villagers challenged the lava flow by playing on a set of small metal gongs in a *bebonang* ensemble; the lava is said to have stopped just short of the village.

Initial press responses to the eruptions saw them as auspicious signs of divine presence. As the death toll mounted and reports of devastation in the countryside came in, however, the commentary shifted. What had provoked the gods' evident wrath? Was it the advanced date for Eka Dasa Rudra? Flaws in preparations, too many corners cut? A punishment for the greed of the aristocracy? Or, as an influential chorus began to insist, the godlessness of the communists?

In the five years leading up to this time, there had been a general movement toward overtly politicizing the performing arts in Bali. PKI and PNI (Nationalist Party) factions emerged in every town. In general, the PKI set itself against the feudal prerogatives of the *triwangsa* castes (*wesia, ksatriya,* and *brahmana*), and tried to establish itself as the champion of the *jaba* peasantry. But many members of the *triwangsa* (including Governor Suteja and the wealthy Puger) were themselves left-leaning; and many of the *jaba* caste were inclined towards the PNI and suspicious of the PKI's ambitions. Political sloganeering and pressures pervaded Balinese life. Even the cockfights later aestheticized and "interpreted" by Geertz featured PKI and PNI roosters, adding another subtext to the fervid betting.

Both parties had programs of support for artists: LEKRA (People's League of Artists) and LKN (Nationalist Artists League). LEKRA, in particular, appealed to the shadow puppeteers (*dalang*) of Bali's Wayang Kulit puppet theatre and the *penasar* of Topeng, supplying new puppets or masks in exchange for support. These performers had long functioned as teachers of moral philosophy. Although the tendency in Wayang and Topeng to treat matters in multivalent and irreverent ways sometimes ran counter to the desire for unambiguous political messages, many artists took up the cause – and the largesse.

One LEKRA-supported shadow puppeteer, known as Dalang Bungkasa, performing at a gathering for the communist mayor of Gianyar, presented a Wayang based on a well-known incident from the *Ramayana* (*Anggada Duta*). In his version the demon King Rahwana talks with Rama's messenger – the red monkey Anggada – reminding the young emissary how Rama unfairly killed his father, questioning faithfulness to such a lord, and mocking Rama's pretensions to godliness and the system of "justice" that Rama administered. In this unique retelling Anggada joined in solidarity with Rahwana against Rama. The familiar epic cannot and did not end this way, but a social critique was powerfully made. The past is indeed important to Balinese performance, but not in a "vectorless" way. The meaning of the past in relation to the present is very much up for grabs; and in the 1960s the stakes – both personal and social – could be very high. Dalang Bungkasa was killed in 1966, and so were many other shadow puppeteers.

The most politicized form of entertainment – and the most popular among the young during this period – was Janger. On the surface this variety show and flirtatious display by young men and women is an unlikely carrier of political energy, but each village had Janger clubs affiliated with PKI and PNI factions. Shows included poeticized trash-talking, and one PKI troupe put on a martial arts display using hammers and sickles. The best chance for propaganda, though, was in the short playlets, or Sandiwara, featured in Janger. These sketches, performed in Bahasa Indonesian, not Balinese, blended melodrama and humor and were blatant agit-prop. PNI troupes performed skits stressing the appropriate functions of various castes in creating a harmonious society and the need to retain "Balinese values" within a new national identity. PKI Sandiwara stressed the inequities of the current social order and the need for a redistribution of land and wealth. It is tempting, but too simple, to label those in the PNI traditionalists and those in the PKI modernists. Neither would see their desires reflected in Geertz's description of a "steady state" outside of time.

Many artists resisted this conversion of the traditional function of moral education in Wayang and Topeng to partisan advocacy. Sometimes the words used could resonate with Geertz's view of Balinese culture: "What makes a whole? If you separate part from part, then everything breaks down. The separate parts may wither and die. Just like a flame. You can't separate the oil from the wick if you wish light and warmth."[33] Avoiding overt political dimensions to performance became much more difficult, though, after September 30, 1965: Gerakan September Tiga Pulu – a date tortured into the acronym GESTAPU. In the official account of that day, there was a deadly, botched attempt on the part of leftist generals to gain control over the military. The coup was ruthlessly suppressed by General Suharto's troops, who eventually managed to seize control of the government from President Sukarno. The roles of Sukarno, Suharto, and the CIA are all contested by historians. What is clear is that the failed coup provided "a pretext for mass murder."[34]

Reportage of the events was sensational. Members of the Gerwani, the PKI women's auxiliary, were said to have danced naked, chopping off genitals and stuffing them in the mouths of murdered conservative generals.[35] However fanciful, these reports from Jakarta resonated powerfully in Bali with images from *Calonarang* performances of the horrific witch and her maddened, transformed female followers, the *leyak*: "Her eyes were red and her body naked. Her hair hung loose in front of her."[36] "Hair down and wild, leg up, tongue extended, her eyes shining like twin suns. That's how a woman transforms herself into a leyak."[37] As Leslie Dwyer observes, "A symbolic resonance was thus constructed between the political left and the magical left, and women's sexuality and men's disempowerment."[38] Gerwani members were targeted for rape, as well as death.

Shortly after the GESTAPU, the killings started in and around Jakarta, and slowly spread east toward Bali. The army arrived in December, forming death squads and encouraging bands of young Balinese males (*tamin*) to "cleanse the land" of "atheism." Army death squads and bands of *tamin* went from compound to compound in the unlit villages of Bali, dragging people from their homes to be slaughtered. Sometimes public executions were staged, with victims treated like suckling pigs at Gulungan feasts before they were killed. This grotesque surrogation was carried to its logical extreme as I Gde Puger, the portly, once powerful force behind the PKI, while still alive, had slices of fat publicly cut from his body.[39]

Sometimes those targeted for death presented themselves for *nyupat*. Governor Suteja, dressed in white, made public confession of his shortcomings and was publicly killed with his own family dagger (*keris*). In Batubulan, Sukawati, and other southern villages, eerie stories are repeated of lines of people dressed in white, walking peacefully with their executioners to the killing grounds.[40] Scenes of dignified surrender to unjust yet inevitable death are common in Balinese myth and theatre:

> JAPYAPRANA: If I am wrong in the eyes of the king, then kill me, please.
> My love, I must leave now to die. Take care.[41]

A pattern of death unique to Bali was the killing of one family member by another. By poison and by sword, father killed son and son killed father, husband wife and wife husband. Rather than be killed by marauding soldiers or *tamin*, or in a public spectacle, those marked for erasure asked to die at the hands of their loved ones, in the family compound, ensuring a better passage to *suarga* (heaven) and return to earth through reincarnation in the same family.[42] Often a meal was shared before the killing. Again, this scenario was foreshadowed and "rehearsed" through performance. In one of the heart-pieces of the Topeng repertoire, Dalem Bungkut, Raja of Nusa Penida, finds that the warrior Jelantik possesses the only weapon (a magical serpent's tooth) that can take his life and end his rule: "Patih Jelantik, let's do this among ourselves, just you and me. Before you match your strength against mine, please share a meal with me. If I die and my soul is ready to be released to heaven, I ask that you provide the cremation ceremony."[43] A second wave of deaths occurred two to three years after 1966. This time, the deaths were suicides, often by those who could no longer bear having killed their family members and neighbors.

While many performers worked to stem the murderous tide with appeals to unity and diversity, others fomented the terror. In Kesiman, on the margin of the capital city, Denpasar, there was ongoing debate about the lavish expenditures required by Balinese ritual practices. Some of the "reformers" argued for the replacement of *gamelan* instruments with guitars.[44] In response, one villager – not a regular performer – enacted the story of Mayadanawa – a shape-shifting Buddhist king who defies Indra and is eventually killed by him. In Kesiman this masked demonic figure became a raging atheistic buffoon, desecrating offerings brought to the temple by kicking them over and pretending to urinate on them: "Hey, you! People of Bali! Why are you giving all those offerings to the gods? The gods are in me! This is your god! ... This is the first real god. Me!"[45] The blasphemy of such speeches had an unmistakable referent, and the performance effectively stirred up murderous feelings against the religious reformers, as well as those who had worked in concert with the PKI.

As the killings continued, gathering up local grudges, even the army commander in Bali saw that things had got out of control.[46] Among some there was a sense, reinforced by suddenly popular Wayang performances that narrated the death of Krishna's entire clan in the *Mahabharata,* that the end times of *Kali Yuga* were at hand, that a final battle between good and evil had been joined. One former leader of a mountain village told me that he ordered the deaths of his family members, believing this to be a divine imperative.

With the slaughter working its way around the island, students and faculty at the recently formed high school of the performing arts (KOKAR) huddled together in a circle, while communist "tendencies" and "indications" were discussed and life and death decisions made. Two teachers were killed in the early days of the massacre, and early in 1966 classes were suspended and the students sent back to their villages. Students and faculty together had just staged *The Ramayana Ballet,* a syncretic work that deployed Balinese, Javanese, and Western techniques to depict the life of an idealized epic hero and *avatar* of Visnu. The student who had assumed the role of Rama was I Made Landra. Before heading home, Landra told friends that he had presentiments of his own death; he had attended meetings of the PKI youth organization in his village and had reason for concern. He, too, was killed. In a grotesque irony, the "traditionalists" killed Rama.

In the midst of the terrible killings, in one of the hardest-hit regions, "Made Pegeg" (not his real name) was appalled to find children of his neighborhood miming executions. One of his own children, obviously disturbed, was spontaneously going into a violent trance. "Pegeg" was himself a participant in the local *Calonarang* group which, in the Pengosekan tradition, turned their swords violently on each other in trance, rather than follow the more familiar pattern of "self-stabbing." "Pegeg" decided that the children would be better off focusing and containing their tension, fear, and aggression in a performative frame, and started a unique children's *Calonarang* group. The spontaneous trance seizures stopped and the children seemed better able to cope with the tumultuous events around them.

New forms of theatre emerged in the wake of the killings. Drama Gong – a genre that deemphasized ritual and dance – recycled some of the conventions of Sandiwara and stressed broad sexual humor. As the playwright and novelist Putu Wijaya noted, while ready for jokes the world of Drama Gong – far more than that of Topeng or Arja – reflected a scene of chaos: it was "touched by craziness."[47] This turn away from political humor was reflected in Wayang and Topeng as well. As one veteran performer stated, "We got very careful about our jokes." Perhaps the most significant initiative was the founding of ASTI (now ISI) as a College of the Arts in 1967, spurred on by the deaths of so many senior artists. Its founding was an attempt to do institutionally what had proven impossible historically: to balance tradition and innovation in a society looking for both a national and a supranational/local identity.

By the time of Geertz's last visit to Bali, officials of Suharto's New Order were using performers for the promotion of government programs such as family planning. Beneath a charming surface lingered unspoken sadness, unresolved tensions, and the dread that the killings could some day begin again. Included in *The Interpretation of Cultures* is a 1972 book review that significantly fails to mention Bali. Geertz notes, however, "a sense that something has happened for which no one was prepared, and about which no one yet quite knows what to say . . . There can be very few Indonesians now who do not know that, however clouded, the abyss is there, and they are scrambling along the edge of it."[48]

Reinterpreting culture

A possible interpretation of events, and one heard, essentially, in Bali, is that Geertz was right in his approach. Balinese culture was too well defined and strongly entrenched to allow the PKI to make lasting inroads. I have heard several Balinese artists say that the great mistake of the 1950s and early 1960s was to allow the arts to become so politicized, and that, when all is said and done, "the Balinese care more about culture (*kebudayaan*) than politics." I have also heard them say that the killings of 1965–6 were a rejection of such intrusive politics. To oppose "culture" and "politics" in this way, however, creates a mistaken impression. These same artists, while often critical of affiliations with specific political parties, continually use their performances to raise social issues that, in the broader sense of the word, are inherently "political." Note, too, the complex interplay of performative traditions, sociopolitical events, and individual actions in the stories related above. What emerges is a pattern of Balinese people making aesthetic, personal, and political choices in a complex field of cross-referenced behavior, where social events are contextualized in and as performance, and where performances both analogically reflect upon and help shape sociopolitical events. In 1995 Geertz wrote, "it is no more possible to escape the situational immediacies of ethnographical knowing ... than it is to escape its temporal bounds, and it is perhaps even more mischievous to pretend to do so ... You may set out to isolate yourself from cosmopolitan concerns and contain your interests within hermetical contexts. But the concerns follow you. The contexts explode."[49] One hears sadness and regret, not only for lives lost, but for a masterpiece diminished.

Do we then simply abandon an interpretive approach to culture as "a license for mischief"?[50] And, if so, at what cost? Leslie Dwyer and Degung Santikarma, while praising Robinson for laying bare the constellations of power at stake and for refusing to see "exoticized cultural difference" as an explanation for the violence in Bali, conclude that only by understanding the semiotic as well as the political roles that ritual aspects played in the violence can we obtain "a clear picture of the events."[51] Despite Robinson's jettisoning of Bali's "cultural" exceptionalism – and, with it, the centrality of performance in Balinese life – it is clear that most of the capsule narratives above are specific to Bali; they could not happen elsewhere – not in the same way. And it is a set – or several overlapping sets – of commonly held, if frequently contested, concerns, stories, and ritual and theatrical practices that make this so.

Fredrik Barth suggests that "culture" is best conceived of, not as a schematic web, but as a set of processes sometimes reflecting tentative consensus and subject to constant contestation.[52] Frequently the stories told above exhibit a modeling of behavior influenced by myth and the precedents of performance. Expanding Geertz's famous aphorism, performance becomes a "model *for*" as well as a "model *of*" not only "religious belief," but also social action.[53] But these stories also show a range of difference in the interpretation and embodiment of the (sometimes contradictory) belief systems underlying Balinese "culture." "The Balinese" shared then and share now a set of references, images, genres, and stories. As Barth argues, they did not and do not subscribe to a uniform "ethos" or "worldview" made from a consistent "stratified hierarchy of meaningful structures."[54]

Barth's observations represent one strand in the recent search by anthropologists to redefine "culture" in a less teleological, ahistorical, impersonal, and "holistic" way, and to seek out a more appropriate set of critical models. Mark Hobart has employed a "dialogic" model inspired by Mikhail Bakhtin's concept of "heteroglossia" that aligns well with Balinese aesthetic practices.[55] Sherry B. Ortner, drawing upon Geertz's implicitly "actor-centered" approach, has supported a greater role for "agency" – recognizing the distribution of power within societies while also accounting for "the pressures of desires and understandings and intentions on cultural constructions" as individuals play their "serious games."[56] The sociologist Jorge Arditi has called for "a theory... capable of accounting, simultaneously, for the unity and autonomy of mental and social structures."[57]

It may well prove useful to think of "culture" as located and constantly contested in sets of individual brains subject to overlapping phenomena (visual, linguistic, narrative, kinetic) and making nonstereotypical sense of these phenomena in relation to constantly shifting (but frequently familiar) circumstances affecting (in sometimes radically different ways) people constituting what might be described as a "distributed network." There is something at stake here besides the dubious upgrade to a newer scientific jargon. The results from the incorporation of this conceptual underpinning may lack some of the grand cohesion of Geertz's Bali, but it may be easier to make a space for individual Balinese people – and for divergent ways of living – within shifting cultural contexts.

Hobart says that he began his study of Balinese culture by asking villagers how he should study Balinese life. Their answer: attend to the theatre.[58] As Barth and Hobart both suggest, Bali is not a puzzle to solve, nor, finally, a "text" to master; it is not a state made "steady" by the interventions of performance, and not a modernist masterpiece. It is, though, a place where, for anthropology, for historiography, and, perhaps, for more people than in most places, performance matters. And that makes it, still, an important place for those who would seek to understand better the role of performance in the construction of societies and lives.

Notes

1. Research for this project has been supported by the Watson Institute and Office of Research, Brown University. For the approximation of 80,000, see "Dewa" (Sue Hok Gie) in Robert Cribb, ed., *The Indonesian Killings 1965–66: Studies from Java and Bali* (Clayton, Victoria: Centre of Southeast Asian Studies, Monash University, 1990), 256. Leslie Dwyer and Degung Santikarma suggest

that 100,000 is more likely; see "When the World Turned to Chaos: 1965 and its Aftermath in Bali, Indonesia," in Robert Gellately and Ben Kiernan, eds., *The Specter of Genocide: Mass Murder in Historical Perspective* (Cambridge and New York: Cambridge University Press, 2003), 290.

2. See Dwyer and Santikarma, "When the World," 300–1.
3. Robert Cribb, "Introduction: Problems in the Historiography of the Killings in Indonesia," in Cribb, ed., *The Indonesian Killings*, 2–43.
4. CIA, Directorate of Intelligence, *Indonesia – 1965, the Coup that Backfired* (Washington, DC, 1968). Names of at least 5,000 PKI leaders and cadres were given to the Indonesian government. See Cribb, "Introduction," 7.
5. Clifford Geertz, "Deep Play: Notes on a Balinese Cockfight," *Daedalus* 101 (1972), 1–37.
6. Clifford Geertz, *The Interpretation of Cultures* (New York: Basic Books, 1973).
7. *Ibid.*, 5, 334, 391, 404.
8. *Ibid.*, 400.
9. *Ibid.*, 335.
10. *Ibid.*
11. *Ibid.*, 334, 379, 403–4. As Geertz notes, Gregory Bateson first used the term "steady state" in reference to Bali. See Bateson, "Bali: The Value System of a Steady State," in Jane Belo, ed., *Traditional Balinese Culture* (New York: Columbia University Press, 1970), 384–401. Geertz considerably expanded on Bateson's observations.
12. Clifford Geertz, *After the Fact: Two Countries, Four Decades, One Anthropologist* (Cambridge, MA: Harvard University Press, 1995), 8.
13. Geertz, *Interpretation of Cultures*, 5, 10, 452.
14. Dwight Conquergood, "Performance Studies: Interventions and Radical Research," *TDR: The Drama Review* 46.2 (Summer 2002), 149–50.
15. Vincent Crapanzano, "Hermes' Dilemma: The Masking of Subversion in Ethnographic Description," in James Clifford and George E. Marcus, eds., *Writing Culture: The Poetics and Politics of Ethnography* (Berkeley: University of California Press, 1986), 51–76.
16. Gannath Obeyesekere, *The Work of Culture: Symbolic Transformation in Psychoanalysis and Anthropology* (Chicago: University of Chicago Press, 1990), 285. For a summary of Geertz's critics, see Sherry B. Ortner, "Introduction," in Ortner, ed., *The Fate of "Culture": Geertz and Beyond* (Berkeley: University of California Press, 1999), 1–14.
17. Geertz, *Interpretation of Cultures*, 208, n. 20. See also René Wellek and Austin Warren, *Theory of Literature* (New York: Harcourt Brace, 1949).
18. Mark Spilka, "The Necessary Stylist: A New Critical Revision," *Modern Fiction Studies* 6 (Winter 1960–1), 329.
19. Geertz, *Interpretation of Cultures*, 453.
20. *Ibid.*, 18.
21. Carol Warren, "Disrupted Death Ceremonies: Popular Culture and the Ethnography of Bali," *Oceania* 64 (1993), 36–56.
22. See Graeme MacRae, "Negara Ubud: The Theatre-State in Twenty-First Century Bali," *History and Anthropology* 16.4 (December 2005), 393–413.
23. Geoffrey Robinson, *The Dark Side of Paradise: Political Violence in Bali* (Ithaca, NY: Cornell University Press, 1995).

24. *Ibid.*, 7–9.
25. See Dwyer and Santikarma, "When the World," and Leslie Dwyer, "The Intimacy of Terror: Gender and the Violence of 1965–66 in Bali," *Intersections: Gender, History and Culture in the Asian Context* 10 (August 2004), 1–17.
26. An exception is Garrett Kam's fictional account, *Midnight Shadows: A Tale of Mysticism and Morality* (Victoria, Canada: Trafford, 2003).
27. Cf. Geertz, *Interpretation of Cultures*, 13.
28. See John Emigh, *Masked Performance: The Play of Self and Other in Ritual and Theatre* (Philadelphia: University of Pennsylvania Press, 1996), 171–206.
29. Balinese performances, while employing known stories and practiced set pieces, are usually improvised. Lacking "playscripts," I have asked senior artists to improvise sections of dialogue within the given circumstances of the 1960s.
30. Victor Turner, *The Anthropology of Performance* (New York: PAJ Publications, 1986), 33–44, 104–7, and Richard Schechner, *Essays on Peformance Theory 1970–76* (New York: Drama Book Specialists, 1977), 140–4.
31. I have relied on interviews with many people, conducted 1975–2005, for the capsule stories that follow. These include I Wayan Suweca, I Nyoman Sumandhi, I Made Bandem, I Wayan Dibia, I Gusti Bagus Nyoman Pandji, Anak Agung Made Djelantik, I Made Sija, Ida Bagus Anom, Ida Bagus Suteja, I Ketut Kodi, I Nyoman Catra, I Nyoman Ceritra, I Ketut Kantor, I Wayan Wija, Kadek Suardana, Putu Wijaya, Luh Ketut Suryani, Tjokorda Gde Dangin, and Ni Nyoman Candri. Others have asked to remain anonymous. There was a time, not long ago, when it was dangerous to tell such stories. I have therefore not yet cited specific unpublished sources for events.
32. Apart from interviews, the account that follows is stitched together from: Anna Mathews, *The Night of Purnama* (Kuala Lumpur, 1983; London: Jonathan Cape, 1985); Adrian Vickers, *Bali: A Paradise Created* (New York: Penguin, 1989), 167; F. L. Bakker, *The Struggle of the Hindu Balinese Intellectuals: Developments in Modern Hindu Thinking in Independent Indonesia* (Amsterdam: VU Press, 1993), 236; and Robert Pringle, *A Short History of Bali, Indonesia's Hindu Realm* (Crow's Nest, Australia: Allen and Unwin, 2004), 172–5.
33. Dialogue by I Gusti Ngurah Windia.
34. John Roosa, *Pretext for Mass Murder: The September 30th Movement and Suharto's Coup D'Etat in Indonesia* (Madison: University of Wisconsin Press, 2006).
35. Cribb, "Introduction," 29, 47.
36. I Made Bandem and Fredrik Eugene DeBoer, *Balinese Dance in Transition: Kaja and Kelod* (1981), 2nd edn (Kuala Lumpur: Oxford University Press, 1995), 112.
37. Dialogue by I Made Sija.
38. Dwyer, "Intimacy of Terror," 9.
39. Cribb, "Introduction," 30.
40. John Hughes, *The End of Sukarno: A Coup That Misfired; A Purge That Ran Wild* (1967), 3rd edn (Singapore: Archipelago Press, 2002), 191.
41. Dialogue by I Gusi Ngurah Windia.
42. Dwyer and Santikarma, "When the World," 297, and several interviews.
43. Dialogue by I Gusti Ngurah Windia.
44. Degung Sanikarma, interview, 2005.

45. Dialogue by I Nyoman Sedana.
46. Robinson, *The Dark Side of Paradise*, 295–6.
47. See Fredrik DeBoer, "Two Modern Balinese Theatre Genres: *Sendratari* and *Drama Gong*," in Adrian Vickers, ed., *Being Modern in Bali: Image and Change* (New Haven: Yale University Press, 1996), 158–78.
48. Geertz, *Interpretation of Cultures*, 323.
49. Geertz, *After the Fact*, 17, 95.
50. Mark A. Schneider, "Culture-as-Text in the Work of Clifford Geertz," *Theory and Society* 16.6 (November 1987), 833.
51. Dwyer and Santikarma, "When the World," 302–3.
52. Fredrik Barth, *Balinese Worlds* (Chicago: University of Chicago Press, 1993), 3–8.
53. Geertz, *Interpretation of Cultures*, 118.
54. *Ibid.*, 7.
55. Mark Hobart, "Live or Dead? How Dialogic is Theatre in Bali?," in Adrian Vickers and I Nyoman Darma Putra, eds., *To Change Bali: Essays in Honor of I Gusti Njurah Bagus* (Denpasar: Bali Post and the University of Wollongong, 2000), 183–212.
56. Sherry B. Ortner, "Thick Resistance: Death and the Cultural Construction of Agency in Himalayan Mountaineering," in Ortner, ed., *The Fate of "Culture,"* 136–63.
57. Jorge Arditi, "Geertz, Kuhn and the Idea of a Cultural Paradigm," *The British Journal of Sociology* 45.4 (December, 1994), 597–617.
58. Hobart, "Live or Dead?," 184–5.

5

SUSAN BENNETT

Universal experience: the city as tourist stage

Point of entry

My destination is "Universal Experience: Art, Life, and the Tourist Eye," an exhibition exploring the phenomenon of global tourism, at the Hayward gallery in London's Southbank Centre.[1] The irony is that I can't find the entrance to the Hayward[2] despite the fact that I'm a native Londoner and have been going to the gallery since it opened in 1968, and despite the fact that I'm now a tourist in London (living away from the city for more than twenty years) and so, apparently, hailed by the exhibition's claim to universality. But, then again, I've never been able to find the entrance to the Hayward. Although the building is easily visible from street level, and stairways and walkways provide helpful signage, the actual entrance is obscure and absorbed into an unrelenting concrete landscape, populated chiefly by the usual skateboarders and other (lost?) cultural visitors.

The Hayward was designed by the Department of Architecture and Civic Design of the then Greater London Council (GLC) to be a significant cultural contribution in the ongoing renaissance of central London in the postwar period. Notably, some of the department's staff were contributors to the 1960s avant-garde architectural magazine *Archigram*, and today the Hayward is often heralded as a textbook example of Brutalist architecture championed by, among others, the Archigram Group.[3] The gallery is elevated above street level, a severe mass of concrete among multilevel surfaces, connecting walkways, and oddly positioned circular staircases; as critics often observe, this part of London's Southbank Centre complex more resembles a public car park than a cultural space. And, in this vein, the Hayward is perhaps best captured by the architectural critic Hugh Pearman: "this is uncompromising concrete at its most heavyweight, most muscular, most brutal. But I do like it, for it is a unique record of the period. It is the Mike Tyson of arts buildings."[4] Others have been less disposed to see this as charming and the Hayward itself has apparently wrestled with its unwelcoming threshold: in 2003 a remodeling provided a new glass-fronted foyer to address access and other issues.[5]

Walking in the (tourist) city

This essay looks at how urban landscapes are revised and reinvigorated when they become marked as tourist attractions. The infrastructure of an area, cultural or otherwise, becomes in effect a series of performances directed at specific audiences with the intention of bringing them pleasure and equally, it must be said, inspiring them to spend. As Richard Schechner has suggested, "To satisfy an enormous and still rapidly growing market of intercultural, international, intracultural, and intranational tourists, performances of all kinds have been found, redesigned, or invented."[6] In this way cities become a subject of performance studies so as to elaborate the relationship between a particular iteration of urban space and those who use it (in Schechner's terms) for leisure globalization.[7] This is, of course, the organizing principle for Barbara Kirshenblatt-Gimblett's *Destination Culture*, where she writes that "tourism stages the world as a museum of itself, even as museums try to emulate the experience of travel. Indeed, museums – and the larger heritage industry of which they are part – play a vital role in creating the sense of 'hereness' necessary to convert a location into a destination."[8] The lens of performance studies is useful precisely because of its attentiveness to this sense of "hereness," or what Alan Blum would call the "scenes" of a city. In Blum's account "the culture of the city is located as much in its topography of scenes as in its formal institutions of 'high art' such as the ballet, opera, theatre district, museums, and galleries."[9] In other words, this is the distinction Schechner makes between "as" performance ("any and all of the activities of human life") and "is" performance ("when historical and social context, convention, usage, and tradition say it is").[10]

The occupation and interrogation of the full variety of a city's scenes constitute Joseph Roach's "vortices of behavior" that "frequently provide the crux in the semiotext of the circum-Atlantic cityscape – the grand boulevard, the marketplace, the theater district, the square, the burial ground – where the gravitational pull of social necessity brings audiences together and produces performers... from their midst."[11] Tourism's distinctive gravitational pull is necessarily vigorous and active in its mobilization of city scenes and active audiences. This crucial function for performance in an economy premised on tourist desire is equally recognized in tourism studies scholarship. Here the attributes of performance are deployed. Tim Edensor explains how locations become destinations:

Different tourist ventures are carried out upon particular stages – on beaches and mountains, in cities, heritage sites, museums and theme parks. These settings are distinguished by boundedness, whether physical or symbolic, and are often organized – or stage-managed – to provide and sustain common-sense understandings about what activities should take place. Indeed, the coherence of most tourist performances depends on their being performed in specific "theatres".[12]

I will return specifically to the Hayward and its "Universal Experience" exhibition, but I want now to look more broadly at the kinds of performances that tourism requires. Judith Adler sets what she calls the "baseline elements of any travel performance" as "space, time, and the design and pace of the traveler's movement through both."[13] Places, cities, regions, and countries in the tourism context are all composed as performances so that they might attract visitors' spectatorship, increasingly a lucrative part of the economy and, in very many cases, a primary engine for employment, growth, and vitality. "Situated in the relationship between tourist and site," writes Edensor, "performances map out individual and group identities, and allude to wider imagined geographies which the stage is part of and may even symbolize."[14] I am interested in how identity and tourism performances intersect in urban space and how, in this context, a performance studies methodology enables strategic rereadings of a city's "scenes." The mapping out of identity required by tourism practices and their audiences might, I suggest, rescript the quotidian with the effect of modeling identity anew.

It is useful to consider first how we have come to understand the modern city and the kinds of performances its streets evoke. The consummate actor for the modern city remains Walter Benjamin's *flâneur*, "the man who walks long and aimlessly through the streets. With each step, the walk takes on greater momentum; ever weaker grow the temptations of shops, of bistros, of smiling women, ever more irresistible the magnetism of the next streetcorner, of a distant mass of foliage, of a street name."[15] This city, then, provokes a masculinist map – interactions between building, space, and actor that work to limit and exclude those not hailed by the *flâneur*'s experience. It is a performance terrain that draws its principles from Benjamin's understanding of the seductions of the Paris arcades: at once a refuge from the harsher realities of industrialism and a site of pleasure and commodification. Such functionality, as Martin Selby has pointed out, is how the consumer came "to associate consumption with pleasure, a crucial aspect of contemporary urban tourism."[16] And, in this way, the *flâneur* takes the city as his stage and promotes his own peregrinations as the necessary action that enlivens the landscape for his consumption.

Of necessity, this performance of *flânerie* has had particular results for women; they appear only, for Benjamin, as one of the many temptations that the *flâneur* strives to resist. As Janet Wolff argues,

> The privilege of passing unnoticed in the city, particularly in the period in which the *flâneur* flourished . . . was not accorded to women, whose presence on the streets would certainly be noticed. Not only that – as many historians of the period have pointed out, women in public, and particularly women apparently wandering without aim, immediately attract the negative stamp of the "non-respectable." It is no accident that the prostitute appears as the central female trope in the discourse of modernity. The problem for women was their automatic identification with this "streetwalker" whenever they walked in the street.[17]

The difficult experience for women – captured succinctly in the aggregation of a "streetwalking" history – is surely not only evident in modernist discourse on the city but also remains fundamental to the actual practice of navigating urban space. For women living in cities (and elsewhere, too), there is, as a daily reality, a self-consciousness about walking. The contemporary artist Helen Scalway has commented,

> I could spend a long time trying to map the street in an A–Z of potential embarrassment, my own and other people's, on the pavements. For women, as anyone may observe (and theoreticians of the city often do), do not usually walk in an obviously purposeless way. They are everywhere, going about their business; their badge of respectability (that is actually vital to their safety) is that they are nearly always either carrying something or pushing something. This pushchair, bag, case, or letter may aid the necessary self-permission for the idle, pleasurable intention of going for a walk.[18]

Scalway's art practice examines her experience of London, as a woman navigating the streets and riding on public transport: "too long in some parts of London can leave me feeling ghost-like; not just disembodied, but actually, more dangerously, not entitled to a body."[19] Thus conventional wisdom inevitably tells us that the experience of the city is far from universal. It is asymmetrical, bifurcated on at least gender lines. Other identities, too, are rendered invisible, fragile, and marginal to the *flâneur*'s experience.

To return to my opening example of the brutalist landscape of the Southbank Centre, its architecture may symbolize London's phoenixlike return after the Second World War, it may celebrate the sculptural qualities of concrete, but it has also been a place where the *flâneuse* loitered only at her peril. More generally, certain areas and neighborhoods as well as the fall of darkness will be peculiarly marked, as potential danger zones on the *flâneuse*'s map. Not forgetting the everyday quality of gendered and other risks in urban environments, it is nonetheless helpful, too, to turn to Michel de Certeau's exemplary essay "Walking in the City" where he writes, "Walking affirms, suspects, tries out, transgresses, respects, etc., the trajectories it 'speaks.' All the modalities sing a part in this chorus, changing from step to step, stepping in through proportions, sequences, and intensities which vary according to the time, the path taken and the walker. These enunciatory operations are of an unlimited diversity."[20] Here is an outline of the performative encounter between cityscape and pedestrian, one that in its "unlimited diversity" suggests, provisionially at least, that the modernist scripts of gender need not always adhere or, at the very least, not just in a singular and coherent narrative. A revisionist, contemporary *flânerie*, occasioned by the economic and cultural ambitions of tourism, might transform the city's streets. As Selby has insisted, we should see "tourism as a cultural process, rather than a product."[21]

Certainly, urban tourism depends on the enthusiasm of audiences for cityscapes and, as Susan Fainstein and Dennis Judd point out, "[c]ities are sold just like any other consumer product... Each city tries to project itself as a uniquely wonderful place to visit, where an unceasing flow of events constantly unfolds."[22] In short, a city needs to attract a mobile and diverse population and make itself (safely) available to a motivated *flânerie*. To illustrate this dynamic relationship, captured by what Edensor sees as the performative turn of tourism, I turn again to London's South Bank district.[23]

Southbank performances

This south side of the River Thames has, of course, a distinguished place in the history of London entertainment: it was no less than the site of the first Globe Theatre, built in 1599 and where many of Shakespeare's plays were originally performed. Proximate to the Globe were The Swan, The Hope, and The Rose theatres as well as a bull ring and a bear garden. As Steven Mullaney has noted, "erected outside the walls of early modern London in the 'licentious Liberties' of the city, the popular playhouses of Elizabethan England occupied a domain that had traditionally been reserved for cultural phenomena that could not be contained within the strict or proper bounds of the community."[24] Its location directly across the Thames from the City of London, but outside its jurisdiction, made this area an early "tourist" destination (audiences arrived via river ferry) and London's first entertainment district. The South Bank was, then, explicitly marked by both its performance venues and its freedom from City laws. And, even in this early modern period, the potential afforded to audiences for a remapping of identity was paramount: "in the metamorphic fears of the city it was not merely players who shifted shapes, confounded categories, and counterfeited roles."[25]

But the South Bank's current status as a cultural district draws, as well, on a much more recent history as the principal site for the 1951 Festival of Britain – an event designed to reassure the resident population that recovery from the Second World War was well underway. The Royal Festival Hall as well as the extensive public art (including Barbara Hepworth sculptures and a Victor Passmore mural) that remained after the 1951 event were subsequently augmented by "high cultural production... contained in this bridgehead location beside Waterloo bridge (reinforced by successive institutions such as the Hayward Gallery and the National Theatre between 1951 and 1968)."[26] According to Peter Newman and Ian Smith, in 1981 "the Greater London Council noted only six sites of 'entertainment' along the South Bank frontage," the rest of the area dominated by public housing, office buildings (County Hall, home of the GLC, and the London headquarters of Shell predominant among them), and largely abandoned nineteenth-century industrial buildings that had once provided infrastructure for an active docks trade.[27] If the South Bank had been vital in late sixteenth- and early seventeenth-century London to the production of what Mullaney calls "ideological mobility and license," most of the rest of its history is much less distinguished.[28] In Peter Ackroyd's view, "the South remained relatively unknown to other Londoners, except as a source of disquiet... as a boundary zone to which London could consign its dirt and its rubbish."[29]

In effect, and despite the postwar revitalization, the South Bank had a long history of identification, for a variety of reasons, as the "wrong" side of the river and was certainly not on a traditional map of London city tourism. The only exceptions came from its longstanding entertainment sites (chiefly the Royal Festival Hall and, later, the Royal National Theatre), generally attracting spectators who arrived and departed by car, taxi, or public transport for mostly evening and weekend events and who did not extend their stay in the area more than a few minutes longer than the performance required. With scant other attractions (such as bars, restaurants, shops, or hotels) in the vicinity and a streetscape that appeared palpably unsafe, there was little motivation to linger.

All this changed, however, with the construction of a new Globe Theatre[30] – a process that took close to thirty years from the formation of the Shakespeare Globe Trust in 1970, to ground breaking in 1987, to the eventual opening a decade later.[31] Although Southwark Council originally argued against building the theatre (it wanted to reserve the site for social housing[32]), by the time the project was completed the Council had revised its policy to "facilitate the provision of new arts, cultural and entertainment and visitor facilities which maximize the benefit and minimize disbenefit to Southwark's residents."[33] This rather churlish acceptance of a new development direction for the area was provoked by a number of new contextual initiatives including residential and commercial renovations of existing buildings and a commitment to locate the new Tate Modern art gallery near by in the former Bankside Power Station. This is a phenomenon that Newman and Smith have identified as "co-locating actors within cultural production,"[34] a strategy that allows for the reinterpretation of space on the scale that has happened on the South Bank.

Anchored by this triumvirate of significant cultural infrastructure – the Southbank Centre, the new Globe Theatre, and the Tate Modern – the neighborhood became a magnet for other activity. County Hall was purchased by a Japanese developer and now comprises two hotels, the London Aquarium, Dalí Universe (a permanent exhibition of more than 600 works by Salvador Dalí), restaurants, a health club, and private residences. Adjacent is the British Airways London Eye, a millennium anniversary project that opened in 2000, the world's tallest observation wheel (at 135 meters) providing a panoptic view across the city and attracting more than twenty million visitors in the seven years since its opening.[35] The architects of the London Eye (David Marks and Julia Barfield) insisted that an "important aspect of the project was the creation of a high-quality public realm space at the base of the wheel, setting the standard for other public space in the area."[36] This is a tactic that has undoubtedly worked, with new restaurant and retail buildings as well as food and merchandise available from less permanent structures set up on a wide promenade along the bank of the Thames and effectively reanimating the previously underappreciated and more sparsely populated landscape. This riverfront footprint stretching between the London Eye/County Hall and the Southbank Centre is now active and busy, day and night, with visitors. Similarly, the walk back to Waterloo Station (for rail, underground, and bus links) is not the bleak adventure it once was, though the two communities who always found a home in this area – the homeless and the skateboarder – are still very much in evidence. But now they are only a contributing aspect to this local scene, part of a much more diverse and definitely more numerous crowd: domestic and international tourists, locals, and other Londoners drawn to the various high and popular cultural experiences, to restaurants and shops, to street performers, to the secondhand booksellers whose tables dot the promenade along with other artisan retailers, and to experience the postmodern reincarnation of old-time, low-brow entertainment in the London Eye, a ferris wheel that rather amazingly makes the South Bank master of a London gaze. The area around the Tate Modern and the Globe Theatre also now boasts the extended trappings of a tourism economy: five hotels, clusters of restaurants (including the Globe's own popular eating venue), retail and service stores, as well as the Millennium Bridge, the city's first new pedestrian bridge across the Thames in more than a century, linking the South Bank back to the City of London (and another premier tourist destination, St. Paul's Cathedral).

The Tate Modern is widely considered London's most famous example of adaptive reuse: "a formerly obsolescent power plant [that] has been transformed into a culture tourism spectacle."[37] Indeed, adaptive reuse is a term that might be appropriately applied to the entire neighborhood as many of its former industrial buildings have been given new purposes. According to Newman and Smith, in 1998 there were more than 100 advertising-related companies located in the South Bank area as well as "30 private galleries and six other part-time hanging spaces over and above four major institutions for the display of visual art... There are also some 23 sites of visitor attraction that collectively can be thought of as forms of heritage promotion."[38] This is an area that has now most definitely arrived, unquestionably a "must see" attraction on any London tourist's agenda. The warehouse buildings are now not just reused as offices and galleries but have also been adapted as residential lofts with design stores, restaurants, rehearsal spaces and Starbucks all comprising part of their street-level façade. Yet the old neighborhood is still powerfully present: the public housing that eventually filled the bombsites that had housed factories and warehouses; businesses such as a tire depot, a repair store for London's ubiquitous black taxis, and a builder's yard; and working-class cafés that offer bacon rolls and mugs of tea for a couple of pounds. Even in its tourism transformation, the South Bank has retained the people and the businesses that were not so long ago its signal *raison d'être*. The district may have been remapped – put on the map, even – but it does not, today, simply cater to a tourism audience. Arguably, its longer-term actors – whether residents, businesses, or skateboarders – have been recast in different roles as part of the streetscape that visitors come to see, albeit at the very same time as their own experiences of the neighborhood may stay tangibly the same.

What is perhaps remarkable in this most recent metamorphosis of the South Bank is its repossession of what had previously seemed an exclusionary architecture of high art – which is to say, the concrete buildings that house the Royal National Theatre, the British Film Institute, and the Hayward (with which I opened this chapter). This pod of cultural infrastructure had refused its surroundings. Yet now that refusal has been negated, appropriated, and claimed by the overarching tourism environment. The Southbank Centre has effectively been remade, given an unprecedented performance within the "universal experience" of tourism. Not that this newfound populism denies high art; it does not. Rather, it is restaged in ways that open up place and space to a variety of people, some of whom live there but most of whom find their way to it in a predetermined agenda of pleasure. In effect, these institutions' status in purveying high art (the "Royal" National Theatre, the "British" Film Institute) becomes an object of consumption for a much wider tourist view. Their spaces become much more than performance stages; now they attract visitors for building tours, for public lectures, for opportunities to eat and drink – and, of course, to spend money in the ubiquitous store. Souvenirs are everywhere and necessary.

Why does this work – because clearly it does – to show the city to itself and to inspire its occupants and its visitors to become actors in a reconfigured landscape, to forge emotional connections to a neighborhood not so long ago more dead than alive? If the answer is simply "culture," how have the Tate Modern and the Globe Theatre succeeded where the Southbank Centre complex once failed? Perhaps it is because the new energy and vitality of this area's cultural presence is refracted through history – not a pure and authentic distillation of "History," but a reimagination of what has always been there, through time, and now cast for a twenty-first-century audience for the purpose of its entertainment. The new Globe is a reminder that when the first English public theatres were built at the end of the sixteenth century, the South Bank was a liminal space, exempt from the City's strictures and as such open to a full demographic of London's population as a "liberty." The contemporary Globe Theatre does not claim to be the real thing (it is not even on exactly the right site), but it is a quotation and a celebration of the advent of a public theatre that attracted a diverse and enthusiastic audience, mapping out new identities that eluded the City's surveillance. The Tate Modern's occupation of a building once central to London's electricity grid (a utility paradigmatically symbolic of modernity) now – with not a little irony – finds itself a vessel for modern and contemporary art's comprehension of and challenges to that same modern condition. Both explicitly invite not (just) elite audiences committed to the consumption of art, but the much wider demographic demanded by economically successful urban tourism. The Tate Modern, it should be noted, has no general admission charge and extends opening hours on Fridays and Saturdays until 10p.m. The Globe Theatre has 700 tickets at £5 each for every performance – a simulation of the groundling experience of Shakespeare's first audiences standing in the Theatre's "Yard." It is surely likely that the success of these two venues influenced the Royal National Theatre's creation of the "Travelex £10 Season" in 2003. Travelex – which advertises itself as "the world's foreign exchange company"[39] – sponsors a number of shows each season, allowing the sale of £10 tickets for two-thirds of the Olivier Theatre seats and two-fifths of the Lyttleton Theatre seats on specific dates.[40]

"Universal Experience"

The South Bank, since the opening of the new Globe Theatre, has promoted an impressive range of new tourism and other performances drawing extensive new audiences. Almost five million people visited Tate Modern in 2006, a 21 percent increase on the previous year, making it the UK's second most visited attraction according to the Association of Leading Visitor Attractions.[41] As a tourism hot spot, then, this area is an ideal setting for an exhibition on the pleasures and pitfalls of tourism. "Universal Experience," the Hayward show with which this chapter started, was described by its curator Francesco Bonami in this way:

> This exhibition is both an experience in itself and a show about experiences; it is about the ways in which global tourism is changing art, architecture, the way we look at images, and the world we inhabit. This transformation is reflected in the practice of the mobile and itinerant group of international contemporary artists whose work is included in *Universal Experience*. The works have been selected and juxtaposed so that the visitor will experience the exhibition as both an adventure and a tourist attraction.[42]

I agree with much of what Bonami suggests: audiences for "Universal Experience" are encouraged to find sheer fun in the many expressions of tourism – the show included the work of more than seventy artists produced in a wide variety of media – and at the same time to understand their complicity in the economic flows of global capitalism. Notwithstanding the joyful spirit of the exhibition – Bonami's "adventure" – it was not without the typical skepticism that attaches to almost all analyses of tourist practices and performances. Some of the exhibits illustrate the environmental degradation that tourism development has wrought across the world. Others pay attention to the less appealing aspects of travel: Doug Aitken's "The Moment" (2004), for example, is an eleven-screen video installation that shows a traveler sleeping in airports, parking lots, and other unwelcoming places. Strangely, perhaps, many of the artists stripped their representations of tourism of tourists or any kind of human presence. As Hans-Peter Feldmann's series of postcards – "Untitled (Eiffel Tower), 1990" – suggests, tourists often prefer images of the iconic places they visit to have "no people in sight so that the viewers can imagine themselves there without the intrusion of other tourists."[43] Overall, however, "Universal Experience" effectively pulled together the inevitable tensions of tourism in a suggestive narrative that always keeps pleasure in sight. Its exhibition at the Hayward, moreover, displayed the complicated performance of tourist audiences in a show that claims to provide a critical, if universal, eye. But the exponential growth of tourism in the world suggests that there is, indeed, a willing spectatorship well able to negotiate the range of performances that tourism provides, even when this includes one that challenges the terms and conditions of this process: tourists, after all, really do want to have fun.

Bonami reminds us, however, that "[t]ourism – in its increasing prevalence, universality even – reduces the complexity of the world."[44] This is likely true but sometimes the very provisionality of the universal experience that tourism promotes to its voracious audiences makes available a possible if only temporary transformative engagement. The South Bank is most definitely no longer designed for the sole possession of the modernist *flâneur*, but hails "streetwalkers" across age, gender, race, and class. To attract the volume of visitors who will sustain not only a significant cultural infrastructure but also the variety of contextual businesses that this infrastructure encourages, South Bank tourism must posit, among other things, a gender-neutral tourist population. And, if only within a prescribed space – the tourist area, but definitely not all of South London – the scripts shift, and this models new ways of walking the city.

Mapping identity

The very nature of tourism is to be a transient pleasure and a time-constrained experience. It is not typical but instead remaps urban settings as places and performances outside the everyday codes of behavior and decorum. This fundamental condition allows for experiential geographies that challenge the tenacity of other maps of the city – Benjamin's *flâneur*'s among them. New maps denote a diversity of what de Certeau called enunciatory operations, a variety of actors' scripts tied loosely to the same tourism plot but that may effectively challenge received ideas about city space.

Even then, the map is perhaps only figurative. After all, gender roles across tourism are not characterized by a liberationist agenda: women occupy the significant majority of tourism jobs, especially those that are low skill and/or low wage.[45] Furthermore, as Cara Aitchison has pointed out in her study of gender and leisure spaces, while "sex tourism frequently generates symbols of women as the 'exotic other', heritage tourism often creates the 'invisibilized other' where emphases upon nationhood, and industrialized or militarized landscapes draw upon a history which renders women invisible from the landscape."[46] On the other hand, tourism has expanded work opportunities for women in many instances, promoting entrepreneurship and financial autonomy.[47]

Women's participation in the production of tourism's performances is, however, not my subject here so, in summary, I turn back to the consumers of those performances for other gender-specific engagements. If the tourism industry generally needs to believe in and market itself to a "universal experience," its continued growth and diversification has become increasingly dependent on fracturing the audience into seemingly limitless subgroups for experiences tailored to the specificities of their identities, both actual and desired. Odaiba – a group of linked islands built as a reclamation project in the Bay of Tokyo – has developed in the past ten years specifically as a tourism shopping and entertainment district for Japan's capital city. Many of its attractions are both expected and familiar: museums (the National Museum of Emerging Science and Innovation, the Museum of Maritime Science), attractions (the Fuji TV building, a hot springs theme park, a 115 meter-high ferris wheel), shops, and restaurants. One – "Venus Fort" – claims to be the world's first shopping and entertainment venue designed specifically for women, with its setting constructed to resemble an eighteenth-century European town.[48] And in the world's most aggressive tourism market, Las Vegas, the "girls weekend" has become an increasingly important target: Howard Lefkowitz, president of the Vegas.com website, notes, "The notion is that it's all men coming here and hiding stuff from their wives. Women come here and do stuff, too, because they think 'They're not going to find out about it in my hometown.'"[49] A little less insidiously, many North American hotel chains offer hotel packages that cater specifically to groups of women visitors.

Mapping identities, real and imagined, is crucial to the business of tourism. Large-scale tourism requires at least the possibility of universal experience, even as it increasingly looks to specific identity subsets to boost profitability. My premise is that this performative act of tourism provides a productive perspective that moves us, albeit temporarily, out of otherwise prescriptive spatial dynamics in the city. Yet, in the end, tourism is never the universal experience it imagined: even those who have the economic, social and other mobilities that allow participation in the tourism economy are never hailed by, nor attracted to, every tourism stage. Notwithstanding this fact, whether from production or reception standpoints, the performances that constitute tourism deserve continued attention. The exhibition at the Hayward and the streetscapes that surround it, as well as the history out of which the South Bank draws its contemporary populations, all contribute to a persuasive terrain for mapping identity, provisionally, imaginatively, and differently. This, in the end, is the potential of the tourist stage.

Notes

1. "Universal Experience" was at the Hayward from October 6 to December 11, 2005. It was originally organized by the Museum of Contemporary Art, Chicago, from February 12 to June 5, 2005. After the Hayward, the exhibition moved to the Museo d'Arte Moderna e Contemporanea di Trento e Roverto (February 10 to May 14, 2006).
2. Originally the Hayward Gallery, a rebranding early in 2007 of the South Bank Centre to Southbank Centre included a change of name to "the Hayward."
3. See Peter Cook, ed., *Archigram* (Princeton: Princeton University Press, 1999). This is a facsimile edition of the Group's manifesto, originally published in 1972. They also maintain a website: www.archigram.net/about.html. Accessed September 21, 2007.
4. See www.hughpearman.com/articles5/hayward2.html. Accessed March 3, 2007. Pearman, a regular contributor to London's *Sunday Times*, maintains the Gabion website to retain his writings on architecture.
5. See www.haworthtompkins.com/. Accessed April 7, 2007. Haworth Tompkins, a distinguished London architectural firm known for its cultural spaces projects, worked in collaboration with the New York conceptual artist Dan Graham to address what the website notes was a lack of "provision for visitor amenities." The foyer extension was completed in October 2003 at a cost of £1.8 million. Other Haworth Tompkins projects include renovations of the Royal Court and Young Vic theatres in London.
6. Richard Schechner, *Performance Studies: An Introduction*, 2nd edn (London: Routledge, 2006), 286.
7. *Ibid.*
8. Barbara Kirshenblatt-Gimblett, *Destination Culture: Tourism, Museums, and Heritage* (Berkeley: University of California Press, 1998), 7.
9. Alan Blum, *The Imaginative Structure of the City* (Montréal and Kingston: McGill-Queen's University Press, 2003), 183.
10. Schechner, *Performance Studies*, 28, 38.
11. Joseph Roach, *Cities of the Dead: Circum-Atlantic Performance* (New York: Columbia University Press, 1996), 28.
12. Tim Edensor, "Performing Tourism, Staging Tourism: (Re)producing Tourist Space and Practice," *Tourist Studies* 1.1 (June 2001), 63.
13. Judith Adler, "Travel as Performed Art," *American Journal of Sociology* 94.6 (May 1989), 1366.
14. Tim Edensor, "Staging Tourism: Tourists as Performers," *Annals of Tourism Research* 27.2 (2000), 326.
15. Walter Benjamin, *The Arcades Project*, trans. Howard Eiland and Kevin McLaughlin (Cambridge, MA: Harvard University Press, 1999), 417.
16. Martin Selby, *Understanding Urban Tourism: Image, Culture and Experience* (London and New York: IB Tauris & Co., 2004), 108.
17. Janet Wolff, "Gender and the Haunting of Cities (or the Retirement of the *Flâneur*)," in Aruna D'Souza and Tom McDonough, eds., *The Invisible "Flâneuse"? – Gender, Public Space, and Visual Culture in Nineteenth-Century Paris* (Manchester and New York: Manchester University Press, 2006), 19.

18. Helen Scalway, "The Contemporary *Flâneuse*," in D'Souza and McDonough, eds., *The Invisible "Flâneuse"?*, 166.
19. *Ibid.*, 168.
20. Michel de Certeau, *The Practice of Everyday Life*, trans. Steven Randall (Berkeley: University of California Press, 1984), 99.
21. Selby, *Understanding Urban Tourism*, 101.
22. Susan S. Fainstein and Dennis R. Judd, "Global Forces, Local Strategies, and Urban Tourism," in Dennis R. Judd and Susan S. Fainstein, eds., *The Tourist City* (New Haven and London: Yale University Press, 1999), 4.
23. As Peter Newman and Ian Smith describe in their article "Cultural Production, Place and Politics on the South Bank of the Thames" (*International Journal of Urban & Regional Research* 24.1 [March 2000], 12), this area extends from Westminster Bridge in the west to St. Saviours Dock in the east, fronting the river through the London boroughs of Lambeth and Southwark.
24. Steven Mullaney, *The Place of the Stage: License, Play, and Power in Renaissance England* (Chicago and London: University of Chicago Press, 1988), vii.
25. *Ibid.*, 51.
26. Newman and Smith, "Cultural Production," 12.
27. *Ibid.*, 12–13.
28. Mullaney, *The Place of the Stage*, 31.
29. Peter Ackroyd, *London: The Biography* (London: Chatto & Windus, 2000), 691.
30. The first Globe Theatre burned down in 1644. Its foundations were discovered in 1989 under a Georgian terrace on Southwark Bridge Road, about 200 yards from the site of the new Globe Theatre. See www.globelink.org/abouttheglobe/architecture/ for further discussion of the location of the original theatre. Accessed May 12, 2007.
31. More information on the history of Shakespeare's Globe can be found on the theatre's website: www.globelink.org/abouttheglobe/. Accessed May 12, 2007. A more detailed account is available in J. R. Mulryne and Margaret Shewring, *Shakespeare's Globe Rebuilt* (Cambridge: Cambridge University Press, 1997).
32. Newman and Smith, "Cultural Production," 18. It should be noted here that the GLC was disbanded by Margaret Thatcher's government across the river at Westminster and that the London Borough of Southwark is now the jurisdiction that oversees this area. Southwark Council had intended the theatre site for council-owned and controlled housing for low- and no-income families and individuals.
33. This quotation is taken from the London Borough of Southwark's "The Unitary Development Plan" of 1995 and quoted in Newman and Smith, "Cultural Production," 20.
34. Newman and Smith, "Cultural Production," 10.
35. Information provided on the website of the London Eye architects David Marks and Julia Barfield; see www.marksbarfield.com/project.php?projectid=10. Accessed May 14, 2007. The website for the London Eye notes an average of 10,000 visitors a day; see www.londoneye.com/AboutEye.aspx. Accessed September 12, 2007.
36. See www.marksbarfield.com.

37. Keith G. Debbage and Dimitri Ioannides, "The Cultural Turn? Toward a More Critical Economic Geography of Tourism," in Alan Lew *et al.*, eds., *A Companion to Tourism* (Malden, MA: Blackwell, 2004), 106.

38. Newman and Smith, "Cultural Production," 13.

39. See www.travelex.com/. Accessed September 12, 2007.

40. Usual ticket prices are in the £20–£40 range.

41. See www.alva.org.uk/visitor_statistics. Accessed September 12, 2007. The Tate Modern's numbers were second only to the Blackpool Pleasure Beach and well ahead of the Tower of London, St. Paul's Cathedral, Tate Britain, Westminster Abbey and the Houses of Parliament. The London Eye's website claims it is "the most popular paid for UK visitor attraction visited by over 3.5 million people a year," www.londoneye.com/AboutEye.aspx. Accessed September 12, 2007.

42. Francesco Bonami, "The Authentic and the Universal," in Bonami, Julie Rodrigues Widholm, and Tricia van Eck, *Universal Experience: Art, Life, and the Tourist's Eye* (Chicago: Museum of Contemporary Art and New York: Distributed Art Publishers, 2005), 14.

43. *Ibid.*, 68.

44. *Ibid.*

45. See Vivian Kinnaird, Uma Kothari, and Derek Hall, "Tourism: Gender Perspectives," in Vivian Kinnaird and Derek Hall, eds., *Tourism: A Gender Analysis* (Chichester: John Wiley & Sons, 1994), 15–18.

46. Cara Aitchison, "New Cultural Geographies: The Spatiality of Leisure, Gender and Sexuality," *Leisure Studies* 18.1 (January 1999), 32.

47. Kinnaird, Kothari, and Hall suggest, however, that this is generally the case only when women's participation "can be accommodated within the prevailing sexual division of labour" ("Tourism: Gender Perspectives," 17). An example here might be running a bed-and-breakfast business out of the family home.

48. See www.japan-guide.com/e/e3008.html. Accessed May 15, 2007.

49. Cited in Kitty Bean Yancey, "Sin City Uncovered," www.usatoday.com/travel/destinations/2007-5-10-naughty-las-vegas_N.htm. Accessed May 12, 2007.

6

DIANA TAYLOR

Performance and intangible cultural heritage

Can performance, normally thought of as "intangible" and "ephemeral," be protected and safeguarded? What would that entail? The two questions, which sound straightforward, are extremely complicated, maybe even irresolvable. When Lourdes Arizpe, an eminent Mexican anthropologist who served as Assistant Director-General for Culture for UNESCO (1994–8), and I met in New York in 2000, these were the questions we asked each other. As someone who has worked on multiple international cultural preservation projects, including UNESCO's World Heritage program, Lourdes Arizpe insisted that protecting intangible cultural heritage was vital – just as great works of art must be conserved, she said, cultural expressions of great significance must also be preserved, particularly those that are rapidly disappearing owing to economic and social change. Furthermore, safeguarding ancient or original forms of expressions allows the preservation of unique creativities that give continuity to meanings and loyalties vital to many groups. Some in UNESCO argued that some societies do not have buildings they want to preserve – no Taj Mahals or Auschwitzes or cathedrals – and thus world heritage sites have been disproportionately located in the "First World." These are signs of cultural power and capital, but underrepresented communities have defining practices and traditions that need crediting and safeguarding. Some are disappearing, while others are changing drastically. Without UNESCO's development of a Convention to Safeguard Intangible Cultural Heritage, communities of practice could not make claims for recognition and support. They would be threatened with extinction. That was Arizpe's commitment to the question.

My investment came from another, albeit related, place. As a performance studies scholar who believes that a community's "intangible" practices (or performances) serve vital aesthetic, epistemic, and social functions, I keenly experienced the seductive hope of somehow protecting or safeguarding them. Communities have developed rich "holdings" and traditions in the arts, medicine, agriculture, and other fields that they transmit through practice.

Intellectual property laws defend knowledge passed on through books, so why not also the knowledge transmitted though embodied behaviors? My book *The Archive and the Repertoire* focuses attention on how humans draw from and contribute to the repertoire – dance, music, ritual, and social practices that I came to understand broadly as "performance" – to produce and communicate knowledge.[1] Unlike the archive that houses documents, maps, literary texts, letters, archaeological remains, bones, videos, films, compact disks – all those tangible items supposedly resistant to change – the acts that are the repertoire can be passed on only through bodies. But while these acts are living practices, they nonetheless have a staying power that belies notions of ephemerality. "Acts of transfer" transmit information, cultural memory, and collective identity from one generation or group to another through reiterated behaviors.[2] That is to say that knowledge, albeit created, stored, and communicated through the embodied practice of individuals, nonetheless exceeds the limits of the individual body. It can be transferred to others. While no gestures are performed exactly the same way twice, this does not mean that people do not perform them again and again, often conveying what onlookers imagine is a supposedly stable meaning. Kneeling at prayer, dancing at a wedding, or singing in a chorus might be thought of as significant communal rather than merely individual practices. Some performances are so culturally specific that activists argue that they have evidentiary power.[3] Indigenous communities, for example, support their claims to lands by demonstrating that the practices they engage in are historically continuous with those enacted by their ancestors. They make lineage and genealogies visible – even in a court of law.

Arizpe and I decided to work together to try to think about how best to "protect" performance/intangible cultural heritage. We formed a working group with scholars from the Hemispheric Institute of Performance and Politics,[4] and invited scholars and artists from different parts of the world to broaden our scope. UNESCO commissioned us to write a manual on Festive Events, Rituals, and Social Practices, one of the five manuals to accompany the 2003 International Convention on Intangible Cultural Heritage (ICH).[5] After our initial meeting at the UNESCO headquarters in Paris, we organized several other discussion forums, including a working group meeting in Cuernavaca, Mexico, that involved other key members of the Hemispheric Institute.[6] We also held a panel discussion of our conclusions at the Hemispheric Institute's "Encuentro" in 2005 Belo Horizonte, Brazil.

Immediately, the complexities, not to say the impossibilities, became evident and few of us in the group were clear about how to address them. Without going into an in-depth description and analysis of the 2003 Convention on ICH, this chapter presents my personal take on the complexities of safeguarding intangible cultural heritage, the multiple contradictions they pose, and the urgency of finding other viable ways of understanding and protecting embodied behaviors understood broadly as "performance." While this is not intended as a critique of UNESCO, that organization's leading role in trying to negotiate international accords makes it an important case study in elucidating the challenges of safeguarding the "live."

UNESCO has been trying for a long time to think about how to safeguard ICH. Shortly after issuing the 1972 Convention Concerning the Protection of the World Cultural and Natural Heritage, discussions began about how to expand that protection to "nonmaterial" or "living heritage."[7] A nonbinding Recommendation on the Safeguarding of Traditional Culture and Folklore was approved in 1989, and in 1990 UNESCO began developing a series of programs with interested state partners: "Living HumanTreasures" in 1993, and the "Masterpieces of the Oral and Intangible Heritage of Humanity" in 1997.[8]

As the titles of the programs indicate, however, the efforts extended the logic and the language of what I call the "archive" into the domain of the "live" – the acts that are the repertoire. While explicitly trying to protect embodied transmission "to facilitate their survival by helping the persons concerned and assisting transmission to future generations," Mounir Bouchenaki, Assistant Director-General for Culture, argued that one of the requisite moves was to "translate intangible heritage into 'materiality.'"[9] The way to safeguard the practices, apparently, was by turning them into something they are not. While bodies are material, the intangible practices to be protected are by definition immaterial, and the act of translation simply multiplies the problems and contradictions. UNESCO defines safeguarding as "adopting measures to ensure the viability of intangible cultural heritage. These measures include the identification, documentation, (protection), promotion, revitalization and transmission of aspects of this heritage."[10]

While several of the methodologies belong to archival work (identification, documentation, and so on), the acts of "revitalization and transmission" that might have allowed for thinking about the "live" could approach practice only as archival objects. The "Living Human Treasures" program, while an important attempt to honor masters of valued practices and encourage them to train others, reflects the difficulties of finding appropriate ways of thinking about the liveness of transmission.[11] Masters (not treasures) perform certain acts and train others. The acts, clearly, are separable from the individual practitioners. People can pass them on. Others can learn them. Performance studies theorists such as Richard Schechner have long recognized that "behavior is separate from those who are behaving," for it can be "stored, transmitted, manipulated, transformed."[12] But these acts of transfer do not render the practices tangible. Rather, as I have argued in my work, they form part of a repertoire of acts kept alive through repeated enactment. These corporeal acts can be repeated, quoted, borrowed, and transformed by other practitioners. So while the strategy of supporting living masters might be one very productive way to pass on embodied knowledge through rigorous performance and training, the bureaucratic transformation of them into treasures turns them into things and erases the centrality of practice. A national living treasure becomes a thing: a breathing world monument, an exemplar of disembodied excellence and universally recognized value, rather than a transmitter of practice. A treasure does not have agency; its value is assigned by cultural arbiters of taste.

The same applies to the term "masterpieces," which reifies certain practices deemed valuable by powerful sectors of society. Masterpieces are safely guarded and preserved objects; while they can be moved, they are usually locked away from daily life. But the UNESCO programs strive to preserve living acts that are central and vital to communal life. Dances, rituals, songs, and other types of performance that require human bodies, energy, virtuosity, and intentionality cannot be objectified and locked away. They are always *in situ*; their meanings come from the context in which the actions take place. They cannot be moved without a thorough recontextualization. Why would people perform in other settings? Who would they perform for? What would their movements communicate? The objectifying approach to the "intangible" creates a series of spatial and temporal dislocations. The "here" and "now" of performance, the body memory of those performing, the meaning of the interaction between performers and participants/spectators become something else – a disembodied, abstract, and universally intelligible cultural product in the language of protection and preservation.

While cultural practices and behaviors are transmitted from one generation to the next and one community to another, the language of tangible "heritage" and "property" skews the debates in several critical ways. Heritage, linked etymologically to "inherited property," stresses the materiality of practices passed down to legitimate owners, the heirs. While ostensibly a form for maintaining the old, its actual function is to produce a new cultural product, a "value-added industry" that converts locations into destinations, as Barbara Kirshenblatt-Gimblett argues in *Destination Culture*.[13] It obviates practitioners and communities as active cultural agents – we inherit cultural places and materials that we might in turn transmit, but not transform. They are not "ours." They pass through us but they belong to an incorporeal everyone: "humanity." The concept of intellectual property – so central to the discussion of embodied culture – is off the table when specific practices become "heritage" and ownership and oversight is transferred to "humanity" as the beneficiary.

In 2003 member states of UNESCO adopted the Convention for the Safeguarding of the Intangible Cultural Heritage. After discussions following their earlier efforts in the 1990s, they made some productive changes. They agreed that the Convention needed to be "of a more binding character" and they chose to focus on protecting "processes" rather than "products" pertaining to ICH. While the earlier language of "living treasures" and "masterpieces" was gone from the definition of ICH, it proved problematic nonetheless:

> The "intangible cultural heritage" means the practices, representations, expressions, knowledge, skills – as well as the instruments, objects, artefacts and cultural spaces associated therewith – that communities, groups and, in some cases, individuals recognize as part of their cultural heritage. This intangible cultural heritage, transmitted from generation to generation, is constantly recreated by communities and groups in response to their environment, their interaction with nature and their history, and provides them with a sense of identity and continuity, thus promoting respect for cultural diversity and human creativity. For the purposes of this Convention, consideration will be given solely to such intangible cultural heritage as is compatible with existing international human rights instruments, as well as with the requirements of mutual respect among communities, groups and individuals, and of sustainable development.

The description, while more focused on practices than the earlier programs, again elides agency. Who transmits these practices? The passive construction ("transmitted from generation to generation") suggests a transhistorical genealogy in which communities participate (they recreate) without being *creators*. ICH is the subject of the sentence; culture supposedly passes through the groups and communities, conferring on them a sense of identity and continuity. The shift in the final part of that sentence, "thus promoting respect for cultural diversity and human creativity," again lacks a clear agent or subject. "The human" is simultaneously invoked and evacuated. Who promotes this respect: ICH? In and for whom? The environments of practice, it seems, exist semiautonomously from the practitioners. The final arbiter this time is not simply "humanity" but human rights agreements that declare (quite rightly, to my mind) that human and animal rights trump cultural rights.

In addition to all the issues of definition and conceptualization surrounding the cultural project of "safeguarding" performance, there were also specific political obstacles. One of the first problems our working group encountered was the organizational and structural framework of UNESCO itself, and its impact on the parameters of the conceptualization of ICH. UNESCO – not a monolithic entity – works with member states (national governments), not with communities or local cultural producers. The states recommend specific practices to be considered by an international jury as ICH that, if accepted as such, the states themselves will need to support. A second problem was that the Convention addressed several divergent audiences simultaneously. It invites "Member States to become aware of their needs and priorities related to their intangible cultural heritage and to formulate and implement safeguarding actions." So while the purpose of the Convention is "to safeguard" ICH, the states are actually the ones assigned the task of implementation. Yet the Convention was also envisioned as a "tool for communities wishing to safeguard their intangible cultural heritage rather than an instrument for researchers," previously the ones who documented, archived, and analyzed practices. Communities, too, then, have to assume the charge of safeguarding. Clearly, "the purposes of the Convention are manifold: apart from directly safeguarding elements of the intangible cultural heritage at the national level, it also wishes to ensure respect for it, to raise awareness of its importance and to provide for international cooperation and assistance. The Convention is intended to contribute to a world sustainability marked by creativity and cultural diversity."

The challenges of developing a manual that would assign agency and be acceptable to the various "stakeholders" – communal, national, international, and, last but not least, the "world" – immediately became evident. At times the goals of interested parties were in direct opposition. While a member state might consider nominating a particular project as ICH to bring national visibility and augment tourism – the economic engine of heritage projects – the cultural producers might on the contrary be seeking ways to sustain a life-affirming practice best performed in relative isolation. How did the selection process function and whose interests did it serve?[14] Was it necessary to "take sides" and, if so, whose side were we on? If tourism changed a practice far beyond its original character, turning it into an economically sustainable attraction or self-conscious performance of itself, had the Convention succeeded in safeguarding it or in destroying it? In cases such as these, what would safeguarding mean? It was not clear what we were supposedly safeguarding practices *from* or who we were safeguarding them *for*. Lastly, what power would the Convention actually have? Although it was considered "binding" for the member states that ratify it, what could be done if one of them decided not to recognize or valorize its own ICH?

The unstable legal standing of the Convention as "instrument" spilled over into other areas in need of clear legal standing: the most urgent was the question of enforceable intellectual property laws pertaining to ICH. In some cases, cultural producers were anxious to protect the use of their traditions and practices from outsiders. Pharmaceutical companies, for example, had exploited traditional healing customs. Native Mesoamerican corn production had been forcefully supplanted by genetically altered and engineered products imposed by state governments in collusion with multinational corporations. First World musicians had stolen songs that they then recorded and sold without attribution. But intellectual property rights – so vital to all discussions of tangible heritage – were not a part of the ICH convention but, rather, had been given over to the World Intellectual Property Organization (WIPO) in Geneva. It was not clear how these encroachments on the intangible might be dealt with – either through existing legal instruments, such as patent law (in the case of pharmaceuticals and corn products) or through intellectual property channels. Cultural producers usually have little or no information about existing resources and the stakes are enormous. What is being stolen or displaced is not simply a particular product but a whole way of thinking, a hierarchy of values, and a knowledge base made visible through practice.

With all these limitations and issues in mind, we met to discuss performance, the intangible practices and behaviors transmitted through reiterated practice. One of our challenges, as Kirshenblatt-Gimblett made clear, was to clarify the ambiguity in the programmatic initiatives on ICH between *doing* the practice (the skill set and conditions required to support performance) and doing something *about* the practice (creating inventories, archives, and documentation). From a performance studies vantage point, we brought some of the pertinent ideas in our field to the debate about sustaining performance.

Instead of the top-down approach used by institutions such as UNESCO, we proposed starting with performance practice. We debated definitions, best practices, sites of cultural exchange and transmission of knowledge and values in relation to the Fiesta de la Virgen de Paucartambo in the Peruvian Andes, the marae (sacred meeting spaces) of Aotearoa, New Zealand, and the Day of the Dead in Mexico, the latter proclaimed ICH in 2005. We looked at the ways that communities express themselves within frameworks of codified behavior. Both individual and social memory depend on a sense of shared recollection, and on activities that make that memory visible in the public sphere, for example anniversary celebrations, birthdays, new years, and so on. The Fiesta of the Virgen, studied by Gisela Canepa-Koch, illustrates how societies enact history.[15] Five thousand masked dancers spend four days a year dancing the history of their area: the time the Natives fought the Mestizos over the Virgen del Carmen, the time the Blacks arrived, the emergence of the ranchers, and the coming of cholera when infected people from the Amazon jungle basin took refuge in the highlands. The dances have continued for hundreds of years even as they undergo change, whether deemed part of a "tradition" or an "invented" tradition (as when women claimed their right to dance based on an oral account of a very old man who said he had heard from one of the ancients that women once danced). These performances make manifest a community's sense of itself as stable and recognizable yet ever changing, especially now in a period marked by migration. It makes clear who can dance (in this case, those whose families have belonged to the community for three or more generations), what standards are required by the community (dancers must commit to dancing for the four days), and who is the social hierarchy (which now, like much else, is contested). Young men who go to work in the capital or abroad have more money, and therefore more clout, than the village elders, who are the traditional custodians of culture. Migration has also led to the Fiesta being performed in Lima, adding another historical layer to the palimpsest. The Fiesta can change significantly even as it maintains a "core" meaning for its participants.

Individual and social memory is also intimately linked to specific spaces that are subject to change in other ways. Our example of the marae, developed by Rangihiroa Panoho, is simultaneously a building and a cultural meeting space for the Maori. It functions along the lines of what Joseph Roach has called "vortices of behavior": churches, marketplaces, theatres, schools, and kitchens in which certain kinds of behaviors and values are learned and certain memories and values are transmitted.[16] The spaces show other tensions. The marae, we observed, could be safeguarded by stressing the conventional behaviors that communities enact in this specific site. However, the marae, just as importantly, is also a site of experimentation. The local space, too, has migrated, as Maori leave their communities. Online marae, for example, have become important virtual meeting places for Maoris living in cities and abroad. The focus has shifted from indigenous community to the individual, from the local village to the global. Would safeguarding the traditional marae (the building) as an environment of practice prove a conservative move in an age marked by demographic transformation?

The Day of the Dead example allowed us to explore how certain cultural performances might change meaning and worldview even as they apparently remain the same. While elders in many parts of Mexico still honor their dead through a ritualized observance that includes a feast and a visit to the graveyard, in some very traditional communities (certain Mayan groups in Chiapas, for example) it proves difficult for families to maintain the gravesites. Sheep and goats often wander into the graveyards, knocking over the crosses as they graze for food. When the Day of the Dead comes around, people clear the bramble and replace the crosses on graves they assume belong to their relatives. Approximation suffices; the intent, rather than strict observance, has to suffice. In other areas children may like the Day of the Dead because it overlaps with Halloween festivities and trick-or-treating promoted on television. Several traditions converge, and individuals participate in ways that often blur distinctions.

As these examples illustrate, we focused on examples from "traditional" communities, in keeping with UNESCO's objective to single out performances by "traditional" and "popular" sectors for protection. Modern societies, supposedly, have archives and museums to ensure that records of their practices are maintained forever, though the practices themselves are no more stable than those from traditional communities. Nonetheless, some of us disagreed with the organization's stance that these forms would disappear without official intervention and preservation. The UNESCO position implies that "intangible heritage" is fragile, short-lived, that it somehow belongs in the past. The supposition that the archival is the only stable form of transmission underwrites much current scholarship and policy-making. The Convention's insistence on recording and documenting practices considered doomed to extinction perpetuates the "salvage ethnographic" impetus of the early twentieth century. The past, cloaked in nostalgia, is endorsed as somehow "truer" and more authentic and real than the present. Scholars such as Pierre Nora have associated the intangible – "[in] gestures and habits, in skills passed down by unspoken traditions, in the body's inherent self-knowledge, in unstudied reflexes and ingrained memories" – with the "milieux de mémoire," which Nora calls the "real environments of memory."[17] The *milieux* constitute the primordial, unmediated, and spontaneous site of "true memory," while the "lieux de mémoire" – the archival memory – is its antithesis, modern, fictional, and highly mediated. The acceleration of the archival impulse (Jacques Derrida's "archive fever")[18] is predicated on the assumption that embodied, intangible transmission, such as speech in an example given by Michel de Certeau, "neither travels very far nor preserves much of anything."[19] But, as I have argued elsewhere, the differences between the repertoire of embodied practice and the archive is not about "true" versus "false," mediated versus unmediated, primordial versus modern, the powerless versus hegemonic. "Performance belongs to the strong as well as the weak; it underwrites de Certeau's 'strategies' as well as 'tactics,' Bakhtin's 'banquet' as well as 'carnival.' The modes of storing and transmitting knowledge are many and mixed."[20] Certain sayings and songs will outlast many a book or photograph, so the codes and structures of the repertoire need to be studied and understood in order to think about how past behaviors and practices continue to be imperative in the present. This is the lesson that modern societies seem to have forgotten, owing precisely to their reliance on archival preservation.

Communities have always had ways of protecting their practices. At times they restrict participation to a specific group of initiatives. At other times performances hide other meaning-making systems within them. Sixteenth-century Catholic priests actually believed that the Amerindians were converting to Christianity when they saw them kneel at prayer.[21] Only later did they come to understand that their object and manner of worship was of an entirely different order. Through our examples and discussions, we explored how social actors reproduce and reinvent themselves through performance practices that allow them to draw from a repertoire of learned, ritualized, and historical practices to adapt to changing conditions. These considerations, so fundamental to thinking about transmission through performance, did not make it into our manual. In keeping with our mandate, the bulk of our efforts went into developing action plans, documentation and archiving strategies, and recommendations for involving more and more stakeholders in best practices. The manual stated that the mechanics of transmission vary widely according to what is being passed on, why, and for whom. But even *transmission* was cast in disembodied, bureaucratic language, defined in the UNESCO glossary as taking place primarily "through instruction and access to documental sources."[22] There was literally no room to analyze the codes and systems of transmission that take place through bodies. Children learn languages through mimetic repetition, while adults learn languages through memorization, practice, and repetition. Actors and dancers internalize a concept and repeat, rehearse, and recreate. Choreographers might draw from earlier repertoires to reenvision and reinvent new work that honors its predecessors even as it breaks new ground. Athletes study past moves and develop techniques of the body to outdo performances by competitors. Military historians might engage in reenactment exercises to discover the concrete choices their subjects made in past battles. Heritage projects, such as "colonial day" in elementary schools, might have children engage in past activities (churning milk to make butter or candle-making) to inculcate them with a sense of historical ownership and continuity.[23] Embodied practices cover a very broad gamut of behaviors: everything from the presentation of the "self" and the performance of everyday life (as Erving Goffman would have put it)[24] to highly codified choreographies of movement that can be copyrighted (such as a Martha Graham dance). The way to understand and preserve practice is through practice, not by converting it into tangible objects or, in the end, manuals.

The bureaucratic approach to safeguarding ICH is paradoxical. On the one hand, it legitimates the notion that cultural practices are valuable and need to be respected and cared for; on the other, the way the safeguards materialize and objectify the "live" fails to understand liveness itself. Still, I cling to my hope that something can be done to counter the predatory political and economic habits that deprive communities of their land, their practices, and their sense of identity. It is impossible, I believe, to safeguard intangible manifestations of cultural heritage without assuring that the stubbornly *material* human bodies, or "cultural bearers" in the language of UNESCO, retain the freedom to function fully within their meaning-making systems. Native languages, for example, are disappearing at an alarming rate because speakers need to know colonial languages in order to survive, few countries offer education in Native languages, speakers endure discrimination if they speak their language, migration has displaced communities of practice, and more. Change all those socioeconomic conditions and the linguistic practices might well continue. But keeping one Native speaker alive to teach others misses the point. The loss of a Native language means far more than the loss of a linguistic system, as regrettable as that may be. It signals the loss of a way of knowing, an approximation to a specific environment and worldview, a way of being in the world. But no convention can safeguard a practice without safeguarding a way of life. Practices thrive as long as people find them meaningful. Nothing else will assure their sustainability.

Performed practices and behaviors offer an alternate history, one based on memory, events, and places rather than just documents. These alternate histories are always illuminating, even in the most literate and democratic societies. They are invaluable, however, in understanding how communities identify and express themselves when, for a myriad reasons, they have limited access to written knowledge, whether they live in semiliterate societies or in periods of dictatorship during which writing is censored. Embodied practice always exceeds the limits of written knowledge because it cannot be contained and stored in documents or archives. Practitioners reaffirm their cultural identity and transmit a sense of community by engaging in these cultural behaviors. Outsiders glean some understanding of a community's values and structure by being there, and participating or watching their performances. Scholars can explore cultural continuities, historical displacements, and erasures by relating modern-day performances to embodied practices that have been alluded to or described in other media (writing, etchings, engravings, and so on). The international community can appreciate the ways in which expressive culture helps individuals and communities make sense of their lives as they migrate and/or adopt new languages and customs, or as they attempt to stay put, delimit their interactions with outsiders, and strive to remain "the same." In any case, individuals and communities are always in contact with others, and increasingly so in a period of globalization. The dangers threatening ICH, we agreed, were encroachment or appropriation by others, neglect by younger generations, or loss of the lands, objects, and traditions associated with the meaning-making systems. Far more worrying and ironic, state and international economic and environmental policies have often proved devastating to the very communities UNESCO sought to safeguard.

In an ironic postscript, UNESCO never published the manual we wrote in the format we presented it in. Although it was never clear what happened, we speculated that bits and pieces of it were transferred to other texts, recombined to make other points. Our work, too, was taken, deauthorized, decontextualized, reconfigured, and presented in bureaucratese as a benefit to humanity.

Notes

1. Diana Taylor, *The Archive and the Repertoire: Performing Cultural Memory in the Americas* (Durham: Duke University Press, 2003).
2. Paul Connerton, *How Societies Remember* (Cambridge: Cambridge University Press, 1989), 38.
3. See Diana Taylor, "Performance and/as History," *TDR: The Drama Review* 50.1 (2006), 67–86.
4. The Hemispheric Institute of Performance and Politics is a consortium of institutions, artists, scholars, and activists dedicated to exploring the relationship between expressive behavior (broadly construed as performance) and social and political life in the Americas. See http://hemisphericinstitute.org.
5. Convention for the Safeguarding of the Intangible Cultural Heritage, 2003 www.unesco.org/culture/ich/index.php?pg=00006. Article 2.2 lists five overlapping domains: (i) oral traditions and expressions, including language as a vehicle of the intangible cultural heritage; (ii) performing arts; (iii) social practices, rituals, and festive events; (iv) knowledge and practices concerning nature and the universe; (v) traditional craftsmanship. At the time we were writing the manual on social practices, rituals, and festive events, the UNESCO plan was to have one manual for each domain, and a general manual that would provide an overview for them all.
6. The working group included Gisela Canepa-Koch, Professor, Facultad de Ciencias y Artes de la Comunicación, Pontificia Universidad Católica del Perú; Leda

Martins, Professor, Nucleo de Estudos em Letras e Artes Performaticas, Universidade do Estado de Minas Gerais, Brazil; Barbara Kirshenblatt-Gimblett, Professor, Department of Performance Studies, New York University; Rangihiroa Panoho, Lecturer, Department of Art History, University of Auckland, New Zealand. The discussions included several other scholars and artists: Zeca Ligiero, Leota Lone Dog, Enrique Nalda, Antonio Prieto, Doris Sommer, Javier Serna, Jesusa Rodríguez, Jill Lane, Milla Riggio, and Silvia Spitta.

7. For information on the 1972 Convention Concerning the Protection of the World Cultural and Natural Heritage, see http://whc.unesco.org/archive/convention-en.pdf.

8. For "Living Human Treasures," see www.unesco.org/culture/ich/index.php?pg= 00061&lg=EN. See note 5 for the URL for the 1997 convention on "Masterpieces of the Oral and Intangible Heritage of Humanity."

9. Mounir Bouchenaki, editorial, "Views and Visions of the Intangible," *Museum International* no. 21–222, http://portal.unesco.org/culture/en/ev.php-url_id= 21739&url_do=do_topic&url_section=201. Accessed October 30, 2007.

10. "Glossary: 'Intangible Cultural Heritage' prepared by an international meeting of experts at UNESCO, 10–12 June 2002," ed. Wim van Zanten (The Hague: Netherlands National Commission for UNESCO, 2002).

11. See "Guidelines for the Establishment the National 'Living Human Treasures' Systems," www.unesco.org/culture/ich/doc/src/00031-EN.pdf.

12. Richard Schechner, *Between Theater and Anthropology* (Philadelphia: University of Pennsylvania Press, 1985), 36.

13. Barbara Kirshenblatt-Gimblett, *Destination Culture: Tourism, Museums, and Heritage* (Berkeley: University of California Press, 1998), 150.

14. For a discussion of the politics of the selection process, see Janet Blake, "On Defining the Cultural Heritage," *The International and Comparative Law Quarterly* 49.1 (January 2000), 61–85 (esp. 74ff.).

15. For more on the Fiesta de la Virgen de Paucartambo, see Gisela Canepa-Koch's *Mascara, Transformacion e Identidad en los Andes: La Fiesta de La Virgen del Carmen Paucartambo-Cuzco* (Lima: Pontificia Universidad Católica del Perú, 1998).

16. Joseph Roach, *Cities of the Dead: Circum-Atlantic Performance* (New York: Columbia University Press, 1996), 26–8.

17. Pierre Nora, "Between Memory and History: Les Lieux de Mémoire," in Geneviève Fabre and Robert O'Meally, eds., *History and Memory in African-American Culture* (Oxford: Oxford University Press, 1994), 284–9.

18. Jacques Derrida, *Archive Fever*, trans. Eric Prenowitz (Chicago: University of Chicago Press, 1995).

19. Michel de Certeau, *The Writing of History*, trans. Tom Conley (New York: Columbia University Press, 1988), 216.

20. Taylor, *The Archive and the Repertoire*, 22.

21. Bernardino de Sahagún, in the *Florentine Codex*, understood that beliefs were transmitted through performance, though he acknowledged that he did not understand the content. The Devil, "our enemy planted, in this land, a forest or a thorny thicket filled with very dense brambles, to perform his works therefrom and to hide himself therein in order not to be discovered ... But only those he

Body politics: the individual in history

7

PHILIP AUSLANDER

Live and technologically mediated performance

> Theatre is different from all other forms of theatrical presentation because it
> is live. ... "At the heart of the theater experience, then, is the
> performer-audience relationship: the immediate, personal exchange; the
> chemistry and magic which gives theater its special quality."[1]

I use this quotation, from an introductory course document prepared by
Professor Kaoime Malloy, to stand for what I shall call the traditional view
of live theatrical performance. The key word is *immediate*, which suggests
that the traditional definition of live performance is founded on an opposition between the immediate and the mediated. From this perspective, the
performer/audience relationship in film, for instance, is thought to be mediated by the camera and the rest of the filmic apparatus; in the theatre, by
contrast, this relationship is seen as direct and unmediated.

Such distinctions are largely commonsensical. Whereas stage actors can
appropriately be considered the "authors" of their performances, film actors
cannot. As the actor Willem Dafoe emphasized when I interviewed him,
film actors basically provide raw material that is shaped into performances
by directors and editors and therefore need not be as concerned about
the through-lines of their performances as stage actors.[2] Audiences witness theatre actors in the moment of performance but see performances by
film actors only long after the actors have done their work. Stage acting is
therefore temporally immediate to its audience in a way that film acting is
not.

Perhaps because of its disciplinary genealogy, performance studies often
exhibits a bias toward live events and a resistance to including technologically mediated ones among its objects of inquiry. Performance studies is
rooted in the fields of theatre studies, anthropology, sociology, folklore,
speech, and oral interpretation, all of which take live events as their major
points of reference, whether those events be aesthetic performances, cultural performances, rituals, or everyday behavior and conversations. Even
though an interest in mass media was implicit in performance studies
from quite early on,[3] only fairly recently did the field begin to draw on

communications and media studies and to consider the kinds of cultural objects with which they engage (for example, television and recorded music) under the rubric of performance. Because the distinction between live and technologically mediated performance remains a fundamental and culturally stratifying one, it is important to interrogate it directly.

Defining the differences between live and technologically mediated performance in terms of the traditional opposition becomes less tenable the more aspects of the question one considers. Speaking of attending the theatre, the playwright and actor Wallace Shawn has said:

> I've been spoiled like a lot of people by watching movies and television, where you can see very well and you can hear what the actors are saying. It's really, really hard for me to sit in row HH and not be able to see the faces of the actors and have to either strain to hear their voices or listen to projected voices which I know are grotesquely unnatural and which make it absolutely impossible for me to take the whole thing seriously.[4]

The situation Shawn describes is not at all unusual; it is something anyone who attends a live event of any kind (theatrical performance, concert, sports event, political rally, and so on) may encounter. Under these circumstances, what becomes of the immediacy, the chemistry, the sense of personal contact said to define the experience of live performance? As Shawn suggests, this experience is not at all unmediated: in the case he describes, it is mediated both by the physical characteristics of the performance space, which can either enhance or undo the potential for contact between performer and spectator, and by his own experience as a film and television viewer. He also implies that the sense of immediacy can actually be stronger when watching film or television than at the theatre.

In other words, we cannot treat the qualities traditionally assigned to live performance that putatively differentiate it from technologically mediated performance as inherent or ontological characteristics. They are, rather, phenomenological and historically defined. They are phenomenological (as opposed to ontological) in the sense that they are not characteristics of the performance itself but things experienced and felt by performers and spectators. One cannot say, for example, that a performance in a small space is necessarily more intimate than a performance in a huge space. It is so only if the participants experience it that way, and there may be forms of mediation taking place that either encourage or discourage participants from having the experience. For example, as Mireya Navarro observed in an article in the *New York Times* on the subject of famous rock musicians who sometimes play concerts for relatively small audiences at high prices, "Intimate is, of course, relative. If the performer usually plays to audiences of 20,000 . . . a concert for 2,000 or so would be downright chummy."[5] The experience of intimacy in such a case results as much from the participants' knowledge and experience of the artist's normal practice as from the circumstances of the performance.

Live performance is historically defined in that both our experience of liveness and our understanding of what counts as a live performance change continually over time in response to the development of new media technologies. Addressing in 1936 what was then the most important new medium, film, Walter Benjamin observed, "human sense perception . . . is determined not only by nature but by historical circumstances as well."[6] Shawn suggests something very similar when he speaks of having been "spoiled" by the spectatorial experience of film and television and of expecting something similar when he goes to the theatre. As a historical being, he cannot treat the theatrical experience simply on its own terms – inevitably, his perception of the theatre, of live performance, is mediated by his experience of technologically mediated dramatic forms. Indeed, most dictionary definitions of the word "live" show how closely our experience of live performance is bound up with our experience of technologically mediated forms. We cannot define live performance without reference to the other kind: "Of a performance, heard or watched at the time of its occurrence, as distinguished from one recorded on film, tape, etc" (*Oxford English Dictionary*, 2nd edn).

It is also the case that, culturally, the categories of technologically mediated performance and live, unmediated performance are not mutually exclusive. As Steve Wurtzler has pointed out, a great many performances blend elements of both, blurring the distinction between them.[7] The particular performance with which he starts his discussion was by Whitney Houston. When Houston sang "The Star Spangled Banner" at the 1991 Superbowl, the audience present at the stadium saw her live body, but heard her recorded voice. She was, in fact, singing live, but her live voice was inaudible and replaced by the recorded one. Such a performance is indisputably technologically mediated but it is also simultaneously live and not-live: it contains elements of both live presence and recording. Liveness, then, is not an absolute condition – it is not the case that a performance either is or is not live. Rather, live elements can be combined with recorded and otherwise technologically mediated ones to produce a hybrid event. As Wurtzler suggests, one can better understand live and technologically mediated performance in terms of a set of temporal and spatial variables in the relationship between performers and audience than as a settled binary opposition, as in the following table.

If liveness were a defining ontological characteristic of certain kinds of events, the definition of what counts as a live event would be stable. In

	Spatial Co-presence	Spatial Absence
Temporal Simultaneity	LIVE I	II
Temporal Anteriority	III	RECORDED IV

Some associated representational technologies/practices:
Position I: Public address, vaudeville, theatre, concert
Position II: Telephone, "live" radio, "live" television
Position III: Lip syncing, Diamondvision stadium replays
Position IV: Motion pictures, recorded radio and television

Source: Steve Wurtzler, "She Sang Live," 89.

fact, this is not at all the case: many performances combine live and nonlive elements, and the concept of liveness is a moving target whose definition changes over time in relation to technological development. The default definition of live performance, Position I in Wurtzler's table, which I call "classic liveness," is as the kind of performance in which the performers and the audience are both physically and temporally co-present with one another. But over time, we have come to use the word "live" to describe performance situations that do not meet these basic conditions. With the advent of broadcast technologies – first radio, then television – we began to speak of live broadcasts. This phrase is not considered an oxymoron, even though live broadcasts meet only one of the basic conditions: performers and audience are temporally co-present in that the audience witness or hear the performance as it happens, but they are not *spatially* co-present. Another use of the term worth considering in this context is the phrase "recorded live." This expression comes closer to being an oxymoron (how can something be both recorded and live?) but represents another concept we now accept without question. In the case of live recordings, the audience shares neither a temporal frame nor a physical location with the performers, but experiences the performance later (this is what Wurtzler calls "temporal anteriority") and in a different place from where it first occurred. The liveness of the experience of listening to or watching the recording is primarily affective: live recordings encourage listeners to feel as if they are participating in a specific performance and to enter into a vicarious relationship with the audience for that performance.

The phrases "live broadcast" and "live recording" suggest that the definition of live has expanded well beyond its initial scope as the concept of liveness has been articulated to emergent technologies. And the process continues, still in relation to technological development. Along these lines, Nick Couldry proposes "two new forms of liveness," which he calls "online liveness" and "group liveness":

> [O]nline liveness: social co-presence on a variety of scales from very small groups in chat rooms to huge international audiences for breaking news on major Web sites, all made possible by the Internet as an underlying infrastructure... [G]roup liveness[:] ... the "liveness" of a mobile group of friends who are in continuous contact via their mobile phones through calls and texting.[8]

Understood in this way, the experience of liveness is not limited to specific performer-audience interactions; it is the feeling of always being connected to other people, of continuous, technologically mediated co-presence with others known and unknown.[9]

The decentered experiences of liveness to which Couldry points are not easily assimilable to a simple performer/audience model; in such interactions, each of us functions simultaneously (or perhaps alternately) as performer and audience member. Although Malloy and Couldry share the premise that liveness is about real-time interactions among human beings, there are crucial differences in their respective understandings of the concept. For Malloy and the writers she quotes, the essence of live performance is unmediated contact between performers and audience, which demands physical co-presence, while Couldry posits liveness specifically as the affective dimension of technologically mediated relationships among human beings. It operates primarily in the temporal dimension rather than the spatial one; its main affect is the sense that one can be in contact with others at any given moment regardless of distance.

However, the word "live" has also come to refer to connections and interactions between human and nonhuman agents. Margaret Morse observes that the imaginary developing around interactive computer technologies entails an ideology of liveness, the source of which lies in our interaction with the machine.

> Feedback in the broadest sense ... is a capacity of a machine to signal or seem to respond to input instantaneously. A machine that thus "interacts" with the user even at this minimal level can produce a feeling of "liveness" and a sense of the machine's agency and – because it exchanges symbols – even of a subjective encounter with a persona.[10]

Liveness is attributed not only to the computer itself but also to the entities we access with the machine. When a website is first made available to users, it is said to "go live." As is true of the computer, the liveness of a website resides in the feedback loop we initiate: it responds to our input to create a feeling of interaction arguably comparable (without being identical) to our interactions with other people.

This discussion began with what seemed to be a well-established binary opposition between live, unmediated performance (represented by theatre) and technologically mediated performance (represented by film). Closer examination quickly revealed, however, that the two terms are best understood not as mutually exclusive possibilities but as points on a grid defined by variations of the performers' and audiences' temporal and spatial relationship to each other. Further analysis suggested that the concept of liveness itself is unsettled and subject to historical redefinition in relation to technological development. Whereas classic liveness involves spatial and temporal co-presence of performers and audience members, subsequent situations that have come to be considered live do not necessarily adhere to those conditions. It seems that spatial co-presence has become less and less important for a performance to be defined as live, while temporal simultaneity has remained an important characteristic, to the point that technologies that enable us to maintain real-time contact with others across distances are thought to provide experiences of liveness.

It may be, however, that we are now at a point at which liveness can no longer be defined purely in terms of either the presence of living human beings before each other or physical and temporal relationships between them. The emerging definition of liveness may be built primarily around the audience's affective experience. To the extent that websites and other virtual entities respond to us in real time, they *feel* live to us, and this may be the kind of liveness we now value.

GuitarBotana

Having proposed that we need to see the relationship between live and technologically mediated forms of performance as fluid rather than bounded by a binary opposition, and that we may experience liveness in our interactions with technological agents, I offer an analysis of a performance that explores this fluidity. *GuitarBotana* (2004), by the classical violinist and composer Mari Kimura, is a work for violin and GuitarBot, a robotic musical instrument designed by Eric Singer and based on the slide guitar. The GuitarBot consists of four independently controlled strings, each of which is "fretted" by a mechanical slide and plucked by a plectrum. It is a rather large and imposing sculptural object that moves when played. It cannot be played directly by human hands but only by using a computer and MIDI (Musical Instrument Digital Interface); the computer can be programmed to play it automatically.[11]

Kimura composed the music and wrote the software for *GuitarBotana*; when performing the piece, she both plays from score and improvises.[12] The GuitarBot's part is also scored. Its software enables it to respond to the violinist's playing in various ways.[13] In some cases, it follows the violinist closely and produces tones to fill out the harmony of the piece. In other instances, it is programmed to disregard random pitches played by the violinist, producing more open-ended situations in which its responses are relatively unpredictable. As composer, Kimura also invites the violinist to improvise while keeping in mind that GuitarBot will respond to the sounds produced in particular ways, depending on the programming that governs the particular section of the piece. It is therefore possible for the violinist and robot to enter into an improvisational dialogue in which the robot responds to the violinist's playing and the violinist responds improvisationally to the robot, and so on, all within the structural constraints of Kimura's composition. When Kimura plays the piece, she interacts physically with GuitarBot very much as she might with a fellow human performer: she faces it, leans and gestures toward it, and her facial expressions look as if she were taking and giving the kinds of performance cues that musicians exchange.

A performance such as this can be analyzed from many perspectives. The musical perspective would tend to focus on *GuitarBotana* as a composition, while the technological perspective would emphasize the design and programming of GuitarBot, and so on. The disciplinary lens of performance studies encourages a comprehensive analysis that would examine these, and all other aspects of the performance, as parts of an overall event. The dismantling of the binary opposition between live and technologically mediated performance that I have been proposing enables such an analysis by providing a means of seeing the commonalities among different aspects of the performance as clearly as the differences.

Although Kimura's status as a live performer is clearly not in doubt, there is an important sense in which her performing is technologically mediated. Kimura describes the experience of performing with GuitarBot as follows:

> I find that performing with the interactive system requires very fast, split-second decisions that are musically coherent overall. In my mind I have a trajectory of what happened before⇒now⇒future when I improvise, or perform any written music, and any given moment must make musical "sense" in relation to the trajectory. In performing with a robot, I assume a dual responsibility – for my own musical trajectory as well as that of this metal partner that doesn't think... So my job as a performer is to merge with the robot in terms of musical thinking during performance... This is what intrigues me as a classical musician, since this kind of new musicality, or new way of listening, has not happened until today.[14]

The mental processes Kimura describes as essential to her performance with GuitarBot are necessitated by the fact that her musical partner is a machine rather than a human being. Even though there presumably has been musical improvisation as long as there has been music, it has never before been the case that a musician must assume responsibility for the musical decisions made by an entity that lacks the capacity to assess its own choices in the light of larger musical objectives. The speed at which the human performer must respond to the robot's output in relation to the desired musical trajectory entails, as Kimura suggests, new modes of listening and playing that are explicitly artifacts of engagement with interactive digital technology. It is worth noting the contrast between Dafoe's comment on film acting and Kimura's on performing with GuitarBot. Both are technologically mediated forms of performance, but whereas Dafoe suggests that film actors are less responsible for the overall trajectory of their performances than stage actors, Kimura suggests that the type of technologically mediated performance in which she is engaged entails assuming greater responsibility for the overall trajectory of the music than is necessary when playing with human musicians.

If Kimura's live performance can be said to be technologically mediated in this way, what of GuitarBot's "performance"? There is a complex philosophical discussion to be had concerning whether or not machines can be considered live performers. Suffice it to say that since GuitarBot executes performances in real time before its audience (it is a technology of production, not a technology of reproduction like a playback system) and is capable of improvisation, thanks to Kimura's software, there is a basis for describing its performance in *GuitarBotana* as live even though the machine is not alive.

It is also the case that Kimura's performance mediates GuitarBot's in a way that parallels the impact on her of performing with a machine. Kimura's goal in the performance is for the audience to perceive GuitarBot as a real musical partner despite the fact that it cannot think for itself:

> My compensating for the robot's or computer's lack of musical "integrity" as the performance goes along should be hidden from, or unnoticeable to, the audience. In short, my aim is that the performance as a whole come across to the audience as if the robot or computer is thinking, feeling, and being sensitive; that it possesses the "rights and responsibilities" of a true musician.

In *GuitarBotana*, then, human performance is technologically mediated in that Kimura must adopt a way of thinking and responding that is determined by the capabilities of digital technology, and machine performance is humanly mediated in that Kimura's interactions with the machine are designed to make the audience perceive it as analogous to a human musician. She thus engages the affective dimensions of liveness on GuitarBot's behalf. As Kimura suggests with her image of "merg[ing] with the robot," these mutual mediations test the boundaries between human and machine, spontaneous and programmed, live and mediated.

Having thus far taken the terms technology and mediation in their most commonly understood senses, I shall now argue for a wider perspective. After all, the primary meaning of the word technology has nothing to do with machines or electronics. It derives from the Greek word *techné*, generally translated as craft or art. A technology is "a particular practical or industrial art" or the study of such arts (*Oxford English Dictionary*, 2nd edn). Performance is a technology in the first sense, as are particular performance practices such as acting, playing musical instruments, dancing, and so on. Performance studies is a technology in the second sense: it is the field that studies the broad spectrum of the practical arts of performance. Rather than seeing *GuitarBotana* as involving a human performer and a robot, we can see it as a performance that merges and juxtaposes different technologies: human performance, machine performance, the violinmaker's craft, musical composition, and digital technology, among others.

Likewise, mediation does not refer specifically to communications media; it means (among other things) "the state or fact of serving as an intermediate agent, a means of action, or a medium of transmission" (*Oxford English Dictionary*, 2nd edn). In my earlier discussion of Shawn's comments on theatregoing, I indicated that Shawn's experience of the theatre is mediated both by his position in the performance space and his experience of watching films and television: these are experiences that intervene between himself as theatregoer and the theatrical event and affect the way he perceives it. There are what we might call internal mediations and external mediations: the internal are aspects of the performance situation itself, such as the nature of the performance space, while the external ones are historical and social factors, such as the impact of television and film on our perception. Even though internal mediations are aspects of the performance itself, they influence the audience's response to the performance as much as external ones. It is also important that the two kinds of mediations interact with one another: it is presumably because his perception has been conditioned by film and television that Shawn finds his physical relationship to the actors in a conventional theatre space unsatisfactory.

It is also not always clear whether a particular mediation is internal or external. For example, Kimura consistently wears a formal black dress, the standard uniform for a female classical musician, when performing *Guitar-Botana*, a work that hardly qualifies as traditional classical music. The black dress is a mediation that Kimura uses to communicate to her audiences that they are to perceive and understand the piece and its performance within the context and tradition of modern concert music rather than as a technological experiment that would be more at home at a robotics conference than at Carnegie Hall.

> I have always maintained that so-called "experimental" work that is presentable and able to sustain an audience deserves and must receive the same level of respect and integrity as music written 200 years ago, never forgetting the fact that many of those works were indeed contemporary and experimental in their time. I consciously try to convey to the audience the fact that Bach, Brahms, Cage, Berio, and Robots belong together in the same evening's program.

The black dress is a technology in the primary sense of that term, a product of a practical art. It is what I am calling an internal mediation, in that it is part of the performance. Yet it is also an external mediation in that it functions as a framing device to inform the audience how to perceive the performance culturally and socially. Not only is the audience to take the music as seriously as they would Bach and Brahms, even though it is performed in part by a machine, but it is also to observe the norms of audience behavior appropriate to a classical music concert, just as Kimura observes the norms for a classical musician in her appearance and onstage behavior.

It is not a big leap from the idea of internal and external mediations to suggest that the concept of performance itself is an external mediation. Calling something a performance places it in a specific, though very broadly defined, category of human action and distinguishes it from other kinds of action. Consider Richard Bauman's definition of performance (which, I stress, is but one of many possible definitions):

> Briefly stated, I understand performance as a mode of communicative display, in which the performer signals to an audience, in effect, "hey, look at me! I'm on! watch how skillfully and effectively I express myself." That is to say, performance rests on an assumption of responsibility to an audience for a display of communicative virtuosity. ... In this sense of performance, then, the act of expression itself is framed as display: objectified, lifted out to a degree from its contextual surroundings, and opened up to interpretive and evaluative scrutiny by an audience both in terms of its intrinsic qualities and its associational resonances ... The specific semiotic means by which the performer may key the performance frame – that is, send the metacommunicative message "I'm on" – will vary from place to place and historical period to historical period ... The collaborative participation of an audience, it is important to emphasize, is an integral component of performance as an interactional accomplishment.[15]

For Bauman, the identifying characteristics of performance include a marked distinction from normal quotidian behavior, a display of skill, and the offering of that display to an audience for its appreciation and evaluation. The fact that a particular action is to be understood as a performance and apprehended that way is signaled by some means to a group of people which is then in a position to behave appropriately as an audience for the action rather than, for example, as mere bystanders. As the example of Kimura's black dress suggests, the signs that signal that an event is to be understood as a performance generally also signal what particular kind of performance it is, thus providing further information to the audience as to what to expect and how to participate. When the full scope of the terms technology and mediation are considered, we see that there can be no such thing as technologically unmediated performance because performance is itself a technology and the idea of performance is a mediation that shapes audience identity and perception of an event.

Conclusion

There are many questions to ponder when considering the relationship between live and technologically mediated performance. Is liveness an objective characteristic of performances? Is there a set of necessary or sufficient conditions that, if met, qualify a performance as live? What degree of technological mediation is permissible before a performance ceases to be live (think of the Whitney Houston example)? Or is liveness primarily an affective experience on the part of the audience rather than a characteristic of the performance – are performances live to the extent that we experience them that way as an audience (in which case, GuitarBot may be a live performer)? If we are willing to admit interactive technologies into the category of the live, what must they be able to do to create the affective experience of liveness? These questions, and many others like them, are ones we must address as we consider the fate of live performance, and the concept of liveness itself, in the twenty-first century.

One of the early projects of performance studies was to develop "a general theory of performance" by looking for "universals of performance" across cultural differences and genre boundaries.[16] While this totalizing approach is probably unfeasible, it nevertheless makes performance studies an ideal platform from which to examine the relationships among live and technologically mediated forms of performance without resorting to the traditional oppositions. Even though performance studies is historically invested in the idea of live presence, it is equally invested in defining performance in expansive and dynamic ways. This latter investment tempers the former one and opens up performance studies to the broad range of performance practices located on the grid mapped by the temporal and spatial coordinates I have discussed. It also allows for the possibility of setting aside the distinction between performances that are technologically mediated and those that are not, in favor of seeing all performances as internally and externally mediated confluences of varied technologies.

Notes

A portion of this chapter is adapted from Philip Auslander, *Liveness: Performance in a Mediatized Culture*, 2nd edn (London: Routledge, 2008).

1. Kaoime Malloy, "Theatre and Film," www.uwgb.edu/malloyk/theatre_and_film. htm. Accessed July 12, 2007. The internal quotation is from Edwin Wilson and Alvin Goldfarb, *Theatre: The Lively Art*, 3rd edn (Columbus: McGraw-Hill College Press, 1999), 19.
2. Philip Auslander, "Task and Vision Revisited: Two Conversations with Willem Dafoe (1984/2002)," in Johan Callens, ed., *The Wooster Group and Its Traditions* (Brussels: P.I.E. – Peter Lang, 2004), 103.
3. See, for example, Richard Schechner, "News, Sex and Performance Theory," in Schechner, *Between Theater and Anthropology* (Philadelphia: University of Pennsylvania Press, 1985), 295–324.
4. Anne Nicholson Weber, comp., *Upstaged: Making Theatre in the Media Age* (New York: Routledge, 2006), 9.
5. Mireya Navarro, "Star Turns, Close Enough to Touch," *New York Times*, July 12, 2007, B1.
6. Walter Benjamin, "The Work of Art in the Age of Mechanical Reproduction," trans. Harry Zohn, in John G. Hanhardt, ed., *Video Culture: A Critical Investigation* (Layton: Peregrine Smith Books, 1986), 31.
7. Steve Wurtzler, "'She Sang Live, But the Microphone Was Turned Off': The Live, the Recorded, and the *Subject* of Representation," in Rick Altman, ed., *Sound Theory Sound Practice* (New York: Routledge, 1992), 87–103. The table on p. 110 is reproduced from p. 89.
8. Nick Couldry, "Liveness, 'Reality,' and the Mediated Habitus from Television to the Mobile Phone," *The Communication Review* 7 (2004), 356–7.
9. Couldry is a communications scholar rather than a scholar of performance. The understanding of liveness to which he responds in his essay developed within communications theory in relation to television, in particular.
10. Margaret Morse, *Virtualities: Television, Media Art, and Cyberculture* (Bloomington: Indiana University Press, 1998), 15.
11. For a technical description of GuitarBot, see Eric Singer *et al.*, "LEMUR GuitarBot: MIDI Robotic String Instrument," *Proceedings of the 2003 Conference on New Interfaces for Musical Expression*, ed. François Thibault (Montréal: Faculty of Music, McGill University, 2003), 188–91.
12. Two videos of Kimura performing *GuitarBotana* are available online. The piece's 2004 premiere is available on *YouTube* at www.youtube.com/watch?v=-9I4ra4B-yg. A studio video by Liubo Borissov of Kimura performing the

piece, as well as still images, are available from http://music.columbia.edu/~liubo/guitarbotana/. Both accessed July 21, 2007. My descriptions are based primarily on Borissov's video.

13. For a technical discussion of Kimura's interactive musical software, see Mari Kimura, "Creative Process and Performance Practice of Interactive Computer Music: A Performer's Tale," *Organised Sound* 8 (2003), 289–96.

14. All quotations are from Mari Kumara, "Re: Query," July 16, 2007, email to the author.

15. Richard Bauman, *A World of Others' Words: Cross-Cultural Perspectives on Intertexuality* (Malden, MA: Blackwell, 2004), 9.

16. The idea of a "general theory of performance" comes from Jon McKenzie, *Perform or Else: From Discipline to Performance* (London: Routledge, 2001), *passim*. The phrase "universals of performance" probably originates with Victor Turner, "Are There Universals of Performance in Myth, Ritual, and Drama?," in Richard Schechner and Willa Appel, eds., *By Means of Performance: Intercultural Studies of Theatre and Ritual* (Cambridge: Cambridge University Press, 1990), 8–18.

8

DELLA POLLOCK

Moving histories: performance and oral history

Oral history studies are fed by many research streams, including folklore, memory studies, trauma studies, anthropology, psychology, communication studies, critical cultural studies, and, increasingly, performance studies, raising the critical question: how do performance analytics change our understanding of and approach to experience narrative (oral history, life history, stories of collective experience)?

Performance and narrative

In the late 1970s, after the publication of Richard Bauman's landmark "Verbal Art as Performance," folklore/vernacular studies attended more vigorously to processes of transmission, shifting the focus of study from the re-presentation of verbal art as fact (or artifact) to the rehearsal of site-specific interaction identified as performance.[1] This shift relied on Bauman's four criteria: competency (demonstrable skill or status as a story-teller); intensity (the sense of a special time, space, and ways of seeing and knowing experience to which performance indicators "key" in audiences); emergence (the unpredictable and uncontrollable shape, affect, and outcomes of time-space aesthetics); and changing structures of social relations (immediate changes among participants heralding change on a larger scale "as if" by proxy). Bauman positioned performance as a critical frame that illumined the authority, reflexivity, and transformative power of some art acts. Thus Bauman encouraged us to answer the persistent question, what *is* performance?, by asking instead: in what ways is it useful to call a particular act or set of interactions "performance"?

In his 1988 *Story, Performance, and Event*, Bauman built on his early work by distinguishing between the narrated event (what is *told* of the past) and the narrating event (the *telling* of it in the present). Reading this as a conventional distinction between content and form, text and performance, however, tends to misidentify performance with "event" and fails to appreciate the tripartite configuration of story, performance, event. To the contrary, Bauman offers a nominal heuristic that advances the inextricability of the *saying* and the *said* and favors performance as the living tissue that connects story and event in tenuous processes of meaning-making.

Barbara Myerhoff made a comparably significant intervention in anthropology, also in the late 1970s, with the publication of *Number Our Days*. Conducting fieldwork at "home," bringing the anthropological quest to the threshold of her own identity, Myerhoff found herself in the midst of shifting subject-subject relations. As a result, the book attends not only to cultural performances – the enactment in rites, rituals, and ceremonies of normative values and selves – but also to embedded performances of culture: the processes by which normative values and selves are made, even minutely crafted. Focusing on the power of life review and narration to draw an element of coherence (if not exactly order) out of chaos, and to establish a personal and social ethos, Myerhoff concludes with a claim for *homo narrans*, defining humanity by a need to narrate as keen as the need to eat or sleep.[2] For Myerhoff, narrative-making is self-making. In his preface to the book, the anthropologist Victor Turner hails Myerhoff's insistence on *homo narrans*, later substituting for it a resounding claim for *homo performans*.[3]

Performance-centered culture

By the late 1980s, the confluence of Richard Bauman and Barbara Myerhoff with work in sociology (C. L. R. James, James Scott), anthropology (James Clifford, James Fernandez, Renato Rosaldo, Michael Taussig, Victor Turner), folklore (Dell Hymes, Dennis Tedlock), critical cultural studies/theory (Frantz Fanon, Mikhail Bakhtin, Jacques Derrida), linguistics (J. L. Austin), theatre studies (Richard Schechner), and performance studies (Dwight Conquergood, Kristin Langellier, and Eric Peterson) was making a crashing wave of what has been called a "performative turn." Narrative trails through this turn as both a problem and a possibility. Bauman enlists the power of narrative transmission for social change. In Myerhoff the possibility of telling a story avails *being* of *becoming*. For both, narrative performance – telling the told, storying storied lives – is a pivotal practice of cultural crisis. Myerhoff, Bauman, and Turner anticipate and influence Conquergood's claim on storied knowledge:

> Knowledge is not stored in storytelling so much as it is enacted, reconfigured, tested, and engaged by imaginative summonings and interpretive replays of past events in the light of present situations and struggles. Active and emergent, instead of abstract and inert, narrative knowing recalls and recasts experience

into meaningful signposts and supports for ongoing action. The recountal is always an encounter, often full of risk. The storyteller struggling for contingent truths – "situated knowledges" – is more exposed and vulnerable than the scientist in pursuit of covering laws and grand theory.[4]

Conquergood largely abandons expressivist and realist models of narrative. Stories do not *reveal* or *refer to* a given world or body of knowledge. They subsume their referents in a re-creative, spatio/temporal "encounter." Accordingly, they are as powerful as they are precarious; knowledge per se is dissolved into contested rhetorics of narrative knowing.

Conquergood draws on and contributes to a performance-centered approach to culture more broadly, an approach that emphasizes core patterns of *repetition* enacted in re-presentation, re-creation, and re-cognition. As Homi Bhabha has famously noted, in its repetitions culture is *"almost the same but not quite."*[5] A performative culture is immanently on the edge of becoming otherwise. It relies for its vitality on the variable repetition that threatens its stability and disrupts the authority of origins – or first stories, foundational premises, original referents.[6] Accordingly, not only does narrative knowledge become subject to narrative knowing but, as Allen Feldman argues, "the whole semiotic relation of legitimation to the concept of origination falls into crisis. Legitimation becomes performative and therefore contingent."[7] A performance-centered approach to culture displaces narrative into practice; defines practice by repetition; finds in the unstable aesthetics of repetition an ethics and politics of possibility; and ultimately then shifts culture itself into the subjunctive register of *what if, as if, could be.*

Oral history performance

How does oral history figure in such a scenario? Oral history began primarily as a method, enabled by the technological innovation and popularization of the tape recorder. Historical researchers first introduced the tape recorder in the 1930s, seeking to supplement archives with otherwise unrecorded materials. In the early 1960s scholars such as Paul Thompson began to discern the radically democratizing potential of oral history, and the possibility not only of filling gaps in official records but also expanding those records to include the stories of people and experiences (labor, strikes, race relations, gendered work, immigration) buried under or excluded from histories of conquest: histories of people who, in effect, lacked papers.[8] Lacking such records, historians were at a loss to verify memory-based claims. The "new" oral history consequently presented political and methodological challenges, requiring historians largely to forgo validation by prior, textual remains; to shift from a text- to subject-centric history; and to give unprecedented favor to perspective and perception.

The terms of historical understanding changed in turn from *validity* to *value*, from *demonstrative* (or evidentiary) to the kind of *narrative* truth that Trinh T. Minh-ha proclaims:

> Literature and history once were/still are stories: this does not necessarily mean that the space they form is undifferentiated, but that this space can articulate on a different set of principles, one which may be said to stand outside the hierarchical realm of facts. On the one hand, each society has its own politics of truth; on the other hand, being truthful is being in the in-between of all regimes of truth.[9]

This entailed investigating the nature of the subject, pursuing a question that concerns many poststructural theorists but that, in the context of oral history, has a peculiarly performative valence. *Who speaks? What difference does speaking make? To what extent is the much heralded agency of the speaker conditioned by prior speech acts? To whom does his or her story belong?* In turn, oral historians began to grapple with the power dynamics intrinsic to the ethnohistorical "encounter," asking, for instance, *how does the performance of the past in the present shape and make historical subjectivity?*

As early as 1982, in his important inquiry into the social in oral history, Samuel Schrager displaced the foundational appeal of the "individual" story authorized and defined by relation to "experience," locating oral history instead in an ongoing history of dialogic relations.[10] According to Schrager, "personal narrative" is something of a misnomer, encouraging us not only to distinguish between the personal and the collective, but to consider the "personal" a kind of endzone of narrative creation. In his view the individual is a teller whose telling is part of a preexisting and unfolding narrative environment. For Feldman, the subject of oral history is always already a political subject. She is the subject of the histories she recounts:

> In a political culture the self that narrates speaks from a position of having been narrated and edited by others – by political institutions, by concepts of historical causality, and possibly by violence. The narrator speaks because this agent is already the recipient of narratives in which he or she has been inserted as a political subject. The narrator writes himself into an oral history because the narrator has already been written and subjected to powerful inscriptions.[11]

For both Schrager and Feldman, the narrator of oral histories is neither an authority-by-experience nor a free agent of historical construction but a moving figure of dialogical (and violent) histories. The body of their narrative, and their embodiment of it, marks and is marked by a forcefield of relationality.

Accordingly, a performance-centered account of oral history understands the oral history as a critical repetition among repetitions; liminal truth – truth storied "in the in-between of all regimes of truth" – as at least complementary to "the hierarchical realm of facts" conventionally favored by the social sciences; the teller as authorized by prior tellings; and the interviewer as directly implicated in a narrative environment that precedes, surrounds, and defines his or her conversations.

In practice this means that the interviewer-as-audience member becomes the measure of the micropolitics and ethics enacted at the relational nadir of the interview process. His or her story is a reflexive account of tactical and sensuous dynamics that embody, in miniature, history working itself out in narrative interaction, on, through, and by interview participants. Already in a conversation begun long before they brought a microphone to the table, the interviewer shares authority with her interview partners, with all the weight of complicity that may entail.[12] Accordingly, the subjunctive quality of telling "true stories," or discovering in dialogue connections between *what could have been* and *what could be*, slips into a normative framework in which possibility becomes potentiality, and what *should have been* becomes *what should be*. Being "in" dialogue thus means engaging in an ethics of thought and relation that may in turn mean intervening in cycles of repetition materialized in performance,[13] and assuming response-ability[14] for the ways in which the story the interviewer-become-narrator tells serves "the in-between of all regimes of truth."

Kate Willink, for instance, reperforms the discourses of whiteness that are themselves replayed in stories told by Mr. Alder, the first white teacher in a previously all-black high school in an eastern North Carolina county after the *Brown* v. *Board of Education* decision mandated school desegregation. In their conversation Mr. Alder eventually arrives at a story about how he "fit in" at the all-black high school: "I *guess I fit in* because I played *basketball*. And I brought my [adult] *team* to play the black high school one time." The game proves to be of a magnitude no one could have predicted. Almost despite himself, Mr. Alder regales its explosive, erotic energy:

Black against white: we were *allllll white*. They were *allllll black*. We were all *older*. They were high school boys.

. . .

You *cannot believe this game. If there has **ever** been an outstanding game ever **played** in Camden County, it was that night that we played them!* . . .

*Those boys were **unbelievable** that night.* I had watched 'em play . . .
I remember one time I think we went six minutes, **nobody** *missed*
a shot. I kept on.
I said, "*We're playing the best I've ever seen us play,*" but I said,
"**These boys are** . . ." (*he doesn't complete his sentence*).
They wanted to beat us so bad.
We won the game on almost a half court shot at the end of
the game . . . The score was a 150–149.
. . .
Those blacks came out and just *hugged us* (*pause*) because they
enjoyed the game.[15]

Mr. Alder's story rehearses the larger-than-life athletic and cultural dramas in which, as Willink notes, "'communities engaged the tensions, possibilities, and contradictions of the world around them'." Willink is a captive witness:

> Listening to Mr. Alder, I am captivated by the back and forth of the game, including six minutes during which "**nobody** *missed a shot.*" Mr. Alder remembers a powerful moment in which an historically divided community came together in a grand show of intimate contact: what was probably the first time some members of the white and black communities ever hugged each other in public.

Mr. Alder quickly cools the narrative heat. As Willink notes, his next comment initially seems a non sequitur: "But they're [black people] just as nice as they could be. I had a lady – I still think a lot of her today. She was a cafeteria manager – she always filled my plate up. I said, 'Miss Hall, you made me start gaining weight, you know that?' I joke – (*We laugh*)." As Willink observes,

> At a second glance, Mr. Alder's humor does more than calm the emotional volatility of the basketball game. It completely puts aside all the radicalness of the scene – a voluntary desegregation of blacks and whites in intimate physical contact, sharing a common passion for the game of basketball. With Mr. Alder's joke about the cafeteria manager and his gaining weight, he separates blacks and whites again – literally by a cafeteria line – into their "proper" places. Thus the joke releases the tension of the moment and its transgressive possibility dissipates. He returns us with laughter to a normative place where "they" are "nice," perform menial labor, are safely divided by service and consumption roles, and literally serve the white man exceedingly well.[16]

In the course of telling "his" story of desegregation, Mr. Alder relies on conventional narrative structures, such as the joke, and customary discourse, such as the cafeteria-line banter, to secure white privilege, even as he challenges its preeminence in the school structure. Playing this out, among other elemental contradictions, Willink discerns the controlling performativities of race – the recurrence of racial privilege in a narrative performance otherwise dedicated to dramatizing its collapse – that govern Mr. Alder's performances of masculinity, authority, and "fit" in the high school, the community at large, and the interview schema.

Mr. Alder performs the tactical, narrative work of exercising agency over histories of raced embodiment. In Rivka Eisner's encounter with co Dinh, a former political prisoner in Vietnam during the Vietnam War, the complexities of embodiment overwhelm narrative structure and agency. Eisner relates a scene of interaction in co Dinh's home in Ho Chi Minh City in which co Dinh was reluctant to speak. Co Dinh had previously, insistently referred Eisner to other women she felt were more appropriate bearers of war and revolutionary history – until she apparently could no longer resist the compulsion to tell. Eisner recounts an eruption of words that, even as they poured forth, fell away against co Dinh's re-presentation of a bullet wound – a scarred gouge in her upper thigh. The first words recorded are Eisner's, as she speaks the scene to which she is now subject:

> RIVKA: Scars, scars . . . oh!
> She is pulling up her pant leg,
> Oh!
> Oh!
> Oh, my god.
> How did she get *that*?
> It's on the inside of her left leg.
> Oh my –
> Oh –

Co Dinh continues through the translator, Nhina:

> CO DINH/NHINA: This leg is a bit shorter.
> At that moment,
> The, the ladies were on the street.
> And they fire –
> They shot –
> And without doctor –
> And they sent her to prison,
> And it got worse.

Soon the three voices overlap. Co Dinh clutches her pant leg, now raised to expose the upper thigh.

> RIVKA: Oh.
> CO DINH/NHINA: It got worse.
> RIVKA: Oh –

Eisner repeats the performance in an elaborated description of the primary relations of which it is comprised:

> Before Nhina and I can process what is happening, we are overtaken. My conversations with the other veterans earlier today were not like this at all. The women told carefully controlled narratives of daring missions, sorrowful losses, patriotic resilience, defiant protests, leading to eventual success. One by one, wearing pastel colored poly-blend pantsuits and sitting properly on the couch, the women let me in on the presence of secrets without fully revealing their substance. Co Dinh's explosion could not be more different. This is bloody. Violent. Emotionally volatile. This is a firestorm, not a story...
>
> Trying to keep up with co Dinh's rapid-fire pace, Nhina's translation echoes co Dinh's urgency with compounding, additive phrases, "*And* they fire – *and* without doctor – *and* they sent her to prison, *and* it got worse, it got worse"... Co Dinh walks out of the kitchen toward me and Nhina. Hurriedly taking up her pant leg, she reveals first a bony knee and then the pale skin of her thigh... Her fingers rest on the edge of a purplish gouge, about five inches below her pubic bone... "Oh my –. Oh –." What is *that*? "How did she get *that*?" There was no warning. I am stunned... now there is no stopping, no turning back. "Oh, my god," I whisper... "They fire – they shot." "Oh. Oh –." I stammer, caught off-guard by what is suddenly happening. Co Dinh's memories, dramatized in the place where bullets pierced her, are piercing me.[17]

Broken, shattered, even astructural, but powerful beyond control, co Dinh's words hijack Eisner's subjectivity in a blast of co-performative reckoning.

In each of these instances, what is said is inseparable from the saying of it. Indeed, understanding "what is said" would be sorely compromised without understanding the complexities and complicities entailed in saying it. Co Dinh's memory act, and Eisner's reiteration of it, suggests moreover that performance may exceed story and event in meaning, affect, and political implication. Similarly, even as Mr. Alder reiterates master codes, he not only reveals their effect on the past but renews their defining arc in the present.

In the saying, the teller is told. The teller enacts a historical self. The past asserts itself through him or her in narrative. The stories each tells are replete with master codes and cultural histories of mastery. While each articulates past and present in the relational drama of teller and listener, each also reiterates the claims of the past on his or her embodied subjectivity. Co Dinh is seized by history; Mr. Alder tries to settle himself – and his listeners – into its provisional comforts.

In each case, the interview is as much a scene of repetition as it is of potential rupture. The listener compels the teller's re-creative agency. The teller recruits the listener into affirmation and reciprocal investment. The negotiation of the past and present – and concomitant possibilities for continuity and change – are embodied in the interaction of the teller and listener as correspondent subjects paradoxically connected by gendered, raced, class, and national difference.

Witnessing

What happens when the intersubjection of the listener becomes a performance in its own right? When the listener becomes a witness to what she has heard? In the turn toward what Conquergood has called "co-performative witnessing,"[18] the listener enacts her dialogical transformation ideally not by "becoming" the teller mimetically but by doubling the teller's subjectivity in the performance of her own. Understood in this way, the performance of oral history becomes a *critique* of defining discourses; a *poeisis* of mutual change; a reparative *intervention*; and a *translation* of the relationship between the teller and listener into that between multiple listeners across boundaries of time and place, such that all are induced into performing a new/renewed ethic of imagination and action.

The performance of oral history is a repetition. Any given performance therefore will/must be "*almost the same but not quite.*" While some repetitions of "what is told" enlist tellers in staged retellings of their histories,[19] most shift the burden of account to primary and secondary listeners (those who heard a teller's account "firsthand" – body-to-body, and those who heard it from or by means of a primary listener). Accordingly, the possibilities for variation increase and the dangers of appropriation, assimilation, even annihilation of the primary teller become acute. In the performance of oral history, repetition belongs to an "other," raising the critical questions: what does it mean to "own" a story and who has the right to tell it? Does repetition in performance by another *take away* the teller's history and betray his or her trust?

Within the frame of a performative culture, the oral history is itself a repetition without stable origins. It is a form of cultural currency that flows among participants. As such, it does not "belong" to any one teller. Its vitality lies in exchange, at the dialogical intersection of teller and listener. This is not to diminish the risks of even unintentionally exploiting the vulnerability of a teller. It is to emphasize a *horizontal* rather than *vertical* economy of performance. In a horizontal economy, a performance of oral history is a tale told *alongside* another.[20] It enacts the intersubjection of interview partners, and their mutual becoming in the fraught negotiation of subjectivity, temporality, memory, imagination, and history. It does not disown the "original" teller, though it does elaborate the displacement of what is ostensibly his or her story into the co-relation of multiple others. The teller is thus doubly burdened – and enabled – by the teller's and an other's histories.

This doubleness defines Emily Mann's project. Variously based on oral histories, court transcripts, news accounts, and conversations, Mann insists that her plays – among them *Still Life* (1981), *Execution of Justice* (1986), and *Greensboro – a Requiem* (1996) – are documentaries. With regard to the documentary style of *Still Life*, a dramatization of conversations with a Vietnam veteran, his wife, and his lover, Mann has said, "Perhaps one could argue about the accuracy of the people's interpretations of events, but one cannot deny that these are actual people describing actual events as they saw and understood them." The play is a documentary in that, as representation, it paradoxically certifies the reality of a prior performance – "actual people describing actual events." It is also a documentary because it transfers Mann's listening experience to audience members: "The play is also a personal document . . . Each character struggles with his traumatic memory of events and the play as a whole is my traumatic memory of their accounts. The characters speak directly to the audience so that the audience can hear what I heard, experience what I experienced."[21] Mann conveys both the violence her interviewees witnessed and the violence committed by witnessing: she was cut through by her interview partners' accounts. She relays a version of that wounding to audiences.[22]

It is important to distinguish here between what might be called *event-based* and *performance-based* trauma. The latter emerges in repetition. Mann describes herself as having been traumatized by her interviewees' memory acts. Hearing about the violence they suffered, what she knew or did not know about the war, violence, and their impact on the intimacies of daily life was thrown into crisis. Doubling their traumatic memories in the performance of her own, she transfers an affective correlate to the *narrative truth* embodied by "actual people describing actual events" – what might be called *narrative pain* – to audience members.

In this case, the circulation of trauma comes with the hope that it will prompt "examination and self-examination," or critique and reflexivity, and lead to the kind of understanding that will allow us to "come out the other side."[23] Mann projects traumatic recovery. Rather than repetition of the same or recursive wounding, the play performs co-witnessing. It redoubles her interviewees' memory acts in her own, testifying at once to "actual people describing *actual* events as they saw and understood them," and the possibility for recreating the conditions of historical trauma.

More recent, popular reckonings with witnessing feature the interviewer in a kind of *mise en scène* of listening. The interviewer is not implied in the relation between "characters" and audience members but enacted in, for instance, the restless co-habitation of multiple interviewees in Anna Deavere Smith's own body (*Fires in the Mirror, Twilight – Los Angeles*) or the staged encounters between investigating members of the Tectonic Theater Company and the residents of Laramie, Wyoming, in *The Laramie Project*.[24] Rather than receiving a report of "what happened," audiences are engaged in the preconditions of critical witness: the shared reflexivity and performative, peculiarly subjunctive ethic characterized by wondering *how could this have happened? how does it happen? could it happen again? how could things be otherwise?* For witness/practitioners, the question then becomes: can staging oral histories bring performativity and performance into such intense collision that comfortable, discursive repetitions burn up in repetition-*beyond*-the-same? And how does or might the performance of witness mobilize this *beyond*?

Performing into the beyond

To the extent that a given performance of oral history performances involves rigorous doubling, it shifts and expands Bauman's primary terms of verbal art as performance with which we began:

1. The authority of the performer rests in his or her display of competency or management of performance skills, typically the special property of designated storytellers or performer historians. In oral history as/in performance, competency as cultural authority to tell is not determined by cultural role, class, or virtuosity but rather is achieved as a matter of "ordinary" relational investment and risk. No account is singular. Exercising multiply-shared authority thus mobilizes an ethical relation "essential to the determination of agency and the possibility of hope."[25]
2. For Bauman, it was the particular prerogative of performance to offer to its participants "a special . . . heightened intensity of communicative interaction which binds the audience to the performer in a way that is specific to performance as a mode of communication." When this happens, "the performer gains a measure of prestige and control over the audience."[26] In recent oral history practice (epitomized in such broadcast/digital innovations as NPR's StoryCorps and the lesser known www.voicethread.com) agency is ordinary; hierarchical "control" is dispersed into widespread possibilities for *enhancing* experience by *knowing* it through *telling* it, or through the vernacular aesthetics of historical re-creation.
3. Bauman claimed that in verbal art, performance meanings or messages do not preexist performance but flow from it in contingent, contextual concert, including, as Cheryl Mattingly argues, that between a patient and

a clinician. For Mattingly, the disconsolate liminality of the patient in life trauma is a stage for co-producing at least barely imaginable narrative futures. In contrast to Myerhoff, Mattingly insists that "coherence is not, perhaps, the most significant thing narrative offers to the afflicted or their healers."[27] For Mattingly, the work of co-creating a compelling therapeutic plot has less to do with coherence than with desire. She thus displaces narrative into a tentative play of dialogue between patient and healer that promises, she argues, "powerful therapeutic plots [that] may foster hope by pointing toward some new telos when old directions are no longer intelligible." Still, resolved to the continually emerging and radically contingent qualities of any one performance among many, Mattingly notes that "this new telos is always in suspense."[28]

4. Considering the qualities of competency, intensity, and emergence, Bauman argues for the power of performance to change structures of social relations. Many scholars and practitioners have relied on the performance of oral history to achieve social change by "breaking silence," amplifying previously unheard voices, and/or entering new stories into the historical record.

But what happens when "behind" the silence is a regressive history of more silence? Or when narrative memory has been stalled by historical trauma?

As Sonja Kuftinec's work in Mostar, a city in an "area now referred to as an absence: 'the former Yugoslavia,'" suggests, the objects of witness may be so haunted by absence that testimony loses direct reference. Bearing witness folds into spectral performativity. Mostar is a ghost town, a figment of "ethnic cleansing": "The spectre of destruction haunts reconstruction, just as the ghost of presence haunts the absences in the urban space. These absences, 'empty' spaces within the city, remain shadowed by spectres of what-was-before and possible-futures-to-come, both engaging in the politics of divisiveness within the city."[29] In this context, what remains to the representational field is to remap the city, to regard the city itself as a performance – a forbidding play of appearance and disappearance – in order to create/recreate a *habitus*, a habitable space, a home. Working with the community-based Cornerstone Theater Company, Kuftinec proceeds to develop a performance based on anecdotes of youth living in the city, a performance that refuses (impossible) nostalgia – that does not try to install memory in the face of devastation but embodies everyday hauntings and the constant, banal work of "negotiating meanings across divisions and through fragments."[30]

Kuftinec's work raises the question of reparation, which Grace Cho puts this way:

How...does one seek reparations for something that is not remembered, indeed is articulated in terms of a repeated failure to remember it? What is being demanded, and of whom, when no party recognizes its offenses? What can be repaired or restored when the violence of which reparations are being sought has not yet come to an end?[31]

These questions drive Peru's leading performance ensemble, Yuyachkani. Yuyachkani rehearses broad-scale, collective trauma and transgenerational memory, repeating history *against* denial and disappearance, *for* survival and change. As Diana Taylor observes, "For Yuyachkani, performance is not about going back, but about keeping alive. Its mode of transmission is the repeat, the reiteration, the yet again of 'performance'... The remembering was always past, present, and seemingly future."[32] Performances of reparation and survival suggest a shift from oral history performance as documentary or testimonial to oral history performance as *ethnokinesis*.[33] For Victor Turner, reembodying cultural performances became a quintessential mode of understanding their significance in the field.[34] The work to which Kuftinec, Cho, and Yuyachkani, among so many others, put their performances, moreover, insists on going beyond either study or certification of a referential real toward embracing the representational real of performance – and the power of performance to sustain, survive, compel, install, and craft memory; not only to write culture (ethnography) but to make and to move it beyond, especially, the spinning wheels of reiterative violence.

This may happen at a local level, with the intent of instigating dialogue about broadly contextual issues such as urban/natural disaster (for example, Danielle Sears Vignes, *Hang It Out to Dry: Katrina Spun Tales*), mass incarceration (Ashley Lucas, *Doin' Time: Through the Looking Glass*), lesbians in the military (Mercilee Jenkins, *A Credit to Her Country*) and justice by execution (Deb Royals, *Still... Life, An Exploration of a Killing State*). It may take the form of legal advocacy.[35] It may also be community-based, inviting community members to contribute primary materials and artistry to the reimagination of collective and contested histories (for example, Shannon Flattery, *Touchable Stories*;[36] Robbie McCauley, *Sugar*). In each case, these performances invoke what D. Soyini Madison calls a "politics of the near,"[37] the intimacies entailed in bringing politics home to and through the body, in remembering, art, and action.

In all these ways the performance of oral history rejects pity and fear, the privatization of public concerns, and/or spectacular dramatization in favor of *critique, poeisis, intervention,* and *translation.* In each of these cases (very selectively cited here), performance goes beyond representation into transformation, beyond mirroring into witnessing and the translation of response-ability. In each case, the shift in oral history that has made it so troublesome to so many – the shift in emphasis from validity to value – is elaborated in a shift in performance from certitude to ethics, from documentation of, for example, histories of violence to performance as the thing itself, the site of inter/multisubjective relays of political concerns from which we can no more avert our eyes than we can refuse our bodies. In sometimes astoundingly beautiful forms, performers of the performance of oral history double its force in their/our bodies, transferring narrative pain with narrative truth, including audience members in a circuitry of affect and power which may be built from ephemeral, fugitive memory but which will not disappear. In the end, all that may remain to remembering is survival. It may be deprived of all objects and even illusions of coherent events. But as Shmuel, Myerhoff's most despondent and reluctant participant, taught her, a life, a whole people, may be wiped out as easily as one might erase a line of writing. Even to the extent that writing "fixes," it ends – it finishes off the life lived, constituting for Shmuel a second death. So he lives, in between inscription and erasure, struggling daily, hourly, not against his own death but the death of memories, memories of others pierced through with irreparable senselessness. So, against every desire and reason, he remembers. So performance persists beyond the archive and the recorded life into the necessary, public reckonings of *ethnokinesis*.

Notes

1. Richard Bauman, *Verbal Art as Performance* (Prospect Heights, IL: Waveland Press, 1977).
2. Barbara Myerhoff, *Number Our Days* (New York: Simon and Schuster, 1978), 272.
3. Victor Turner, *On the Edge of the Bush: Anthropology as Experience* (Tucson: University of Arizona Press, 1985), 167.
4. Dwight Conquergood, "Storied Worlds and the Work of Teaching," *Communication Education* 42.4 (1993), 337, citing Donna Haraway, "Situated Knowledges," in Haraway, *Simians, Cyborgs and Women: The Reinvention of Nature* (New York: Routledge, 1991), 183–201.
5. Homi K. Bhabha, *The Location of Culture* (New York: Routledge, 1994), 89.
6. See Rebecca Schneider, "Hello Dolly Well Hello Dolly: The Double and Its Theatre," in Patrick Campbell and Adrian Kear, eds., *Psychoanalysis and Performance* (New York: Routledge, 2001), 94–114, and "Never, Again," in D. Soyini Madison and Judith Hamera, eds., *The Sage Handbook of Performance Studies* (Thousand Oaks: Sage Publications, 2005).
7. Allen Feldman, *Formations of Violence: The Narrative of the Body and Political Terror in Northern Ireland* (Chicago: University of Chicago Press, 1991), 4.

8. Paul Thompson, *The Voice of the Past: Oral History* (Oxford: Oxford University Press, 1988).
9. Trinh T. Minh-ha, *Woman, Native, Other: Writing Postcoloniality and Feminism* (Bloomington: Indiana University Press, 1989), 121.
10. Samuel Schrager, "What is Social in Oral History?," in Robert Perks and Alistair Thomson, eds., *The Oral History Reader* (New York: Routledge, 1998), 285.
11. Feldman, *Formations of Violence*, 13.
12. Michael Frisch, *A Shared Authority: Essays on the Craft and Meaning of Oral and Public History* (Albany: Syracuse University of New York Press, 1990).
13. See Elin Diamond, "Introduction," in Diamond, *Performance and Cultural Politics* (New York: Routledge, 1996), 4–5.
14. See Kelly Oliver, *Witnessing: Beyond Recognition* (Minneapolis: University of Minnesota Press, 2001).
15. Kate Willink, "Domesticating Difference: Performing Memories of School Desegregation," *Text and Performance Quarterly* 27.1 (2007), 33.
16. Kate Willink, *ibid.*, quoting Pamela Grundy, *Learning to Win: Sports, Education, and Social Change in Twentieth-Century North Carolina* (Chapel Hill: University of North Carolina Press, 2001), 5, 33, 33–44.
17. Rivka Eisner, chapter 3, "Re-Staging Revolution and Remembering Toward Change: National Liberation Front Women Perform Prospective Memory in Vietnam" (PhD dissertation, University of North Carolina at Chapel Hill, 2008).
18. Dwight Conquergood, "Performance Studies: Interventions and Radical Research," *TDR: The Drama Review* 46.2 (2002), 145–56.
19. See Pam Schweitzer, "Many Happy Retirements: An Interactive Theatre Project with Older People," in Mady Schutzman and Jan Cohen-Cruz, eds., *Playing Boal: Theatre, Therapy, Activism* (New York: Routledge, 1994), 64–80; Rena Fraden, *Imagining Medea: Rhodessa Jones and Theater for Incarcerated Women* (Chapel Hill: University of North Carolina Press, 2001); and Alicia Rouverol, "Trying to Be Good: Lessons in Oral History and Performance," in Della Pollock, ed., *Remembering: Oral History Performance* (New York: Palgrave Macmillan, 2005),19–44.
20. See Hugo Slim and Paul Thompson, *Listening for a Change: Oral Testimony and Community Development* (Philadelphia: New Society Publishers, 1995), 9–10.
21. Emily Mann, *Testimonies: Four Plays* (New York: Theatre Communications Group, 1997), 35.
22. See Rivka Eisner, "Remembering Toward Loss: Performing *And so there are pieces . . .* ," in Pollock, ed., *Remembering: Oral History Performance*, 123ff.
23. Mann, *Testimonies*, 35.
24. Anna Deavere Smith, *Fires in the Mirror: Crown Heights, Brooklyn, and Other Identities* (New York: Anchor Books, 1993), and *Twilight – Los Angeles, 1992 on the Road: A Search for American Character* (New York: Anchor Books, 1994); and Moisés Kaufman, *The Laramie Project* (New York: Vintage, 2001).
25. Judith Butler, *Giving an Account of Oneself* (New York: Fordham University Press, 2005), 21.
26. Bauman, *Verbal Art as Performance*, 434.
27. Cheryl Mattingly, *Healing Dramas and Clinical Plots: The Narrative Structure of Experience* (New York: Cambridge University Press, 1998), 107.
28. *Ibid.*, 108.

29. Sonja Kuftinec, "[Walking Through A] Ghost Town: Cultural Hauntologie in Mostar, Bosnia-Herzegovina or Mostar: A Performance Review," *Text and Performance Quarterly* 18.2 (1998), 83. See also Kuftinec, *Staging America: Cornerstone and Community-Based Theater* (Carbondale: Southern Illinois University Press, 2003).

30. *Ibid.*, 89.

31. Grace Cho, "Performing an Ethics of Entanglement in Still Present Pasts: Korean Americans and the 'Forgotten War,'" *Women and Performance* Special Issue, "Reparations," ed. Joshua Chambers-Letson and Robert G. Diaz, 16.2 (2006), 305.

32. Diana Taylor, *The Archive and the Repertoire: Performing Cultural Memory in the Americas* (Durham: Duke University Press, 2003), 208.

33. With debt to Dwight Conquergood's projection of the movement of performance from mimesis to poeisis to kinesis in "Beyond the Text: Toward a Performative Cultural Politics," in Sharon Dailey, ed., *The Future of Performance Studies: Visions and Revisions* (Washington, DC: National Communication Association, 1998), 25–36.

34. Victor Turner, with Edie Turner, "Performing Ethnography," in *The Anthropology of Performance* (New York: PAJ Publications, 1986), 139–55.

35. Note Conquergood's interventions into trials of Hmong refugees living in Albany Park in the late 1980s, reported in, for example, Terry Wilson, "Judge Tells Tribesmen to Study U.S.," *Chicago Tribune*, 30 June 1988, "Chicagoland" section, and Conquergood, unpublished MS., prepared for the Center for Urban Affairs and Policy Research, Northwestern University, May 23, 1988.

36. Shannon Jackson, "Touchable Stories and the Performance of Infrastructural Memory," in Pollock, ed., *Remembering: Oral History Performance*, 45–66. See also www.touchablestories.org.

37. D. Soyini Madison, "My Desire is for the Poor to Speak Well of Me," in Pollock, ed., *Remembering: Oral History Performance*, 149.

9

SHANNON JACKSON

What is the "social" in social practice?: comparing experiments in performance

"In my innermost heart I am a Minimalist with a guilt complex."
– Santiago Sierra[1]
"Touchable Stories began in 1996 with the idea of using the talents of
contemporary artists to help individual communities *define their own voice*
and give it public expression."
– Shannon Flattery, Touchable Stories website (italics in original)[2]

The above quotations come from two artists whose work differs enormously,
yet both artists' work has been called "social practice." As I noted recently
in the "Lexicon" special issue of *Performance Research,* social practice is a
term that has allegiances with a number of movements in experimental art
and performance studies.[3] Those allegiances bring to mind other terms that
share some kinship with social practice: activist art, social work, protest performance, performance ethnography, community art, relational aesthetics,
conversation pieces, action research, and other terms that signal a social turn
in art practice as well as the representational dimension of social and political
formations. However, "social practice" is also embedded in a longer history
of terms that have not always enjoyed triumphant celebration in the history
of aesthetics: literal art, functionalist art, dumbed-down art, social realist
art, victim art, consumable art, and related terms that have been coined
to lament the capitulations to accessibility and intelligibility that can occur
when art practice and social practice – aesthetics and politics – combine.
How should we come to terms with this difference? Do the barometers for
assessing aesthetic innovation differ so enormously from those that assess
social innovation?

The tensions and opportunities in conducting an interdisciplinary analysis of social practice, an interdiscipline that integrates experimental aesthetic
movements with the traditions of social science and social theory, are regularly felt in the field of performance studies. The cross-disciplinary site of
performance studies provides a forum for asking some very pointed questions about different critical barometers. Is, for instance, the visual artist's

sense of the social in conceptual art comparable to the folklorist's sense of the social? Do they have the same commitments to historical contextualization? Are they similarly or differently interested in the medium of embodiment, voice, gesture, and collective assembly? Similarly, we might ask whether a shared interest in participation provides a link between a social movement theorist and a Boalian forum theatre-maker. Do they have the same barometers for gauging efficacy? For understanding human action? As someone whose first book examined social reform in the cultural performances of the settlement movement, who now finds herself regularly teaching courses in contemporary experimental art, I am continually compelled by cross-disciplinary tensions and questions.[4] Often they confuse me. By exploring different techniques and effects within the category of "social practice," this chapter seeks to make explicit some of the contradictions and competing stakes of interdisciplinary scholarship and experimental art-making in performance studies. Firstly, I offer an account of both contemporary and past debates in aesthetic theory around the social in art practice, arguing for the usefulness of the term "heteronomy" in understanding both experimental art and social selves. I then reflect on how two artists, Santiago Sierra and Shannon Flattery of Touchable Stories, offer different models for engaging the legacies and debates of social practice.

Social aesthetics and its debates

The visual art critic Claire Bishop's essay "Antagonism and Relational Aesthetics," published in *October* in 2004, set off a great deal of discussion in the experimental art world, including a fairly lacerating response from one of the artists she critiques, Liam Gillick. Bishop's continued reflection appeared subsequently in *Artforum*, along with a variety of explicit and implicit responses in that journal and others.[5] Their concerns are symptomatic of the kind of discourse and confusion that emerges whenever a discussion of politics and aesthetics is underway, especially over how such discussion provokes and is provoked by a categorical crisis around performance as both an aesthetic form and a social one.

Bishop's *October* essay and her *Artforum* piece express themselves in slightly different terms, but together they create oppositions among different critical paradigms and art movements. Generally, Bishop seeks to support what she calls the "antagonist" possibilities of art practice. Antagonism is the term she uses to argue for the necessity of a criticality and a resistance to intelligibility that is, in her view, necessary for aesthetics and, again in her view, neutralized when art starts to tread into social territory. Art practices that seek to create a harmonious space of intersubjective encounter – that is, those that "feel good" – risk neutralizing the capacity of critical reflection. Furthermore, art practices that seek to ameliorate social ills – that is, those that "do good" – risk becoming overly instrumentalized, neutralizing the formal complexities and interrogative possibilities of art under the homogenizing umbrella of a social goal. As her argument unfolds, certain artists – such as Rirkrit Tiravanija and Liam Gillick – end up on the "bad" feel-good side of her critical equation; Tiravanija's renowned use of gallery space as a site for food preparation and festive circulation does not leave room for a critical antagonism. Meanwhile, the "do-gooding" impulses of other social practices in Liverpool, Los Angeles, San Sebastian, Rotterdam, and Istanbul are critiqued for their uncritical gestures of "responsibility." Bishop's critiques are leveled most heavily at Oda Projesi, a Turkish artist collective that moved into a three-room apartment in Istanbul and proceeded to visit their neighbors and invite them over, eventually sponsoring children's workshops, parades, potlucks, and other events that sought to create a context for dialogue and exchange. Indeed, their practice might be called a contemporary instance of settlement work. At the same time, other artists such as Santiago Sierra, Thomas Hirschorn, Francis Alÿs, and Alexandra Mir end up on Bishop's "good" antagonistic side. She reconsiders Hirschorn's well-publicized contribution to "Documenta XI" in 2002, *Bataille Monument,* a piece that was sited in a local bar and on the lawn shared by two housing projects in Norstadt, a suburb miles away from the "Documenta" venue in Kassel. Defending him against accusations that Hirschorn appropriated a local space without gaining a sufficiently deep understanding of its local politics, Bishop foregrounds the degree to which Hirschorn's decisions and structures created a space of disorientation for "Documenta" spectators, one that disallowed any notion of "community identity" to form and simultaneously "re-admitted a degree of autonomy to art."[6]

In creating a critical barometer for making these determinations, Bishop invokes Chantal Mouffe, whose social theory argues for the necessity of antagonism within and between large-scale social sectors. Bishop thereby equates a (post)socialist theory of antagonism with the felt antagonism of a spectator's encounter with appropriately edgy art material.[7] By opposing antagonistic and nonantagonistic art, Bishop seeks to foreground the extent to which "ethical judgements" and a "generalized set of moral precepts" govern the goals and analysis of such work in lieu of aesthetic criteria.[8] Moreover, the social mission of social art overdetermines its structure, creating a desire for functionality and efficacy that neutralizes art's capacity to remain outside the instrumentalist prescriptions of the social. While Bishop's arguments are not exactly the same – sometimes Bishop does not like art that is feeling good and sometimes she does not like art that is doing good – together, the essays reassemble a familiar lexicon for understanding (and casting judgment upon) a social practice. Such a critical barometer measures an artwork's place among a number of polarizations: 1) social celebration versus social antagonism; 2) legibility versus illegibility; 3) radical functionality versus radical unfunctionality; and 4) artistic heteronomy versus artistic autonomy. The thrust of Bishop's "discontent" is that "the social turn" in art practice is in danger of emphasizing the first terms in this series of pairings over the critical, illegible, useless, and autonomous domains that art must necessarily inhabit in order to be itself. Bishop draws some new lines in the sand in some very old debates about aesthetics and politics. She condemns art that uses references that are easily consumed and accessible, calls for social goals that aspire to "effective" social change, and collaborates to invest overly in a "Christian ethic of the good soul" to engage in an "authorial self-sacrifice" to communities and societies. Instead, she argues that "The best collaborative practices of the past ten years address this contradictory pull between autonomy and social intervention, and reflect on this antinomy both in the structure of the work *and* in the conditions of its reception."[9]

It is hard for me to disagree with the phrasing of the last sentence. Indeed, the fact that Bishop elsewhere advocates art practices that "attempt to think the aesthetic and the social/political *together,* rather than subsuming both within the ethical" seems to dovetail with the kind of coincidence between the social and the aesthetic that I find myself perpetually seeking. In fact, I would imagine that a number of readers of this volume would claim to be similar seekers. So where are these judgments coming from? Where have terms like intelligibility and unintelligibility become polarized? Why is the other-directed work of social art cast as a capitulation to the "Christian ethic of the good soul" (a religious equation that surely is the fastest route to damnation in critical humanities circles)? Finally, what is meant by the ideas of autonomy and heteronomy in all these aesthetic debates about social practice?

I would imagine that the above snapshot of Bishop's work might pique curiosity in a performance studies student trained in the field of social movements, or another working in the field of folklore, or another experienced in the practice of critical ethnography. All might consider themselves scholars of the "social" and all might consider themselves to be interested in artistic interventions into the social. At the same time, such students might be less inclined to see anything radically rewarding in the "feel-bad" artists that Bishop favors. Let me briefly try to suggest a lineage for debates like the one I have described; by doing so, I hope to be able to reorient and revise a visual arts critique such as Bishop's, yet I also hope to show how the formal language of the field of the visual arts offers performance studies a certain kind of critical traction in understanding social practice as an extended form.

Even to use a phrase like "extended form" is to invoke an aesthetic vocabulary, one that has sought over the course of the twentieth and twenty-first centuries to understand how the claims of the social altered the conventional parameters of the art object. Of course, the conventions of nineteenth-century aesthetics argued that art achieved its greatness to the degree that its representations transcended its material substrate, rising above its raw material and its social apparatus of production. This is one way of casting an early aesthetic opposition between "autonomy" and "heteronomy." Such terms have a varied etymology, but for the purposes of this debate the etymology that seems most helpful is the one that aligns autonomy with "the condition of being self-governing" and "heteronomy" with "the condition of being governed by an external rule." Transcendent art achieved the former state by appearing to exist independently from its material; that is, it seemed to exist autonomously from the conditions of its making. In many ways the debates of twentieth-century aesthetics have revolved around whether, how, and to what extent an art form could have such status and/or achieve such an autonomous effect. For some, the achievement of transcendence was only sublimation: the achievement of autonomy merely the disavowal of the "external rules" that perpetually structured all social life, including the social life of aesthetics. Early twentieth-century workers' movements were one of many places where the social role of art was reimagined in heteronomous terms, whether in the appropriation of vernacular forms, the institution of social realism as a progressive aesthetic, or the Constructivist reimagining of the affinity between artistic labor and social labor.

It was after the Second World War, however – upon seeing how the fascist aesthetic use of the vernacular and the Stalinist enforcement of realist aesthetics had rationalized purges of all varieties – that Theodor Adorno questioned the social effects of so-called heteronomous art. In essays such as "Commitment" and "The Autonomy of Art," Adorno's main figure for condemnation was not a celebrated hero of either fascist or Stalinist regimes but, famously, the leftist, avant-garde theatre-maker Bertolt Brecht.[10] Adorno roundly criticized "Brecht's didacticism" and argued that the playwright's desire to be socially engaged had in fact blunted his efficacy.[11] Brecht's desire to be useful had produced an instrumentalization of aesthetics. His desire to be accessible had produced a legibility of plot and character that only "trivialized" politics into easy good and bad oppositions.[12] For Adorno, Brecht's entire "oeuvre" was a capitulation to the "crudely heteronomous demands" of the social that ultimately divested aesthetics of its reason for being. It is important to note that Adorno – and Brecht – were just as likely to encounter critics who argued the opposite. Unlike Adorno, Georg Lukács, as well as a variety of leftist comrades, did not find Brecht's work "too intelligible"; rather, they found it to be not intelligible *enough* to be of social use. Meanwhile, Walter Benjamin argued that Brecht was the ur-example of an aesthetic practice that was at once socially engaged and formally innovative, not an instrumentalization of aesthetics.

This variation in interpretation notwithstanding, it should be noted that Adorno's defense of autonomy was made in somewhat new terms. He was concerned with how much the call for socially intelligible art rationalized intellectual closure:

> Today the curmudgeons whom no bombs could demolish have allied themselves with the philistines who rage against the alleged incomprehensibility of the new art ... This is why today autonomous rather than committed works of art should be encouraged in Germany. Committed works all too readily credit themselves with every noble value, and then manipulate them at their ease.[13]

Rather than a celebration of aesthetic transcendence, aesthetic autonomy was crucial in order to preserve a space of criticality, a question mark amid the piety, righteousness, and neat dualisms of "committed" art. "Even in the most sublimated work of art there is a hidden 'it should be otherwise.'"[14] This willingness to occupy a place of refusal was for Adorno the most important goal of aesthetic practice. It meant questioning the social pull to "accommodate to the world" – refusing social conventions of intelligibility and utility – however well intentioned and morally just their causes seemed. However much Adorno's legacy in modernist aesthetics was celebrated or repudiated in the last half of the twentieth century, his language echoes in a variety of critical circles. Questions around intelligibility and unintelligibility persist in circles that grapple with the modernist preoccupations in the postmodern embrace of ambiguity. Questions around autonomy and heteronomy persist in circles that grapple with the extension of art into social space. Finally, questions around the utility and futility of art persist in circles that grapple with the social and formal dimensions of social art practice.

Similar kinds of preoccupations have propelled subsequent twentieth-century art experimentation. Marcel Duchamp famously entered with a different politics to ask a similar formal question about the autonomy of the art object, installing everyday objects in art museums to expose art as an effect heteronomously produced by the conventions of the museum. Perhaps the most significant movement credited and blamed with presaging the conversation on social art is Minimalism and all varieties of post-Minimalist extensions. Artists such as Donald Judd, Sol LeWitt, Tony Smith, and Robert Morris were heralded as the "fathers" of this movement and were, of course, the figures most famously trounced in Michael Fried's notorious 1967 essay on Minimalist "theatricality," "Art and Objecthood." Employing a reductive sculptural vocabulary – one that rejected both figuration and abstraction to utilize specific geometrical forms such as the cube, the line, the polyhedron, the parallelepiped, and the serial repetition of such forms – Minimalist artists created such "specific objects" in part to expose the conditions of viewing to the spectator who received them. As legions of critics have noted subsequently, Fried's impulse to call such techniques "theatrical" had to do with his discomfort with such self-aware forms of spectatorship and with the durational experience they produced. For example, "[l]iteralist sensibility is theatrical because, to begin with, it is concerned with the actual circumstances in which the beholder encounters literalist work . . . the experience of literalist art is of an object *in a situation* – one that, virtually by definition, *includes the beholder*."[15] Fried went on to quote the sculptor Morris on "Specific Objects" to comment on the artist's desire to turn aesthetic experience into a self-conscious spatialized experience for the spectator:

> The better new work takes relationships out of the work and makes them a function of space, light, and the viewer's field of vision. The object is but one of the terms in the newer aesthetic. It is in some ways more reflexive because one's awareness of oneself existing in the same space as the work is stronger than in previous work, with its many internal relationships. One is more aware than before that he himself is establishing relations as he apprehends the object from various positions and under varying conditions of light and spatial context.[16]

While Morris wished to make clear the degree to which such situations decentered the spectator – "I wish to emphasize that things are in a space with oneself, rather than . . . [that] one is in a space surrounded by things" – Fried refused to accept the importance of the distinction:

> Again, there is no clear or hard distinction between the two states of affairs: one is, after all, *always* surrounded by things. But the things that are literalist works of art must somehow *confront* the beholder – they must, one might always say, be placed not just in his space but in his *way* . . . It is, I think, worth remarking that "the entire situation" means exactly that: *all* of it – including it seems the beholder's *body* . . . Everything counts – not as part of the object, but as part of the situation in which its objecthood is established and on which that objecthood at least partly depends.[17]

Although Fried does not use the word "heteronomy" in this essay, what is striking is his degree of discomfort with the externally derived claims of the "situation," claims that placed demands of an external order that could only be experienced as confrontation or inconvenience ("in his *way*"). The "everything" which "counts" saturated the viewing experience, provoking not only an awareness of a new medium – the *body* of the beholder – but, as a result, an awareness of the art object as "dependent." The interdependency of art and spectator, art object and situation, thus disallowed an experience of aesthetic autonomy. Interestingly, Fried – like Adorno, and not unlike Bishop – turned to theatre and to a theatrical vocabulary to critique the social encumbrances and interdependencies of heteronomous art.

Much has been made of the legacy of Minimalism to the emerging performance art. While their techniques deviated dramatically from the reductive Minimalist form, much experimental, often gallery-based, performance shares the goal of producing this kind of spectatorial self-consciousness in an extended space. The beholder's recognition of embodiment extended to the art object itself and ultimately to the body of the artist who further unsettled the boundaries of visual art practice by inserting the body of the visual artist (for example, Vito Acconci, Chris Burden, and Karen Finley). While occasionally the formal preoccupations behind this extension are forgotten in the sensationalism surrounding some performance art interventions, much performance art of the late twentieth century is helpfully understood as post-Minimalist experimentation. Performance art has been said to "break the frame" of visual art, which is not only to claim a generalized rebellious impulse but also to suggest that such breaking exposes the frame, making participants aware of the supporting apparatus of aesthetic experience by disallowing its bounded obfuscations.

I hope that, by this point, the reader understands my interest in reviewing some episodes in the history of twentieth-century aesthetics. Such histories assist us in navigating the different disciplines that contribute to this conversation. This kind of experimentation in self-reflexivity in art practice and art criticism developed in the same decades in which other academic fields began to grapple with the apparatus of scholarly production and scholarly writing. Although very different in their politics, gestures, and styles, the impulses of critical ethnography, of situated knowledge-making, and of self-reflexivity in cross-cultural writing partook of a similar desire to understand the conventions by which our most treasured experiences, pleasures, and ideas are made. As the twentieth century gave way to the twenty-first, both art practices and new scholarship in the humanities and social sciences wrestled with a variety of "social" issues that made the need for this self-consciousness particularly urgent. Civil rights movements across the globe, Western and transnational feminisms, and postcolonial and anti-Orientalist reflection on the representation of otherness promoted not simply new knowledges and new art-making but forms of practice that asked participants to reflect on *how* they had come to know and to call attention to the assumptions and conventions that had kept them from knowing and experiencing differently.

In other words, in the past few decades, both art-making and social inquiry have been induced to avow their heteronomy, the degree to which their making and their thinking were "governed by external rules," that is, contingent and interdependent with a world that they could not pretend to transcend. It is in recognition of this shared impulse that I find myself most interested in trying to see how we can cast the question of "social practice" – in aesthetics, in the humanities, and in the social sciences – as the heterogeneous pursuit of a shared formal problem.

Social practice: two cases

I opened this chapter with epigraphs from two artists who are "very different" yet linked by the social turn of their aesthetic practice. Santiago Sierra, a Spanish artist currently based in Mexico City, has an international reputation in the contemporary art world. He has participated in annual festivals and biennials and received major commissions from a range of art organizations in both elite cosmopolitan cities and locally engaged galleries and museums in Latin and South America. Shannon Flattery is the founder and artistic director of Touchable Stories, a Boston-based community arts group that creates multiyear, interactive, site-specific oral history installations in neighborhood community spaces. According to their curators, spectators, and reviewers, both artists address social issues of marginalization, especially those of poverty, labor, immigration, exile, urbanization, and environmental injustice. However, to compare one artist who calls himself "a Minimalist with a guilt complex" with another who seeks to give marginal sectors of society the opportunity to "define their own voice" is to compare different artistic methods of social engagement, even if both produce a consciousness of artistic heteronomy and social interdependency. As I will suggest below, Sierra produces such effects through an aesthetics of reduction while Flattery does so through an aesthetics of expansion. While Flattery's practice exemplifies an ethic of critical ethnography in its methods of extended collaboration and intermedia incorporation, Sierra's social engagements are in some ways "antisocial," exposing the reductive operations of social inequity by mimicking their forms. At the same time, both artists cultivate an awareness in spectators of their systemic relation to the social issues addressed and to the durational, spatial, and embodied structures in which that address occurs.

Let me consider first the experience of duration, as it came forward from Minimalist experiments and as it has been reworked by Sierra. The durational consciousness produced by the Minimalist object was an effect disparaged in Fried's essay and celebrated by Minimalism's proponents. Whereas

Fried condemned the "endlessness" of Minimalist sculpture, Morris lauded durational experimentation to such a degree that he found himself turning to collaboration with time-based artists of performance and even adding another signature essay, "Notes on Dance," to his critical writing. In the latter essay Morris emphasized the structural nature of time. Duration was less something to be manipulated than a structure to be exposed; silences were used not so much as "punctuations" but "to make duration itself palpable."[18] Sierra utilizes duration in a way that both extends Minimalist technique and calls its bluff. Consider, for instance, his 1999 piece "Paid People," created for the Museo Rufino Tamayo in Mexico. Here 465 people were hired to stand over the entire floor space of the museum's primary display area (five people per square meter). As the crowd of people stood, expecting to receive an hourly minimum wage for their effort, spectators came to watch the bodies trying to be still while simultaneously being aware of the ticking of time. The basic structure of the piece thus addresses the conventions by which labor is organized under the phrase "time and materials." In a structure where the only material is the hired worker's body, the notion of time as something bought comes more startlingly into view. But it also shows the degree to which the Minimalist interest in "time's palpability" has a class basis. The piece exposed the degree to which time is already quite palpable to those who watch the clock for a living. Thus the piece not only avowed duration as a structuring influence on the artwork but also exposed duration as itself governed by the external rules of the wage system. Subsequent pieces such as "Eight People Paid to Remain Inside Cardboard Boxes" (Guatemala City, 1999), "A Person Paid for 360 Continuous Working Hours" (New York, 2000), or "430 People Paid 30 Soles" (Lima, 2001) reused a similar basic structure, while other projects such as "250 cm Line Tattooed on Six Paid People" (Havana, 1999) or "160 cm Line Tattooed on 4 People" (Salamanca, 2000) raised the stakes of the exchange in hiring people who allow themselves to be tattooed. Indeed, in Sierra's open reuse of hired labor as the foundation for his pieces, time emerges not only as a natural force that the artwork can no longer transcend (à la Minimalism) but as a social force heteronomously dependent on the asymmetries of capitalist economics. Duration is all the more palpable when it is exchanged for a wage.

The reduction – indeed, some would say, the replicated dehumanization – of Sierra's practice is nearly the opposite of the kind of rehumanizing impulses at work in pieces by Touchable Stories. Whereas Sierra's pieces transform "collaboration" into a hiring relationship and make little mention of the histories of participants – and never their names – Touchable Stories conducts roughly eighteen months of research – meeting neighbors, sitting in on civic meetings, holding community dinners, and collecting hundreds of hours of oral histories to serve both as the inspiration for an exhibit and as the aural medium in an installation. The process of living among the people it seeks to represent supports the creation of large site-specific installations that are called "living mazes," sited in church basements, community centers, and former retail spaces donated for two years by individuals and groups living in the marginalized neighborhoods of Dorchester, Central Square, and Allston, Massachusetts and, most recently, in Richmond, California.[19] In each of its "living mazes," small groups move through interactive installations, listening to the voices of taped oral histories as they open drawers, turn knobs, pull curtains, and linger on pillows to encounter stories of migration, relocation, gentrification, violence, and loss.

As different as this gesture is from the work of Sierra, we could say that "duration" is still an integral structure in the Touchable Stories practice. However, understanding its durational investments requires that we look in different places. Indeed, "time" is a word that repeatedly emerges in much Touchable Stories documentation, but here the emphasis is on the artists' willingness to spend time on understanding issues and worlds of great complexity. Here the durational commitment to shared time and space is in fact the underlying structure of Touchable Stories' practice, a willingness to commit time – indeed to commit, as Flattery does, to self-relocation in a new neighborhood space for years – in order to allow one's predetermined sense of the issues and arguments to change as well as to create a collaboration with community members that has a provisional relationship of trust. Touchable Stories thereby shares in an ethic of participatory ethnography as so many of its practitioners have theorized it, committing to a degree of sensuous knowing over time. Interestingly, it is this durational and spatial commitment that a critic like Bishop finds unaesthetic in groups such as Oda Projesi and other "social turns" with which she is "discontented."[20] Adorno, too, might well have found this durational commitment to be a capitulation to the "crudely heteronomous demands" of the social, but it seems to me that the challenge here is to allow duration to have a different kind of aesthetic palpability.[21] Even if Flattery's ethic of participation can be analogized to the practices of the ethnographer, the settlement worker, or the activist, it seems important to notice the specificity of her desire to do so under her self-identification as an artist. While her attempt to know others with more complexity and intimacy might read to some as instrumentalization of the art process, we might also note the degree to which this form of participation is differently "endless" in a Touchable Stories project. The multiyear collaborations seem not to end even after the installation has come down. Just as we might analyze the experimental durational structures of the endurance performances of Marina Abramovic or Linda Montano, we might notice that the durational commitment to shared time-space is a *technique* of the social artist, that it is a commitment made whose consequences are unforeseen and – by virtue of an implicit social contract – will be received and incorporated by the process and its structure. Moreover, this experience of duration is part of a larger gesture of collaboration that is not only an "authorial self-sacrifice," as Bishop would have it, but also a more radical experiment in authorial release to the external claims of others, one that might be asking a basic question about how far the avowal of aesthetic heteronomy can be pursued.

Similar kinds of exercises in reorientation would be necessary to compare other elements in the work of Sierra and Touchable Stories. Sierra works with Minimalist forms such as the cube, the line, and the parallelepiped, but situates them differently through the incorporation of wage laborers. In a piece that seemed to comment on both the Minimalist form and the desire to "do good," Sierra's "90 cm Bread Cube" (2003) was a solid bread cube baked in specific dimensions and offered as charity in a shelter for homeless people in Mexico City. Documentation shows people gathered round to slice off parts of the cube onto paper plates, the geometry of the cube undone by the claims of its marginalized consumers. Sierra also works with the Minimalist desire to avow the force of gravity; indeed, his work can be placed in a direct genealogy with Minimalism's emphasis on sculpture over painting and the tendency in that movement to privilege artworks that oriented themselves toward the ground plane of the floor rather than the antigravitational plane of the wall. Orientation toward the floor – without a pedestal – was seen as an avowal of the art object's relationship to the natural external rule of gravity – opposing itself to painting's attempt to overcome gravity with hooks, wires, and frames on a wall. In pieces like "Object Measuring 600 × 57 × 52 cm Constructed to be Held Horizontally to a Wall" or "24 Blocks of Concrete Constantly Moved During a Day's Work by Paid Workers," Sierra evokes the Minimalist impulse toward gravitational avowal as inherited from the large, heavy geometrical installations of Donald Judd, Sol LeWitt, Richard Serra, and others.

However, Sierra's engagement with the social politics of gravity is different; indeed, by hiring workers to move such large, heavy Minimalist forms, he exposes the antigravitational labor required to install a gravitational aesthetic intervention. Here the gravitational – like the durational – has a class basis, forcing an acknowledgment of the long classed history that governs the social management of gravity. Like duration, gravity has always been palpable for the class historically hired to do the most heavy lifting. Finally, we can see a similar relationship of reuse and revision when it comes to another Minimalist trope: seriality. As a term that exposes the steady operation of time and that uses repetition to question the myth of originality, the serial reproduction of similar forms appears throughout Sierra's work; once again, however, the "moved constantly" of such repetitions exposes seriality as enmeshed in the repetitive forms of labor that were never given the status of "authorship" in the first place.

Finding such kinds of Minimalist genealogies in the practice of Touchable Stories would require a reorientation and a willingness to look in different places for an engagement with gravity, seriality, futility, and the limits of the intelligible. It might begin with a form – the suspended collection of glass jars – that has become a recurrent motif in all Touchable Stories' projects. Jars hang at slightly different eye levels in a series; inside, viewers find miniature photographs of old buildings transferred to transluscent paper, usually illuminated through the back light of a nearby wall. While listening to stories of neighborhood spaces that have since been destroyed, visitors linger before the jars, holding them to identify the doorframes, signposts, and other features that tell them which disappeared building they are viewing. The installation functions at many levels. It evokes the rhythms of encounter found in a gallery or museum, calling forth the steady flow of people as they move from one image to the next in a row. However, the images are suspended from the ceiling, allowing circular movement around the image as one might encounter a sculpture. The antigravitational suspension from on high emphasizes the airspace underneath and allows for another kind of interaction – touch, the careful holding of the object itself. Meanwhile, that formal suspension sets off and is set off by the contents inside; the seeming weight and immobility of the building is countered by the ease of its uprooting; a social history of uprooted urbanization is thus made palpable by an aesthetic form that lifts all too easily, presented in a glass jar that is both precious and easily broken. While this kind of seriality is surely a sentimental one, the cumulative effect creates a heightened spatial consciousness on several levels, allowing the boundaries of the art object to extend into the spectators' space – "in his *way*?" – while simultaneously provoking reflection upon the spectators' own spatial location in a longer urban history, a history on which that spectatorial location "depends."

Having offered some sample readings of the work of two very "different" artists, it is simultaneously important to observe how "different" such readings could be. To emphasize this fact is not simply to withdraw into a generalized relativism as a critic but also to foreground the different kinds of precedents and object histories that structure an encounter with a social practice. Such variation seems to affect and afflict practices that seek to think "aesthetics and politics together." Just as Brecht became a figure who received contradictory forms of critique, so the works of both Sierra and Touchable Stories have endured all varieties of critique, ranging from every position on the poles to which I referred above: social celebration/social antagonism, radically unfunctional/radically functional, unintelligible/intelligible, autonomous/heteronomous. For some, the slicing up and doling out of Sierra's "90 cm Bread Cube" was an attempt to be functional; for others, it was a parody of such a gesture. The contrast raises the question of how we might compare such a meal with the kind of "community dinners" that Touchable Stories sponsors as part of its process. For some, Touchable Stories' glass-jar displays convey the literal history of a neighborhood too explicitly. For others, the miniaturization and absent didactics do not convey enough information. Too intelligible? Too unintelligible? For some, Sierra is an advocate for the poor; for others, he is simply a cynic. For some, Touchable Stories instrumentalizes aesthetics in service of social progress. For others, its commitment to maintaining an aesthetic space over two years in a site that could be put to "real use" only confirms aesthetic futility. Such differences demonstrate the very different metrics and barometers that critics and viewers bring to bear on social practice, an exceptionally hybrid form. But such differences might also be the occupational hazard of heteronomous engagement. For my part, I find it helpful to keep eyes and heart trained on the particular ways in which this conjunction can form and transform, the numerous ways in which the avowal of heteronomy can have simultaneously aesthetic precision and social effects. Such an approach, however, means acknowledging the degree to which art and humans are not "self-governing." And it means deciding to believe that an awareness of that interdependency can yield both innovative aesthetic forms and an innovative social politics.

Notes

1. Touchable Stories, www.touchablestories.org. Accessed September 7, 2007.
2. Quoted in Eckhard Schneider, "300 Tons," in Schneider, *Santiago Sierra: 300 Tons and Previous Works* (Germany: KUB, 2003), 33.
3. Shannon Jackson, "Social Practice," *Performance Research* 11.3 (September 2007), 113–18.
4. Shannon Jackson, *Lines of Activity: Performance, Domesticity, Hull-House Historiography* (Ann Arbor: University of Michigan, 2000).
5. Claire Bishop, "Antagonism and Relational Aesthetics," *October* 110 (Fall 2004), 51–79; Liam Gillick, "Contingent Factors: A Response to Claire Bishop," *October* 115 (Winter 2006), 95–107; and Claire Bishop, "The Social Turn: Collaboration and its Discontents," *Artforum* 44 (February 2006), 178–83.
6. Bishop, "Antagonism and Relational Aesthetics," 74, 75.

10

AMELIA JONES

Live art in art history: a paradox?

Until the 1990s, the discipline of art history, as developed in Europe and North America from the nineteenth century onward, refused to acknowledge the crucial role of the body in the production and reception of works of art. Art history and its discursive and institutional corollaries, the art gallery, the auction house, and much of art criticism, thus systematically ignored the body, even (after 1960) in the face of the development of an explosive interest in representing, enacting, or otherwise foregrounding the body as central to the experience of visual culture. This chapter addresses why this was the case and explores how shifting emphases on the body in the production and reception of visual arts practices in the post-Second World War period insistently wore away at the occlusion of the body in art discourses and institutions. It will then examine the fact that, in the 1990s, a new generation of art historians and critics had began to theorize the central importance of the body as a crucial matrix, ground, and activating source for meaning and value in the visual arts and visual culture in general.[1]

The suppression or erasure of the live or inhabited body in institutionalized versions of art discourse and in art institutions has a long history in Euro-American culture. It is linked to the belief systems articulated in Western theories of aesthetics – beliefs that, in turn, became embedded in the very structures of thought relating to the institutions for teaching, displaying, and making the visual arts. Aesthetics developed in Western philosophy as a model for navigating the connection between a certain class of objects in the world and the perceiving (as well as feeling and judging) human subject. Immanuel Kant's 1790 *Critique of Judgement*, a (if not *the*) formative text in the development of what would become modernist conceptions of aesthetics, thus argues that it is aesthetic judgment that functions as a bridge to link the human subject to the object. Aesthetic judgment "is the faculty of thinking the particular as contained under the universal"; it is the means through which the specific aesthetic object is apprehended through the individual senses (the "particular," as enacted through the embodied subject)

151

and understood as well as given supposedly "universal" (objective) value through a structure of shared beliefs about value and meaning.[2]

The paradox in Kantian aesthetics is that the judgment must be both subjective (it obviously takes place through an individual human's senses, first and foremost) and objective (it must be universalizable in order to have any value at all). For the judgment to have validity, Kant argues, it "must involve a claim to validity for all men."[3] Kant was well aware of the paradoxical nature of aesthetic universality, noting that "[t]he necessity of the universal assent that is thought in a judgement of taste, is a subjective necessity which, under the presupposition of a common sense is represented as objective." He further notes that "we tolerate no one else being of a different opinion" when we judge something as aesthetically beautiful and thus as art – we strategically present our "private feeling" as a "public sense," and our assertion is "not that every one *will* fall in with our judgement but rather that everyone *ought* to agree with it."[4]

Contrary to modernist readings of Kant, then, his model of aesthetics actually acknowledges the contingency of aesthetic judgment as well as, albeit indirectly, the *embodied* nature of our encounter with the aesthetic image or object.[5] Such subtlety, however – Kant's tenuous attempt to maintain the tension between the subjective and objective – was repressed in Euro-American aesthetics as it developed in the nineteenth and twentieth centuries in favor of a radically reductive model favoring the art critic as a subject who was inherently objective, a subject (as it were) without a body. By the early to mid twentieth century, the modernist art critics Roger Fry, writing in London, and Clement Greenberg, working in New York, had articulated an increasingly reified critical model based on *formalism*, defining art as that which fulfilled a very specific set of formal standards which could be interpreted objectively by a trained and "disinterested" (and so nonsubjective and effectively disembodied) critic.

For Fry and other formalists loosely following Kant, the aesthetic became a special category of experience defined in relation to a special group of objects.[6] The critic defined himself as above the fray of the market precisely through his "disinterested" relationship to these objects. This notion of aesthetics produced a specialist subject whose subjectivity (interestedness, bodily attachment) was masked by the notion of the work as having an intrinsic meaning and value to be discerned by a disinterested specialist viewer who was implicitly defined as a transparent conduit through whom the hallowed significance of the work would be magically transmitted.

For Greenberg, the success of a modernist work of art was to be determined by the specialist art critic who could determine how well the work adhered to its own medium's specificity. In a well-known argument, Greenberg thus noted:

> The essence of Modernism lies, as I see it, in the use of the characteristic methods of a discipline to... entrench it more fully in its area of competence... It quickly emerged that the unique and proper area of competence of each art coincided with all that was unique to the nature of its medium... It was the stressing... of the ineluctable flatness of the support that remained most fundamental in the processes by which pictorial art criticized and defined itself under Modernism.[7]

The determination of whether or not a work succeeded in this way was made *by the critic* (Greenberg, of course, took this role himself throughout his career). It would be predicated on a simplified logic of Kantian aesthetics, whereby the critic was implicitly positioned as disinterested – that is, not invested in a bodily way in the work (rather than, as in Kant, conflicted by his *subjective* sensorial relationship to the work and his desire to compel "universal" assent with his judgment by posing it as *objective*). Greenberg's influential model of aesthetics thus denied the role of the senses and embodiment, strictly disavowing the role of the body in determining the meaning and value of the work of art. By the 1950s, Greenberg's model was hegemonic in the New York art world, itself the new postwar center of visual arts practice and discourse in Western culture.[8]

The tendency for art history, art criticism, and museum practice and discourse to ignore or suppress the role of the body in the making, display, and interpretation of works of art can be linked quite clearly to the assumptions built into these discourses and practices, which developed out of a narrow interpretation of European aesthetics. In addition to the closures around the body because of the prohibition against acknowledging the role of the senses and the particularity of "subjective" vision and reasoning in relation to the work of art, the body threatens these systems in other ways. The early twentieth-century avant-gardists began to probe the limits of visual arts discourses and particularly the then burgeoning private art market (which developed with the rise of capitalism and industrialism, replacing the patronage system once the European monarchies had been deposed or disempowered) by mobilizing the *live* body in particular.

Most notably, in the early twentieth century the Dadaists – coming from literary, theatrical, and visual arts backgrounds – staged outrageous theatrical public events in the First World War period in Central Europe and Paris. For example, the "Greatest Ever Dada Show," staged in 1919 at the Saal zur Kaufleuten in Zurich (Switzerland held a position of neutrality during the war and had thus been a mecca for artists escaping conscription), included speeches on abstract painting, outrageously "modern" dances by African-style masked figures, and poetry readings, including a text by organizer Tristan Tzara read simultaneously (but not synchronistically) by twenty participants.[9] Hugo Ball's famous performances of poetry at Zurich's Cabaret Voltaire during the war involved his donning bizarre outfits such as a funnel with a cone hat as he sonorously intoned nonsense poetry. The performative and cross-disciplinary character of such cultural events produced a cacophonous range of live bodies performing often outrageous, confrontational and/or incomprehensible visual and verbal expressions.

For art history to accommodate such practices would be for the discipline, and its corollaries the art gallery, art museum, and broader art market, to acknowledge that the "value" placed on visual art works through the codified structures of aesthetic judgment were contingent on bodies that, in this case, could not be suppressed. One's appreciation for, or revulsion from and desire to avoid, acts such as Ball's poetry readings were intimately linked to the senses and emotions attached to them. The reactions of the audience to such raucous events *had* to be openly embodied – it would be ridiculous to pretend that one could judge Ball's poetic performance in a disembodied or "disinterested" way as called for by formalist criticism (and equally ridiculous to suppose that such radically cross-disciplinary works were "entrenching" in a formal or stylistic area of competence, as Greenberg's model demanded).

The mobilization of the live body strategically destroyed the pretensions of objectivity on which the various institutions and discourses of Euro-American art based their authority. Such works could not be accommodated into a discipline whose logic – in order to support the art market, with its assumption that the value of the artwork was objectively determined – demanded the erasure of spectatorial desire from interpretation. The Dada performances were completely erased from official histories of art until the late 1970s, though they did have a kind of subterranean historical afterlife, informing an alternative strand of modernism as it developed into postmodernism after 1945.[10] In fact, the publication of several books shortly after the war, including Robert Motherwell's epochally important 1951 anthology *The Dada Painters and Poets* and Robert Lebel's 1959 book *Marcel Duchamp*, testified to a growing interest even among the Abstract Expressionists, among whom Motherwell was counted, in modes of creative production that were not strictly "formalist."[11]

However, this performative and/or embodied strand of art practice and theory remained for the most part marginalized. Even as artists from the Happenings and Fluxus movements (see below) began to explore the power of the live body to break down the boundaries between artist, artwork, and audience in the late 1950s and 1960s, Greenberg's conception of modernism became more powerful, and more entrenched, as the decade unfolded. For example, while Minimalist artists and theorists such as Robert Morris and Donald Judd produced large-scale sculptural forms that demanded recognition of the body as it navigated in relation to these forms, Michael Fried infamously extended Greenberg's tenets in his 1967 article "Art and Object-hood" to argue that Minimalist (or, as he called them, "literalist") works are unsuccessful because they are "theatrical" (concerned with "the actual circumstances in which the beholder encounters literalist work"); they are "ideological" (as opposed to the "wholly manifest" objects of modernism, as defined by Greenberg's tenets); "anthropomorphic" (versus the putative self-sufficiency of successful modernist art); "corrupted and perverted by theatre"; and, ultimately, "antithetical to art."[12]

Morris, who privileged Minimalism in his writing and his practice and openly admitted to the works' overt solicitation of the viewer's body, wrote in his important "Notes on Sculpture, Part 2" (1966), "[t]he awareness of scale is a function of... comparison... Space between the subject and the object is implied in such a comparison... it is just this distance between object and subject that creates a more extended situation, for physical participation becomes necessary." Morris continues, arguing for the large scale of Minimalist works as a strategic method of spectatorial engagement: "Things on the monumental scale [place]... kinesthetic demands... upon the body."[13] The fervor of Fried's attack on Minimalism (paralleled by vit-riolic references in Greenberg's 1960s writings on Minimalism and other "new" modes of artistic production that arguably opened the work to the body)[14] indicates the intensity of what was at stake in these debates. They were not just arcane discussions about whether or not Minimalism was "good" art, but raised crucial questions about what it means to engage with the visual arts as a whole. Artists working in the 1960s began to insist that "art" inevitably involved the body, not just because it could be experienced only through the senses but because the body was invested emotionally and even erotically in anything believed to be a work of art. Radically open-ing the work to the body of the artist, to its environment and to the bodies around it, new approaches to the visual arts threatened to collapse the entire edifice of value on which the art market (with its corollaries art history, art criticism, and the art gallery/museum) is built. Their introduction of the body into (or "as") the work of art in relation to an embodied specta-tor could be said to define a major structural shift away from modernist beliefs, which continued to rest on a narrow view of eighteenth-century aesthetics.

Yoko Ono's 1964 *Cut Piece*, for example, which involved her sitting on a stage in Kyoto (and in 1964 and 1965 in Tokyo and New York) and inviting members of the audience to cut off her clothing, demanded a relationship of reciprocal action with audience members. The fear and anxiety potentially provoked in these "participants" by being asked or encouraged to enact a kind of visual/tactile "rape" on a female body (and, in the New York context, one who was marked as ethnically "other" to the bodies inhabiting the white-dominated art world) activated not only an obvious "interestedness," but a revulsion that complicated the entire conception of the aesthetic as a project invested in the making and interpretation of beautiful things with inherent value, as discerned by "disinterested" judges.

Even earlier, however, at the same time that Greenberg's conception of modernism became dominant across the English-speaking art world, certain artists and theorists had begun to resist the rigid terms of his concept of modernism. As early as 1952, the art critic Harold Rosenberg published his important article "American Action Painters," in which he challenged Greenberg's erasure of the body through lengthy descriptive passages defining contemporary art in relation to a performative painting body. While Rosenberg never states Jackson Pollock's name directly, his essay clearly pivots around the idea and the image of the body of Pollock painting, a body that was becoming internationally visible through the publication of photographs of him in action and the circulation of a 1951 film by Hans Namuth showing the artist in the act of painting.[15] As Rosenberg famously described the embodied act of painting that was becoming popular in postwar New York, "[a]t a certain moment the canvas began to appear to one American painter after another as an arena in which to act... What was to go on the canvas was not a picture but an event."[16]

Rosenberg was one among several (mostly artists) who began in the 1950s to open the door for a new way of thinking about what the Abstract Expressionists, and particularly Pollock, were doing. Far from Greenberg's disembodied account of modernist painting, Rosenberg insisted on painting as an *act*, a process, involving bodily movement through space and time (and thus engaging a spectatorial body as well). Rosenberg's model was paralleled by developments in the visual arts that were, at the time, subterranean but have come to have epic significance in more recent histories of the period – those written since 1990, when art history scholars have addressed more consciously the repression of the body in dominant strands of modernism.[17]

In these revisionist accounts various art movements and practices that had been marginalized in the Greenbergian system have been excavated and written into histories of contemporary art. In the early 1950s, for example, at the experimental Black Mountain College in the mountains of North

Carolina, a group of innovative artists, musicians, writers, and dancers, including the musician John Cage and his romantic as well as creative partner, the dancer Merce Cunningham, worked together on projects merging two modes of performance, music and dance, with the visual arts. For a famous 1952 event, *Theater Piece #1*, they collaborated with Buckminster Fuller, Franz Kline, and the young art student Robert Rauschenberg to work across media in a distinctly performative way. *Theater Piece #1* consisted of "a multi-focus event in which simultaneous, unrelated activities would be taking place both in front of and around the audience": Cage delivering a lecture, his music being played by David Tudor, Cunningham dancing, and Rauschenberg playing scratchy records with photographs and movies projected onto his innovative "White Paintings," canvases simply covered with white paint.[18]

In retrospect, and once inscribed into histories of contemporary art, it is clear that *Theater Piece #1* was a watershed project in the development of an alternative kind of contemporary visual art – one that, unlike Greenberg's exclusively medium-based and disembodied modern painting, not only accommodated the live body and the art-making process, but highlighted them – making the performative body central to the art experience. In so doing, this alternative mode of practice opened the visual arts to temporality and to the vicissitudes of interpretation: for a body in process, producing art as action rather than final product opened art to the audience in new ways. A closed view of what the "art" meant could no longer be assumed if the art was in process, being created in relation to an audience, and potentially incorporated into it. Produced at virtually the same moment as Rosenberg was publishing his essay, and at a moment in which Greenberg's model of modernism was clearly dominant, *Theater Piece #1* insistently broke down the boundaries Greenberg was so adamant about maintaining between the different arts, as well as activating space and the bodies both making and viewing the work within that space.

Artists working in France and Japan, inspired in part by the example given in the photographic and filmic images of Pollock painting, also ruptured the neat divisions that Greenberg's model labored to maintain. In the early 1950s the French painter Georges Matthieu began staging performances (live or, in his studio, to be photographed) in which he flung paint on a vertically hung canvas.[19] Also in the early 1950s, in Tokyo, Gutai (meaning "concrete," and pointing to the concrete use of the body and extending tools and materials to make art) was founded. Gutai, a group of artists led by Yoshihara Jiro, began to stage performative events, producing two- or three-dimensional works as acts before audiences and documenting these acts for posterity through photographs and films. Gutai insistently turned visual arts practice into a time-based, live performative act explicitly involving a visible and laboring body. This turn to the struggling live body as a creative force could be seen as a strong response to the devastation wrought in Japan by the two atom bombs at the end of the Second World War.[20]

In a parallel move Allan Kaprow and several colleagues began developing performance works that they called "Happenings" in the late 1950s. In 1958, two years after Pollock's untimely death in a car crash, Kaprow published a hugely influential article entitled "The Legacy of Jackson Pollock," in which he took off on the terms Rosenberg had established six years earlier to elaborate a particular reading of Pollock as explicitly performative. Kaprow noted that "[w]ith Pollock . . . the so-called dance of dripping, slashing, squeezing, daubing, and whatever else went into a work placed an almost absolute value upon a diaristic gesture."[21] Kaprow was clear about the necessity for the viewer of Pollock's work to take on an equally active, embodied role vis-à-vis the works:

> I am convinced that to grasp a Pollock's impact properly, we must be acrobats, constantly shuttling between an identification with the hands and body that flung the paint and stood "in" the canvas and submission to the objective markings, allowing them to entangle and assault us. This instability is indeed far from the idea of a "complete" painting. The artist, the spectator, and the outer world are much too interchangeably involved here.[22]

Kaprow brilliantly departs from Rosenberg and aggressively shifts the terms through which Pollock's work, and postwar abstract painting in general, could be understood. As he notes of Pollock's works, "they cease to become paintings and became environments," leaving us "at the point where we must become preoccupied with and even dazzled by the space and objects of our everyday life, either our bodies, clothes, rooms, or, if need be, the vastness of Forty-second Street."[23] Kaprow's important contributions to the Happenings movement, such as *18 Happenings in 6 Parts* (1959), performed at the Reuben Gallery in New York City, exemplify his putting these arguments into practice, which short-circuited Greenberg's separation of the arts into areas of "competence" and the erasure of the bodies of interpreters or spectators. In *18 Happenings* Kaprow divided the gallery into separate parts by sheets of plastic on wood frames, and gave members of the audience a program and cards directing them when to appear in which of the three spaces. Audience members were drawn in as active participants in the work, which was only loosely scripted and took place across space and time.

These alternative voices and practices from Rosenberg to the Black Mountain group to Gutai and Kaprow were marginalized in hegemonic art history surveys and the major galleries such as the Museum of Modern Art in

New York. Until the 1990s, these discourses and institutions promoted a combination of Greenberg's formalism and a traditional conception of the history of modern art as beginning with French Romanticism or Impressionist experiments and ending with Pollock's drip paintings.[24] An alternative version of post-Second World War art not only emphasized the body and the process of making art, but put an embodied, time-based, and spatially open concept of art-making (which included the bodies of the audience members) at the forefront of what visual arts could be thought to be about. In a sense these theorists and artists returned the body to aesthetics, pointing toward what would be an explosion of performative and body-oriented art practices in the 1960s and 1970s. This put the lie to a particular concept of aesthetics as insistently disembodied. The reintegration of the body into "art" put pressure on discourses, practices, and institutions of the visual arts which, in turn, finally began to accommodate questions of embodiment and works that invoked the body.

Following the innovations of the Black Mountain group and the early Happenings and Fluxus artists, who began producing live performative works around 1959/1960, other artistic practices and critical voices began to emerge in the 1960s and early 1970s to challenge the hegemony of a disembodied Greenbergian formalism.[25] Artists such as Carolee Schneemann, loosely connected with the Fluxus group in the early 1960s, produced radical performative works such as *Meat Joy*, performed three times in 1964, first at the First Festival of Free Expression held at the American Center in Paris (organized by Jean-Jacques Lebel, the son of Duchamp scholar Robert Lebel and a key figure in European Fluxus), then in London, and finally at the Judson Memorial Church in New York City. In *Meat Joy* Schneemann, who began as a painter but was moving into installation, live art and filmmaking, mobilized almost naked male and female bodies in an orgiastic tableau of writhing flesh, smeared with meat juices and accompanied (in her words) by tapes of "Paris street sounds [including] . . . the cries and clamorings of rue de Seine vendors selling fish, chicken, vegetables, and flowers beneath the hotel window where I first composed the actual performance score."[26] Schneemann's insistence not only on the presence of the body but on its messiness, fleshiness, and eroticism pointed to a radical shift in thinking about the visual arts. Not only were the visual arts capable of moving beyond what Greenberg had termed their "areas of competence," and in so doing perhaps maintain an even more powerful charge and sense of political and social value, but potentially they involved a complete dissolution of boundaries between artist, artwork, and spectator, as well as an overt enactment of the erotics of making and viewing. In the later 1960s and into the 1970s, European theorists such as François Pluchart and Lea Vergine, sparked by the effusion of performative works being presented across Europe in the 1960s by artists associated with Fluxus and Jean-Jacques Lebel's events, began writing about "body art" or "performance art"; meanwhile, the Americans Ira Licht, Cindy Nemser, and Willoughby Sharp, the latter of whom edited the important experimental arts journal *Avalanche*, articulated a theory and early history of "body works" or "Body Art."[27] In particular, Sharp devoted a number of issues of *Avalanche* either to body art in general or to the work of specific artists exploring various media (such as Vito Acconci) who deploy their bodies within and as the work of art.[28]

Such was the impact of this critical writing (and of course the "body works" inspiring it) that in 1984 a major exhibition was mounted at the Whitney Museum of American Art in New York addressing the previously subterranean cross-media and body-oriented works of this alternative strand of post-1945 art; curated by Barbara Haskell, it was entitled "Blam! The Explosion of Pop, Minimalism, and Performance 1958–1964." In the 1990s, an increasing number of scholarly books and exhibitions began to address the history of a subterranean, performative dimension to post-1945 art and/or explicitly to historicize body and performance art, as well as surfacing issues of embodiment around the movements previously viewed as extensions (whether in a positive or critical sense) of a disembodied formalist practice such as Pop Art or Minimalism.[29]

Even as the discourses and institutions supporting and positioning the visual arts in Euro-American culture began to acknowledge the role of the body and performance in modern and contemporary practice, performance studies was developing as a cross-disciplinary field of inquiry at institutions such as (most notably) the Tisch School of the Arts at New York University, where the important graduate Department of Performance Studies was founded in 1980.[30] Linked to Tisch, the first Performance Studies conference was organized by Peggy Phelan, then at Tisch, and her PhD students and held in New York City in 1995. While by its very nature performance studies, addressing performative arts across media, is cross-disciplinary, the tenets of the official performance studies organization (which has come to be called "Performance Studies international" or PSi) and most of the scholars attached to it largely came from theatre studies and to a lesser extent anthropology (the department at Tisch was co-founded by a theatre studies scholar, Richard Schechner, who was influenced by the work of the anthropologist Victor Turner). It is notable that within official performance studies departments and on behalf of PSi there has been a certain blindness until quite recently in relation to scholarly work coming out of the visual arts and addressing body art, performance art, and/or aspects of performativity and visuality. While groundbreaking scholars such as Phelan could cross over into writing about the visual arts, the work of art historians writing about performance was until the early 2000s largely invisible within performance studies scholarship.[31]

The disciplinary "blindness" in relation to the body and the visual thus goes both ways. While art history, art criticism, and the art gallery and museum – blinded by the imperatives of European aesthetics – literally could not "see" works invoking or even directly employing the body as live or even in represented form (especially photographic or filmic) until around 1970, performance studies was unable to accommodate or recognize the performance and scholarly work coming out of the visual arts until the 2000s. The *body* is clearly the crux of the first kind of blindness; as I have noted, Western aesthetics in effect made it impossible to acknowledge the role of the body in the making, display, and interpretation of works of art – particularly the body viewed or experienced as *performative*, whether live or in representational form (from the performative images of Gutai to the live Fluxus works of the 1960s).

The inability of performance studies to account for visual arts scholarship (even as some performance studies scholars, such as Phelan and Rebecca Schneider, have addressed visual arts practices in their writing)[32] has perhaps had less to do with the body and more to do with the schism between art history and performance studies as they are situated in universities. While art history still tends to be institutionally a more or less conservative, market-driven, and traditional discipline that is often resistant to acknowledging the explosive role of the body in breaking the bounds of traditional aesthetics in post-1945 practices, performance studies has been articulated as a new cross-disciplinary initiative whose founding impulse came in part from the antidisciplinary logic of cultural studies and whose political impulse has often been stated as resisting the market imperative, including the tendency to categorize creative productions according to medium. Thus, the performance studies scholar Barbara Kirshenblatt-Gimblett notes that to study performance "as an artform that lacks a distinctive medium (and hence uses any and all media), requires attending to all the modalities in play. This distinguishes performance studies from those that focus on a single modality – dance, music, art, theatre, literature, cinema."[33] In addition, the tendency for performance studies scholars to have some background in theatre studies (rather than a familiarity with art history) has meant that it has emphasized theatrical and narrative performance over the often more static or installation-oriented kinds of body art produced by those trained in the visual arts.

In the year 2007, at which point I am writing this chapter, this double failure of art history to attend to body and performance art and of performance studies to address art historical accounts of body and performance art is beginning to be mitigated. This is thanks to two efforts: younger generations of art history scholars insist on interrogating the limitations of traditional concepts of what constitutes art and doing justice to the rich complexity of what people who called themselves artists (working as they did across film, dance, music, visual arts, theatre, and other modes of production from the 1950s onward) were up to in the post-1945 period; meanwhile, practitioners increasingly see the usefulness of models of meaning, value, and history provided across the disciplines of art history and performance studies. Many across the two areas of study are also beginning to recognize that the conservatism of post-Second World War art critical models (based largely on Greenberg's theories) was in part responsible for motivating the radical shift away from a closed model of aesthetics in the visual arts. It was, after all, *visual artists* who had the greatest stake in breaking down conventional conceptions of aesthetics as these continued (and still, to this day, continue) to support the art market and its corollaries.

The failure of live, performance, and/or body art to destroy these structures once and for all, which points to their uncanny ability to absorb anything (even the "live" or ephemeral) as a commodity, should not devalue the project of insistently inserting, performing, enacting, and/or representing the body as central to the visual field. Rather, it should make it all the more imperative that disciplines such as art history, or "cross" disciplines such as performance studies, acknowledge the complexities of how such practices take place and are culturally positioned, then discursively and institutionally given meaning and value.

Notes

1. For a detailed discussion of body art, see my book, *Body Art/Performing the Subject* (Minneapolis: University of Minnesota Press, 1998).
2. Immanuel Kant, *The Critique of Judgement* (1790) (London: www.kessinger.net, n.d.), 12.
3. *Ibid.*, 36.
4. *Ibid.*, 61.
5. In this sense, as Luc Ferry argues, Kantian aesthetics, conceived as a model wherein the beautiful object provokes consensus among subjects, gives rise to *intersubjectivity*. See Luc Ferry, *Homo Aestheticus: The Invention of Taste in the Democratic Age* (1990), trans. Robert de Loaiza (Chicago: University of Chicago Press, 1993), 27.
6. See Roger Fry's "An Essay in Aesthetics" (1909), reprinted in Charles Harrison and Paul Wood, eds., *Art in Theory 1900–1990* (Oxford: Blackwell, 1992), 78–86, and Caroline Jones's critical history of formalism in "Form and Formless,"

in Amelia Jones, ed., *Companion to Contemporary Art Since 1945* (Oxford: Blackwell, 2005), 127–44.

7. Clement Greenberg, *Modernist Painting* (1960), rpt. in Gregory Battcock, ed., *The New Art* (New York: Dutton, 1973), 68, 79.

8. Caroline Jones addresses the suppression of the sensory body in Greenbergian modernism in *Eyesight Alone: Clement Greenberg's Modernism and the Bureaucratization of the Senses* (Chicago: University of Chicago Press, 2006).

9. On this performance, see John Stevenson, "Dada/Theatre" (1986), at www.tranquileye.com/theatre/dada_theatre.html. Accessed March 8, 2007.

10. Mel Gordon, *Dada Performance* (New York: PAJ Publications, 1987), and Roselee Goldberg, *Performance Art: From Futurism to the Present*, 2nd edn (New York: Thames and Hudson, 2001).

11. Robert Motherwell, ed., *The Dada Painters and Poets* (1951), 2nd edn (Cambridge, MA: Harvard University Press, 2005), and Robert Lebel, *Marcel Duchamp* (London: Trianon Press, 1959).

12. Michael Fried, "Art and Objecthood" (1967), rpt. in Gregory Battcock, ed., *Minimal Art: A Critical Anthology* (New York: E. P. Dutton, 1968), 116–47 (esp. 125).

13. Robert Morris, "Notes on Sculpture, Part 2" (1966), rpt. in Morris, *Continuous Project Altered Daily: The Writings of Robert Morris* (London and Cambridge, MA: MIT Press, 1993), 13–14. It is no accident that Morris was active in experimental dance and performance in the 1960s, literally proposing his body as a site of spectatorial engagement. For an excellent overview of this trajectory in Morris's career, see Maurice Berger, *Labyrinths: Robert Morris, Minimalism, and the 1960s* (New York: Harper & Row, 1989).

14. Clement Greenberg, "Avant-Garde Attitudes: New Art in the Sixties" (1969), rpt. in *Clement Greenberg: The Collected Essays*, ed. John O'Brian, *Volume IV: Modernism with a Vengeance* (Chicago: University of Chicago Press), 292–302.

15. See Jones, *Body Art/Performing the Subject*, 53–102.

16. Harold Rosenberg, "American Action Painters," *Artnews* 51 (December 1952), 22.

17. Rebecca Schneider, *The Explicit Body in Performance* (New York: Routledge, 1997); Kathy O'Dell, *Contract with the Skin: Masochism, Performance Art and the 1970s* (Minneapolis: University of Minnesota Press, 1998); and Jones, *Body Art*.

18. Mary Emma Harris, *The Arts at Black Mountain College* (Cambridge, MA: MIT Press, 1987), 226, 228.

19. Kristine Stiles, "Uncorrupted Joy: International Art Actions," in Paul Schimmel, ed., *Out of Actions: Between Performance and the Object 1949–1979* (Los Angeles: Museum of Contemporary Art, 1998), 287.

20. Alexandra Munroe et al., *Japanese Art after 1945: Scream Against the Sky* (New York: Harry Abrams, 1994).

21. Allan Kaprow, "The Legacy of Jackson Pollock" (1958), rpt. in Kaprow, *Essays on the Blurring of Art and Life*, ed. Jeff Kelley (Berkeley: University of California Press, 1993), 3–4.

22. *Ibid.*, 5.

23. *Ibid.*, 6, 7.

24. Clement Greenberg, "American Type Painting" (1955), rpt. in Greenberg, *Art and Culture* (Boston: Beacon Press, 1961), 208–29.
25. Fluxus artists opposed commercialism and high art aesthetics; Fluxus performances were typically succinct and conceptual, pranklike, and intermedial.
26. Carolee Schneemann, "Meat Joy," in *Carolee Schneemann: Imagining Her Erotics* (Cambridge, MA: MIT Press, 2002), 62.
27. Willoughby Sharp, "Body Works," *Avalanche* 1 (Fall 1970), 14–17; Cindy Nemser, "Subject-Object Body Art," *Arts Magazine* 46, no. 1 (September–October 1971), 38–42; Lea Vergine, *Body Art and Performance: The Body as Language* (Milan: Skira 2000); François Pluchart, *L'art corporel* (Paris: Editions Rodolphe Stadler/Galerie Stadler, 1975); and Ira Licht, "Bodyworks," in *Bodyworks* (Chicago: Museum of Contemporary Art, 1975), n.p.
28. Special Issue on Vito Acconci, *Avalanche* 6 (Fall 1972).
29. Sally Banes's *Greenwich Village 1963: Avant-Garde Performance and the Effervescent Body* (Durham: Duke University Press, 1993) was an important addition to this alternative history, studying the interconnections among dance, music, performance, and the visual arts in New York in the early 1960s. The 1993 exhibition "In the Spirit of Fluxus" took place at the Walker Art Gallery in Minneapolis and was accompanied by a scholarly catalogue, *In the Spirit of Fluxus*, edited by Janet Jenkins (Minneapolis: Walker Art Center, 1993). The 1998 exhibition "Out of Actions: Between Performance and the Object 1949–1979," curated by Paul Schimmel, marked a new stage in the institutionalization of the history of body- and process-oriented contemporary art in the art museum. By the 1990s, a wave of books began to redress the absence of a consideration of the body in histories of contemporary art. In addition to Schneider, O'Dell, and Jones (see note 17), see also Henry Sayre, *The Object of Performance: The American Avant-Garde Since 1970* (Chicago: University of Chicago Press, 1989); Jane Blocker, *Where is Ana Mendieta? Identity, Performativity and Exile* (Durham: Duke University Press, 1999), and *What the Body Cost: Desire, History, and Performance* (Minneapolis: University of Minnesota Press, 2004); Jennifer Doyle, *Sex Objects: Art and the Dialectics of Desire* (Minneapolis: University of Minnesota Press, 2006); and Kristine Stiles, "Performance," in Robert Nelson and Richard Shiff, eds., *Critical Terms for Art History*, 2nd edn (Chicago: University of Chicago Press, 2003), 75–97.
30. The Department of Performance Studies was created out of the graduate arm of the Department of Drama. The department's website claims unequivocally: "The Department of Performance Studies is the first program in the world to focus on performance as the object of analysis." See http://performance.tisch.nyu.edu/page/home.html. Accessed June 11, 2007.
31. It is interesting to note that the Wikipedia entry for "performance studies" lists only scholars trained in theatre studies or performance studies – none of the art historians noted here is mentioned. See http://en.wikipedia.org/wiki/Performance_Studies. Accessed June 11, 2007. Richard Schechner sketches the history of the first decade of performance studies in his book *Performance Studies: An Introduction* (London: Routledge, 2002), 1–21. Schechner takes full account of the crucial continuum between performance practice and theory in performance studies, and of the anthropological dimension of its attention to "other" performative practices beyond the "Western" (1–2), but

does not reference the visual arts at all as a context for the making or theorizing/ historicizing of performance practices. Notably, he leaves out art history from his list of disciplines from which performance studies draws its interpretive strategies: "social sciences, feminist studies, gender studies, history, psychoanalysis, queer theory, semiotics, ethology, cybernetics, area studies, media and popular culture theory, and cultural studies" (2). This is not in any way to demonize Schechner, whose importance to performance studies is unarguable, but to point to the way in which art historical approaches (and the visual arts in general as a context for performative works) have until recently been absent from "official" performance studies discourse. For a thoughtful rumination on the first decades of performance studies, which, nuanced as it is, reinforces the conception that it has nothing to do with the visual arts (aside from brief references to Vincent Van Gogh and the art historian Rosalind Krauss [8, 9]), but instead derived entirely from theatre studies, anthropology, and cultural studies, see Peggy Phelan, "Introduction: The Ends of Performance," in Jill Lane and Peggy Phelan, eds., *The Ends of Performance* (New York: New York University Press, 1998), 1–19. Phelan must be given full credit, however, for being one of the performance studies scholars who is the best versed in histories and theories of visual arts practices.

32. Schneider, *The Explicit Body*, and Peggy Phelan's survey essay in Helena Reckitt, ed., *Art and Feminism* (London: Phaidon, 2001), 14–49.

33. Barbara Kirshenblatt-Gimblett, "Performance Studies," adapted from a report written for the Rockefeller Foundation, 1999. See www.nyu.edu/ classes/bkg/issues/rock2.htm. Accessed June 11, 2007. Rpt. in Schechner, *Performance Studies*, 3.

11

E. PATRICK JOHNSON

Queer theory

The word "queer," like the word "performance," has a vexed historical trajectory. Once a pejorative slur targeted at gender and sexual nonconformists, queer is currently also a hip signifier of postmodern identity. To embrace "queer" is to resist or elide categorization, to disavow binaries (that is, gay versus straight, black versus white) and to proffer potentially productive modes of resistance against hegemonic structures of power. This deployment of queer, then, exemplifies the traits of performance in that "its definitional indeterminacy, its elasticity, is one of its constituent characteristics."[1]

In academic circles queer has become a catalyst for theorizing not only gender and sexuality in ways that detach them from singular or rigid identitarian markers, but also a way to discuss race and class in antiessentialist ways. A poor, fifty-year-old, African American female rugby player from the southern United States might be considered "queer," for instance, because each of the adjectives that describe her do not comport with the traditional ideas of who plays rugby. According to this logic, this particular player is queer because she is anomalous, odd, or strange in the world of rugby. It is this oddity and strangeness that queer theorists would use to argue that all identity is fraught because it is always already mediated through language and ceded to those who have the power to control representation. Thus this player's queerness can be taken as subversive because her presence in the rugby league – a sport typically populated by white middle-class men – transgresses the image of the "rugby player" in the social imaginary and potentially deconstructs power relations within the context of rugby as a sport. Through the slide from personal pronoun to active verb (for example, "I *am* a queer" to "The actor *queered* the character"), the term has been reappropriated to activate a way to theorize subjectivity, social relations, and culture in general.

This chapter maps the relatively short history of queer theory as an academic discourse, methodology, and mode of intellectual inquiry. I suggest that three fields of study – gay and lesbian studies, cultural studies, and performance studies – all provided the groundwork for the emergence of queer theory and its own subsequent codification as queer studies. The tripartite of gay and lesbian studies, cultural studies, and performance studies – all considered anti- or transdisciplines – undergirds the queer project, but with varying degrees of productivity, tension, and backlash. Yet the interanimation of these fields of study provides fecund ground for innovative pedagogy, research, and scholarship that continue to have an impact on other disciplines in the academy.

What's in a name? Queer versus gay and lesbian

In the introduction to their 1993 anthology *The Lesbian and Gay Studies Reader*, co-editors Henry Abelove, Michèle Aina Barale, and David M. Halperin write:

> It was difficult to decide what to title this anthology. We have reluctantly chosen not to speak here and in our title of "queer studies," despite our own attachment to the term, because we wish to acknowledge the force of current usage. The forms of study whose institutionalization we seek to further have tended, so far at least, to go by the names "lesbian" and "gay." The field designated by them has become a site for inquiry into many kinds of sexual non-conformity ... Moreover, the names "lesbian" and "gay" are probably more widely preferred than is the name "queer."[2]

The fact that the editors felt compelled to provide a justification for their disavowal of "queer" in their title indicates that by 1993 the force of queer theory/studies had already begun to have an impact on the well-established field of "gay and lesbian" studies. It is also ironic, then, that the volume contains Judith Butler's essay "Imitation and Gender Insubordination" (first published in 1991).[3] That essay critiques the use of "lesbian" as an identity category because embracing such an identity not only forecloses occupying multiple subject positions, but also, according to Butler, colludes with homophobic and heterosexist discourses to maintain the status quo. Butler suggests that "identity categories tend to be instruments of regulatory regimes, whether as the normalizing categories of oppressive structures or as the rallying points for a liberatory contestation of that very oppression." Ultimately, Butler argues that she is "not at ease with 'lesbian theories, gay theories.'"[4]

And why should she be? One year before the publication of "Imitation and Gender Insubordination," Butler penned the now canonical *Gender Trouble: Feminism and the Subversion of Identity*, which changed the landscape of gender and sexuality studies forever. *Gender Trouble* advocated expunging the category "woman" altogether as a "subject" of feminism, challenging feminist theorists to rethink rallying around female "identity" in exchange for a more politically nuanced strategy of political resistance. She writes:

> Within feminist political practice, a rethinking of the ontological constructions of identity appears to be necessary in order to formulate a representational politics that might revive feminism on other grounds. On the other hand, it may be time to entertain a radical critique that seeks to free feminist theory from the necessity of having to construct a single or abiding ground which is invariably contested by those identity positions or anti-identity positions that it invariably excludes. Do the exclusionary practices that ground feminist theory in a notion of "women" as subject paradoxically undercut feminist goals to extend its claims to "representation"?[5]

While the "revival" of feminism is what Butler had in mind with her radical rethinking of identity politics, *Gender Trouble* instead became the catalyst for rethinking "gay and lesbian" studies – from its nomenclature to its historical grounding in homosexual identity. Indeed, identity as politically inefficacious found traction among many who believed, like Butler, that "gay and lesbian" restricted and legislated the boundaries of gender and sexual difference too narrowly. A movement based on a single identity, these theorists believed, would always fall short because of the ways in which its rhetoric failed to expose the malleability of all identity claims, including heterosexuality. Once heterosexuality was exposed as an invention, then the binaries of gay/straight, homosexual/heterosexual, man/woman could no longer be used to uphold hegemonic regimes of power.

Because of its seemingly nonidentitarian connotations as "queer" – as term and as theory – seemed to be the saving grace by which to escape from the quagmire of identity politics. And after Butler's follow-up monograph in 1993, *Bodies That Matter: On the Discursive Limits of "Sex,"* a text in which she built upon the theorizing in *Gender Trouble*, but with an eye toward theorizing sexual difference and gender performativity, queer was mobilized as the latest and greatest new chic by-product of the "post-identity" era.

Indeed, queer theorists, as opposed to gay or lesbian theorists, began to crop up everywhere, embracing the political potential of this nonessentialist signifier. Some queer theorists argued that their use of "queer" was more than just a reappropriation of an offensive term. Cherry Smith, for example, maintains that the term entails a "radical questioning of social and cultural norms, notions of gender, reproductive sexuality and the family."[6] Others underscore the playfulness and inclusivity of the term, arguing that it opens up rather than fixes identities. According to Eve Kosofsky Sedgwick, "What it takes – all it takes – to make the description 'queer' a true one is the impulsion to use it in the first person."[7] Michael Warner offers an even more politicized and polemical view:

> The preference for "queer" represents, among other things, an aggressive impulse of generalization; it rejects a minoritizing logic of toleration or simple political interest-representation in favor of a more thorough resistance to regimes of the normal. For academics, being interested in queer theory is a way to mess up the desexualized spaces of the academy, exude some rut [express sexual excitement], reimagine the public from and for which academic intellectuals write, dress, and perform.[8]

The foregoing theorists identify "queer" as a site of indeterminate possibility, a site where sexual practice does not necessarily determine one's status as queer. Indeed, Lauren Berlant and Warner argue that queer is "more a matter of aspiration than it is the expression of an identity or a history."[9] Accordingly, the straight-identified critic Calvin Thomas appropriates Butler's notion of "critical queerness" to suggest that "just as there is more than one way to be 'critical,' there may be more than one (or two or three) to be 'queer.'"[10]

As one might imagine, this "anything goes" approach to gender and sexuality studies did not sit well with those who believed that rather than opening up political possibilities, queer theory actually diluted the specificity of LGBT (lesbian, gay, bisexual, transsexual) life and politics. If anyone or anything could be queer, some believed, then on what ground would those who are materially discriminated against stand? Moreover, at the moment when queer theory gained momentum in the academy and forged a space as a legitimate disciplinary method, much of the scholarship produced in its name elided issues of race and class. In *Bodies That Matter,* Butler anticipates the contestability of "queer," noting that it excludes as much as it includes but that such a contested term may energize a new kind of political activism.[11] The critique of queer theory came hard and fast, led mostly by lesbians, gays, bisexuals, and transgendered people of color who often ground their theorizing in a politics of identity, and therefore frequently fall prey to accusations of "essentialism" or "anti-intellectualism." Galvanizing around identity, however, is not always an unintentional "essentialist" move. Many times, it is an intentional strategic choice.[12] Cathy Cohen, for example, suggests that "queer theorizing which calls for the elimination of fixed categories seems to ignore the ways in which some traditional social identities and communal ties can, in fact, be important to one's survival."[13] The "communal ties" to which Cohen refers are those which exist in communities of color across boundaries of sexuality. As the black transgendered

British activist Helen (charles) asks, "What happens to the definition of 'queer' when you're washing up or having a wank? When you're aware of misplacement or displacement in your colour, gender, identity? Do they get subsumed . . . into a homogeneous category, where class and other things that make up a cultural identity are ignored?"[14] What, for example, are the ethical and material implications of queer theory if its project is to dismantle all notions of identity and agency? The deconstructive turn in queer theory highlights the ways in which ideology functions to oppress and to proscribe ways of knowing, but what is the utility of queer theory on the front lines, in the trenches, on the street, or anyplace where the racialized and sexualized body is beaten, starved, terminated from employment – indeed, when the body is the site of trauma?

The critique of queer theory based on race and class spawned a host of articles, books, and anthologies – many of which were published from the mid 1990s to the present. Evelynn Hammonds's essay "Black (W)holes and the Geometry of Black Female Sexuality" (1994), was one of the first to push back against the force of queer theory. Hammonds writes, "When I am asked if I am queer I usually answer yes even though the ways in which *I* am queer have never been articulated in the *body* of work that now is queer theory."[15] Hammonds's larger intervention in this debate is the way in which she calls attention to the void (the "hole") of work on black women's sexuality within queer theory. David Eng and Alice Hom's *Q & A: Queer in Asian America* calls attention to the dearth of work on Asian Americans in queer studies, and in Asian American studies on Asian sexualities, noting that "this project of considering race and homosexuality together is all the more urgent in light of the ways in which contemporary queer politics has shaped itself both inside and outside of the academy."[16] José Muñoz's *Disidentifications: Queers of Color and the Performance of Politics* makes a similar intervention by showcasing the work of queer performers of color who are mostly absent from the scholarship of queer theory. Muñoz argues that "most of the cornerstones of queer theory that are taught, cited, and canonized in gay and lesbian classrooms, publications, and conferences are decidedly directed toward analyzing white lesbians and gay men."[17] Following on the heels of Muñoz, Roderick A. Ferguson's *Aberrations in Black: Toward a Queer of Color Critique*, codifies the conjoining of race and sexuality as a methodology of its own: "queer of color analysis," which he defines as "a heterogeneous enterprise made up of women of color feminism, materialist analysis, poststructuralist theory, and queer critique."[18] And most recently, my own co-edited volume with Mae G. Henderson, *Black Queer Studies: A Critical Anthology*, mines the fields of black studies and queer studies "to demonstrate how both might be pressed into the service of a larger project – one imbricating race, class, gender, and sexuality."[19] As noted above, *Black Queer Studies* follows a plethora of critical writings, artistry, and theories that critiqued the exclusionary history of queer theory.[20] These critiques have generated various racialized modes of queer studies: black queer studies, Latino/a queer studies, Asian queer studies, etc.

The cultural turn: queer theory and cultural studies

The cultural turn in literary studies in the late 1970s and early 1980s emerged in response to growing pressures from subaltern epistemologies that had yet to be acknowledged in traditional academic departments or taken into account in theoretical and methodological approaches to cultural or social phenomena. Those who circled the wagons around rigid disciplinary boundaries and who desperately tried to hold onto a single object and method of study as a marker of what constituted a discipline (for example, a literary text was the object of study and literary exegesis was the method), had to concede that the canon (both in the sense of an elite list of must-read/must-study works and the attendant approaches to such reading and studying) was as vulnerable to what Barbara Herrnstein Smith might call "contingencies of value" as any other body of cultural production.[21] Factor in a burgeoning desire to establish gender and sexuality studies as a legitimate field of study, alongside a growing activist group of gay and lesbian faculty at universities around the United States, and the conservative ground of the academy gradually began to shift.

Queer theory was one product that emerged out of the twists and "turns" in the academy. While cultural studies opened the door for queer theorists to focus on "queer" representation in popular culture and within the realm of cultural production more generally, cultural studies "purists" rejected the appropriation of its methods and objects of study, as they deemed some queer theorists' methods too "experiential." According to Donald Morton, there are two brands of cultural studies; one brand "'describes' various emerging, suppressed cultural groups and its goal is to give voice to their previously un- or little-known 'experience,' to let them 'speak for themselves.'"[22] William G. Tierney's book, *Academic Outlaws: Queer Theory and Cultural Studies in the Academy*, is exemplary of this kind of (queer) cultural studies approach. Tierney devotes most of the Introduction to discussing the politics of book dedications and the underlying heteronormative assumptions they make about readers. This premise is a jumping-off point to engage broader questions about the relationship between gay and lesbian research and "the way lesbian and gay people get defined in the daily life of the university." Tierney writes, "At first glance it may appear self-indulgent

E. PATRICK JOHNSON

to have gone on at length about the dedication of a text to the fellow whom
I have loved and lived with for the past decade. Yet a goal of this book
is to outline how the lives we live and the matter of with whom we live
help determine what counts for knowledge, which in turn becomes tied to
institutional policies and framed as parameters of power."²³ To some, however, Tierney's employment of personal experience to highlight the subaltern
position of the gay and lesbian subject within larger institutional structures
is unsatisfactory: simply "speaking" does not provide a material platform
to *intervene* in the very structures that suppressed these "silenced" voices in
the first place.

The other branch of cultural studies, which Morton refers to as "critical
cultural studies," *is* invested in such interventions. Morton explains:

> Unlike experiential cultural studies, whose mode is "descriptive" and whose
> effect is to give the (native) bourgeois student of culture the pleasure encounter
> with the exotic "other," the mode of critical cultural studies is "explanatory"
> and its effect is to alter the settled and exploitative relations between bourgeois
> reader and her/his "other." The point of critical cultural studies is not simply to
> "witness" cultural events but to intervene in them, that is, to produce socially
> transformative cultural understandings.²⁴

This critique of experience grows out of a desire to effect change at the
macro rather than micro level of culture by focusing on the "materiality
of culture as the historical conditions and the social and economic – the
material – structures which in fact produce that 'experience.'"²⁵

The distinction between "experiential" and "critical" cultural studies that
Morton makes is well made, but is actually old news. Steeped in the Birming-
ham School of materialist Marxism, the critical cultural studies that Morton
champions necessarily focuses on political economic structures and systems
of power and the ways in which ideology creates and maintains social subjects. But this approach is not necessarily anathema to experiential critical
cultural studies, as such. Gayatri Chakravorty Spivak's now canonical question, "Can the Subaltern Speak?," reminds us not only that the answer
is "yes," but also that the insertion of the subjugated subject's voice may
intervene in capitalist modes of production that promote material effects
and social change.²⁶ After all, legally speaking, "speech" is not defined
solely as what a person *says* with words, but also what a person *does* –
such as marching in a protest, burning the American flag, etc.²⁷ Thus
the drag queens, transgendered people, and transsexuals who initiated the
Stonewall riots of 1969 engaged in a form of speech, grounded in their experience that impacted the material rights of the queer community for years to
come. These protestors enacted both experiential cultural studies and critical

cultural studies because they understood "'politics' ultimately as a struggle over access to the material base of power/knowledge/resources."[28]

This binary between experiential and critical cultural studies seems odd, given the antibinary deployment of queer theory. And while Morton's anthology, *The Material Queer*, is supposed to be exemplary of *critical* cultural studies as opposed to *experiential* cultural studies, the volume's first chapter, by Warner, is based on his "experiences" of being "a teenage Pentecostalist" and the grandson of a Southern Baptist preacher. It is through the expression of his first person account of being raised in a fundamentalist religious community that he argues the similarities of queer culture and fundamentalist religion, but obviously with different aims.[29] From where I stand, Tierney's use of autobiography to address the status of the queer subject in academic research and in the academy does not seem so different from Warner's use of autobiography to establish the relationship between queer subjectivity and religious dogma. Both employ experiential knowledge and both scholars' theorizing has material consequences. The more productive strategy, I believe, is not to place a hierarchical or binary frame on experiential and critical knowledge, but rather to put the two in dialogic tension.

The advent of cultural studies offered a new inter- (anti-?) disciplinary way to produce knowledge. The lure of this approach was the escape from overdetermined theories and methods that produced many of the same answers while spawning no new questions. The open-endedness of cultural studies' methods and objects of study was fertile ground from which something like queer theory could emerge. Indeed, Simon During's elaboration on the ways in which cultural studies is an engaged critical praxis could be said of queer theory/studies:

> First . . . it is not neutral in relation to the exclusions, injustices and prejudices that it observes. It tends to position itself on the side of those to whom social structures offer least, so that here "engaged" means political, critical. Second . . . it aims to enhance and celebrate cultural experiences; to communicate enjoyment of a wide variety of cultural forms in part by analyzing them and their social underpinnings. And third . . . it aims to deal with culture as a part of everyday life, without objectifying it.[30]

The political implications undergirding these various modes of engagement represent the spirit and intellectual muscle with which progenitors of queer theory cultivated its foundational premises: knowledge production is bound to power relations and culture is the site at which the struggle to produce that knowledge occurs. If queers can deconstruct the master narrative of heteronormativity and not only insert the queer subject, but also discern the systemic and economic systems by which the queer was excised in the first place, then queer theory, like cultural studies, will have done its job.

Like many of the theories that arose in the wake of postmodernism, however, the always already fragile glue that held these theories together assured that there would be fractures, fissures, and foreclosures. Cultural studies and queer studies are no exceptions, and both still experience splintering as scholars and students generate and introduce new ways of theorizing what constitutes "culture" and "queer." The fact that nonqueer academics and nonacademic queers employ queer theory speaks to the contestation of cultural and queer studies. The interanimation of these two epistemologies, if they continue down the path they have gone so far, will continue to spark new strategies of theorizing identity and culture.

The performative turn: queer theory and performance

The cultural turn was not eclipsed by the performative turn occurring almost simultaneously across disciplines. Part of this turn to performance was a reaction to text-based methodologies that reinforced hegemonic notions of the Other, especially in literary studies. As Dwight Conquergood argues, "performance is a more conceptually astute and inclusionary way of thinking about many subaltern cultural practices and intellectual-philosophical activities."[31] Thus the elasticity of a performative methodology not only elucidated the "free play" of postmodern signification, it also became a way to access and highlight alternative epistemologies – queer ones among them.

Indeed, Butler's theorizing in *Gender Trouble* and *Bodies That Matter* drew heavily on the trope of performance as a way to develop her theory of gender performativity. Using the British philosopher J. L. Austin's theory of the performative, the proposition that in certain contexts saying something constitutes doing something (for example, "I do" during a marriage ceremony), along with Jacques Derrida's theory of iterability, or the notion that any recognizable form can be copied and therefore cited multiple times, Butler developed a theory of gender as performance, as a set of citations of previous performances of gender such that the repetition and reiteration of these performances calcify, making them seem "natural." As the discussion of queer theory and gay and lesbian studies above demonstrates, the embrace of the performance trope gels nicely with that of queer, in all its indeterminacy and malleability.

As "natural" bedfellows, queer theory and performance theory carry out their promiscuity in productive and destructive ways. Like the critique waged by queers of color about the absence of work on race and class in queer theory/studies, performance theorists have sometimes critiqued queer theorists for appropriating performative discourse, while privileging the concept of performativity over performance, as well as advancing queer performativity as if no theories of performance existed before its popularity in the academy. While Butler is one culprit, there are others – mostly literary scholars – who are guilty of disavowing a whole body of scholarship on performance theory. Conquergood lays bare the stakes of this move when he asks, "What are the costs of dematerializing texts as textuality, and disembodying performance as performativity, and then making these abstractions interchangeable concepts? What gets lost in the exchange, in the 'reworking of performativity as citationality'?"[32] Conquergood's questions arise out of concern that theorists like Butler who, in their zeal for a radical internment of weary, worn identity politics, calcified essentialism, and outdated gender theory, simply champion performativity as a salvo against all that came before its emergence as a critical trope. Indeed, Conquergood and others warn that the concealed deconstructive lens of performativity may ask performance theorists to cede too much ground. Instead, Elin Diamond suggests that "Performativity... be rooted in the materiality and historical density of performance."[33] The rootedness that Diamond speaks of here suggests a return to performance as a critical praxis, or more specifically, to live performance as a site for social change. As Sue-Ellen Case muses, "It is confounding to observe how a lesbian/gay movement about sexual, bodily practices and the lethal effects of a virus [HIV/AIDS]... would have as its critical operation a notion of performativity that circles back to written texts, abandoning historical traditions of performance for print modes of literary and philosophical scrutiny."[34]

Some queer performance theorists have taken up the charge not to allow performativity to upstage performance in this theory melodrama. Taking Diamond's and Case's cues, queer performers and critics have cast performativity and performance in coeval starring roles, and produced scholarship that takes queer performance as the stage on which to place performance and performativity in dialogic and dialectic tension. In so doing, they confirm Diamond's argument that "as soon as [queer] performativity comes to rest on a performance, questions of embodiment, of social relations, of ideological interpellations, of emotional and political effects, all become discussable."[35] Much of the early work of this nature (post Butler) came from lesbian critics like Case and Jill Dolan. Even before Butler came onto the scene, Case had already established herself as a critic of lesbian performance and critical theory with her influential essay "Toward a Butch-Femme Aesthetic," in which she analyzes the lesbian theatre troupe Split Britches' performance of *Beauty and the Beast* to suggest lesbian camp as a site of female agency.[36] Her later work builds on this foundation by necessarily avoiding the lure of queer performativity by staying true to her generation's commitment to a particular set of politics of social change that is uneasy about disavowing every aspect of identity politics. In *The Domain-Matrix*, for example, Case points out that for all its heft, queer performativity actually reinscribes scriptocentrism: "In fact, one might argue that the project of performativity is to recuperate writing at the end of print culture."[37] The irony for Case, however, is that despite this act of recuperation, critiques of performance in favor of performativity end up relying on performance to wage its critique in the form of reading: "There is a model of performance lurking behind these several critiques of it – one that actually 'embodies' those who write about theater. While they seek to confute performance and its assumptions, they themselves continue to perform in a way that replicates what they would contradict by reading academic papers . . . Reading a paper is academic performance."[38]

Dolan's work has always privileged the interplay between staged performance, queerness, and critical theory. In her collection of essays, *Presence and Desire*, Dolan takes (lesbian) sexuality as the central lens through which to enact readings of performance practices that challenge normative sexuality and gender. In the Introduction she writes, "Even as antimetaphysical theories such as deconstruction and poststructuralism move feminist critics away from their earlier valorizations of the female body onstage, I'm not ready to give up the intense pleasure I find in a powerful female performer."[39] Neither Case nor Dolan is willing to give up on part of the nomenclature that their generation acknowledged as the political bulwark of radical theatre: "lesbian and gay." Although accommodating "queer" theatre by adding it to "lesbian/gay theater," almost ten years after the publication of her *Presence and Desire*, Dolan suggests in the Introduction to Alisa Solomon and Framji Minwalla's edited volume, *The Queerest Art: Essays on Lesbian and Gay Theater*, that the advent and cachet of queer as a term and the performances gathered under its name do not call for an erasure of the history of "gay and lesbian" performance: "I hope that . . . we'll celebrate the achievements of gay and lesbian theater and performance, along with the queer version, so that we can remember our history."[40] The lesbian theatre historian Lisa Merrill recasts that history by actually queering it, by rewriting and revising the heteronormative master narrative of women's theatre history in her critical biography of the nineteenth-century actress Charlotte Cushman, whose "circle of female spectators" cloaked her lesbianism only from those who were unwilling to "see" it. Merrill not only recuperates Cushman's lesbian past and contribution to gay and lesbian theatre, but her methodical archival research among Cushman's letters to and from her women "friends" instantiates the performance/performativity dialectic as Merrill's own subjectivity as a lesbian performance scholar becomes a part of the archive that now stands in for Cushman's "body" of work.[41]

From this brief overview, one might think that only lesbian artists and critics have produced work on queer performance. Quite the contrary. Most notably, David Román's *Acts of Intervention: Performance, Gay Culture, and AIDS* in some ways echoes the critique that Case and Dolan wage against queer performativity. In *Acts of Intervention* Román employs queer theory to argue that gay performance – from Broadway to activist protests – intervened in and confronted the AIDS epidemic. He demonstrates how gay theatre contests dominant meanings and disrupts hegemonic discourses by providing material ways in which these performances altered the ways in which institutions such as the government, at the national level, and everyday folk, at the local level, discussed the epidemic. Rather than engage in the polemical stance that characterizes much queer theory, Román deploys what he calls "critical generosity" in recognition that "criticism can be much more than simply a procedure of critique or means for qualitative analysis."[42] As opposed to "critical generosity," in *Disidentifications* Muñoz takes a decidedly polemical stance by writing against the grain of the mostly Eurocentric queer theory that he suggests has marginalized the contributions of queers of color. Also unlike Román, Muñoz in some instances takes on, and in other instances embraces, poststructuralist, postcolonial, and Marxist theorists to develop his theory of "disidentification," "a strategy that tries to transform a cultural logic from within, always laboring to enact permanent structural change while at the same time valuing the importance of local or everyday struggles of resistance."[43]

Disidentification as a theory and method comes closer to Butler's queer performativity than all the other texts mentioned; thus it does not position a subject as outside ideology or disavow the notion that agency or volition are constituted by the very structures that they attempt to embrace or resist. On the other hand, Muñoz's work does depart from Butler and others in that he offers as a rejoinder to his theoretical abstraction "real" performances by queers of color to demonstrate how they "disidentify" with the social structures in the process of queer "worldmaking," or "the ways in which performances – both theatrical and everyday rituals – have the ability to establish alternative views of the world."[44] Like Muñoz, my own work in *Appropriating Blackness: Performance and Politics of Authenticity* draws heavily from poststructuralist and, to some extent, psychoanalytic theory to theorize the multivalences of racialized performance.

Specifically, *Appropriating Blackness* engages notions of authentic blackness vis-à-vis cultural and theatrical performances of race and the discourses of authenticity that those performances enable. The first three chapters of the book focus on the queer performativity of race in the dialogics of gender, sexuality, and class. Race, or blackness, however, is the privileged criti-cal lens; as I argue, "performance may not fully account for the ontology of race."[45] The work differs from Román and Muñoz in that it engages ethnographic methods to theorize not only the other's relation to racial and queer performativity, but also my relation to my performance in the field, and the "dialogic performatives" that such self-reflexive methodologies evince.[46]

What I have tried to map out here is less a history of queer theory, per se, than its frisky relations with other inter/antidisciplinary fields of study. What cultural studies, gay and lesbian studies, performance studies, and queer studies all have in common is a history of contestation, revision, and political engagement. Each emerged in the wake of a theoretical lacuna needing to be filled, but all left their constituents wanting – for that is the gift and curse of a theory with no disciplinary base. Queer theory, in particular, has been successful in resisting codification as a discipline, since, to my knowledge, there is only one academic queer studies department, located at City College of San Francisco.[47] On the other hand, there are more than a few departments and programs around the country that have "performance studies," "cultural studies," and "gay and lesbian studies" (also "LGBT," "Women's Studies," or "Gender and Women's Studies") in their titles. It is unclear whether queer theory/studies' resistance to codification is a part of its own built-in immunity or if it is due to institutionalized homophobia. I suspect it might be a bit of both. Whatever the case, queer theory has enabled a whole generation of scholars, critics, and performers to press out the boundaries of criticism, conventional methodologies, and performance practice, resulting in a fecund site of knowledge production. The future twists and turns of queer theory will rely in part on its progenitors, who just might reap the queer fruit they have sown.

Notes

1. Annamarie Jagose, *Queer Theory: An Introduction* (New York: New York University Press, 1996), 1.
2. Henry Abelove, Michèle Aina Barale, and David M. Halperin, eds., *The Lesbian and Gay Studies Reader* (New York: Routledge, 1993), xvii.
3. The essay first appeared in Diana Fuss's anthology, *Inside/Outside: Lesbian Theories, Gay Theories* (New York: Routledge, 1991), 13–31.

4. Judith Butler, "Imitation and Gender Insubordination," in Abelove, Barale, and Halperin, eds., *The Lesbian and Gay Studies Reader*, 308.
5. Judith Butler, *Gender Trouble: Feminism and the Subversion of Identity* (New York: Routledge, 1990), 5.
6. Cherry Smith, "What is This Thing Called Queer?," in Donald Morton, ed., *The Material Queer: A LesBiGay Cultural Studies Reader* (Boulder, CO: Westview, 1996), 280.
7. Eve Kosofsky Sedgwick, "Queer and Now," in Sedgwick, *Tendencies* (Durham: Duke University Press, 1993), 9.
8. Michael Warner, "Introduction," in Michael Warner, ed., *Fear of a Queer Planet: Queer Politics and Social Theory* (Minneapolis: University of Minnesota Press, 1993), xxvi.
9. Lauren Berlant and Michael Warner, "What Does Queer Theory Teach Us about X?" *PMLA* 110 (May 1995), 344.
10. Calvin Thomas, "Straight with a Twist: Queer Theory and the Subject of Heterosexuality," in Thomas Foster, Carol Siegel, and Ellen E. Berry, eds., *The Gay '90's: Disciplinary and Interdisciplinary Formations in Queer Studies* (New York: New York University Press, 1997), 83.
11. Judith Butler, *Bodies That Matter: On the Discursive Limits of "Sex"* (New York: Routledge, 1993), 228–9.
12. For more on "strategic" essentialism, see Diana Fuss, *Essentially Speaking: Feminism, Nature & Difference* (New York: Routledge, 1989), 1–21; Teresa de Lauretis, "The Essence of the Triangle, or Taking the Risk of Essentialism Seriously: Feminist Theory in Italy, the U.S. and Britain," *differences: A Journal of Feminist Cultural Studies* 1.2 (1989), 3–37; and Sue-Ellen Case, *The Domain-Matrix: Performing Lesbian at the End of Print Culture* (Bloomington: Indiana University Press, 1996), 1–12.
13. Cathy Cohen, "Punks, Bulldaggers and Welfare Queens: The Radical Potential of Queer Politics?," in E. Patrick Johnson and Mae G. Henderson, eds., *Black Queer Studies: A Critical Anthology* (Durham: Duke University Press, 2005), 34.
14. Helen (charles), "'Queer Nigger': Theorizing 'White' Activism," in Joseph Bistrow and Anglia R. Wilson, eds., *Activating Theory: Lesbian, Gay, Bisexual Politics* (London: Lawrence and Wishart, 1993), 101–2.
15. Evelynn Hammonds, "Black (W)holes and the Geometry of Black Female Sexuality," *differences: A Journal of Feminist Cultural Studies* 6.2/3 (1994), 126 (italics in original).
16. David L. Eng and Alice Y. Hom, eds., *Q & A: Queer in Asian America* (Philadelphia: Temple University Press, 1999), 12–13.
17. José Muñoz, *Disidentifications: Queers of Color and the Performance of Politics* (Minneapolis: University of Minnesota Press, 1999), 10.
18. Roderick A. Ferguson, *Aberrations in Black: Toward a Queer of Color Critique* (Minneapolis: University of Minnesota Press, 2004), 149, n.1.
19. Johnson and Henderson, eds., *Black Queer Studies*, 3.
20. Most notably, Essex Hemphill, ed., *Brother to Brother* (New York: Alyson, 1991), and Delroy Constantine-Simms, *The Greatest Taboo: Homosexuality in Black Communities* (New York: Alyson, 2000).

21. See Barbara Herrnstein Smith, *Contingencies of Value: Alternative Perspectives for Critical Theory* (Cambridge, MA: Harvard University Press, 1991).

22. Morton, ed., *Material Queer*, xvi.

23. William G. Tierney, *Academic Outlaws: Queer Theory and Cultural Studies in the Academy* (Thousand Oaks: Sage Publications, 1997), xviii.

24. Morton, ed., *Material Queer*, xvi.

25. *Ibid.*

26. Gayatri Chakravorty Spivak, "Can the Subaltern Speak?," in Cary Nelson and Lawrence Grossberg, eds., *Marxism and the Interpretation of Culture* (Urbana: University of Illinois Press, 1988), 271–313.

27. See Judith Butler, *Excitable Speech: A Politics of the Performative* (New York: Routledge, 1997).

28. Morton, ed., *Material Queer*, xvii.

29. Michael Warner, "Tongues Untied: Memoirs of a Pentecostal Boyhood," in Morton, ed., *Material Queer*, 39–45.

30. Simon During, *Cultural Studies: An Introduction* (New York: Routledge, 2005), 1.

31. Dwight Conquergood, "Beyond the Text: Toward a Performative Cultural Politics," in Sheron J. Dailey, ed., *The Future of Performance Studies: Visions and Revisions* (Annandale, VA: National Communication Association, 1998), 26.

32. *Ibid.*, 25.

33. Elin Diamond, "Introduction," in Diamond, ed., *Performance and Cultural Politics* (New York: Routledge, 1996), 5.

34. Case, *The Domain-Matrix*, 17.

35. Diamond, "Introduction," 5.

36. See Sue-Ellen Case, "Toward a Butch-Femme Aesthetic," *Discourse* 11.1 (Winter 1988–9), 55–73.

37. Case, *The Domain-Matrix*, 17.

38. *Ibid.*, 23.

39. Jill Dolan, *Presence and Desire: Essays on Gender, Sexuality, and Performance* (Ann Arbor: University of Michigan Press, 1993), 1.

40. Jill Dolan, "Introduction: Building a Theatrical Vernacular: Responsibility, Community, Ambivalence, and Queer Theater," in Alisa Solomon and Framji Minwalla, eds., *The Queerest Art: Essays on Lesbian and Gay Theater* (New York: New York University Press, 2002), 5.

41. See Lisa Merrill, *When Romeo Was a Woman: Charlotte Cushman and Her Circle of Female Spectators* (Ann Arbor: University of Michigan Press, 1999).

42. David Román, *Acts of Intervention: Performance, Gay Culture, and AIDS* (Bloomington: Indiana University Press, 1998), xxvi.

43. Muñoz, *Disidentifications*, 11–12.

44. *Ibid.*, 195.

45. E. Patrick Johnson, *Appropriating Blackness: Performance and the Politics of Authenticity* (Durham: Duke University Press, 2003), 9.

46. D. Soyini Madison defines the dialogic performative as "encompassing reflexive knowledge, that is, the ethnographer not only contemplates her/his own actions (reflective), but s/he turns inward to contemplate how s/he is contemplating her actions (reflexive)" (321) and as "always embodied and purposeful within

a designated time and space that evokes the imaginary" (322). See her essay "The Dialogic Performative in Critical Ethnography," *Text and Performance Quarterly* 26.4 (2006), 320–4.

47. City College of San Francisco claims that it has the only department of Queer Studies in the United States. See www.ccsf.edu/Departments/Gay_ Lesbian_Bisexual_Studies/. Accessed April 6, 2007.

FURTHER READING

Anderson, Benedict, *Imagined Communities: Reflections on the Origin and Spread of Nationalism* (New York: Verso, 1991).

Auslander, Philip, "At the Listening Post, or, Do Machines Perform?," *International Journal of Performance Arts and Digital Media* 1 (2005), 5–10.

"Humanoid Boogie: Reflections on Robotic Performance," in David Krasner and David Z. Saltz, eds., *Staging Philosophy: Intersections of Theater, Performance, and Philosophy* (Ann Arbor: University of Michigan Press, 2006), 87–103.

Liveness: Performance in a Mediatized Culture, 2nd edn (London: Routledge, 2008).

Austin, J. L., *How to Do Things with Words* (1962) (Cambridge, MA: Harvard University Press, 1975).

Bandem, I Made and Fredrik Eugene DeBoer, *Balinese Dance in Transition: From Kaja to Kelod* (1981), 2nd edn (Kuala Lumpur: Oxford University Press, 1995).

Banes, Sally, *Dancing Women: Female Bodies on Stage* (New York, London: Routledge, 1998).

Greenwich Village 1963: Avant-Garde Performance and the Effervescent Body (Durham: Duke University Press, 1993).

Subversive Expectations: Performance Art and Paratheatre in New York, 1976–85 (Ann Arbor: University of Michigan Press, 1998).

Writing Dance in the Age of Postmodernism (Middletown: Wesleyan University Press, 1994).

Barthes, Roland, *Image, Music, Text*, trans. Stephen Heath (New York: Hill and Wang; London: Fontana, 1977).

Battier, Marc, ed., *Aesthetics of Live Electronic Music*. Special issue of *Contemporary Music Review* 18 (1999).

Bauman, Richard, *Story, Performance, and Event: Contextual Studies of Oral Narrative* (New York: Cambridge University Press, 1986).

Verbal Art as Performance (Prospect Heights, IL: Waveland Press, 1974).

Bennett, Susan, *Theatre Audiences: A Theory of Production and Reception*, 2nd edn (London: Routledge, 1997).

Berthoz, Alain, *The Brain's Sense of Movement*, trans. Giselle Weiss (Cambridge, MA: Harvard University Press, 2000).

Bharucha, Rustom, *The Politics of Cultural Practice: Thinking Through Theatre in an Age of Globalization* (Hanover: Wesleyan University Press, 2000).

Bishop, Claire, ed., *Participation* (London: Whitechapel and MIT Press, 2006).

Blau, Herbert, *To All Appearance: Ideology and Performance* (London: Routledge, 1992).

Blocker, Jane, *What the Body Cost: Desire, History, and Performance* (Minneapolis: University of Minnesota Press, 2004).

Boal, Augusto, *Legislative Theatre: Using Performing to Make Politics*, trans. Adrian Jackson (New York: Routledge, 1998).

Theatre of the Oppressed, trans. Charles A. and Maria-Odilia Leal McBride (New York: Theatre Communications Group, 1979).

Bourdieu, Pierre, *Distinction: A Social Critique of the Judgement of Taste* (Cambridge, MA: Harvard University Press, 1984).

The Field of Cultural Production: Essays on Art and Literature (New York: Columbia University Press, 1993).

Bourriaud, Nicholas, *Postproduction – Culture as Screenplay: How Art Reprograms the World* (Dijon: Les Presses Du Réel, 2005).

Relational Aesthetics (Dijon: Les Presses Du Réel, 1998).

Broadhurst, Susan and Josephine Machon, eds., *Performance and Technology: Practices of Virtual Embodiment and Interactivity* (Basingstoke: Palgrave Macmillan, 2006).

Burrill, Derek Alexander, "Out of the Box: Performance, Drama, and Interactive Software," *Modern Drama* 48.3 (2005), 492–511.

Butler, Judith, *Bodies That Matter: On the Discursive Limits of "Sex"* (New York: Routledge, 1993).

Gender Trouble: Feminism and the Subversion of Identity (New York: Routledge, 1990).

Giving an Account of Oneself (New York: Fordham University Press, 2005).

Cage, John, *Silence: Lectures and Writing* (Cambridge, MA: MIT Press, 1961).

Carlson, Marvin, *The Haunted Stage: The Theatre as Memory Machine* (Ann Arbor: Michigan University Press, 2001).

Performance: A Critical Introduction (1996), 2nd edn (London: Routledge, 2004).

Places of Performance: The Semiotics of Theatre Architecture (Ithaca, NY: Cornell University Press, 1989).

Carver, Gavin and Colin Beardon, eds., *New Visions in Performance: The Impact of Digital Technologies* (Lisse, The Netherlands: Swets and Zeitlinger, 2004).

Case, Sue-Ellen, *The Domain Matrix: Performing Lesbian at the End of Print Culture* (Bloomington: Indiana University Press, 1996).

"Toward a Butch-Femme Aesthetic," *Discourse* 11.1 (Winter 1988–89), 55–73.

Clifford, James, *The Predicament of Culture* (Cambridge, MA: Harvard University Press, 1988).

Writing Culture: The Poetics and Politics of Ethnography (Berkeley: University of California Press, 1986).

Cohen-Cruz, Jan, ed., *Radical Street Performance: An International Anthology* (New York: Routledge, 1998).

Connerton, Paul, *How Societies Remember* (Cambridge: Cambridge University Press, 1989).

Conquergood, Dwight, "Performance Studies: Interventions and Radical Research," *TDR: The Drama Review* 46.2 (2002), 145–56. Rpt. in Henry Bial, ed., *The Performance Studies Reader* (New York: Routledge, 2004), 311–22.

"Storied Worlds and the Work of Teaching," *Communication Education* 42.4 (1993), 337–48.

Davis, Tracy C., *Stages of Emergency: Cold War Nuclear Civil Defense* (Durham: Duke University Press, 2007).

Davis, Tracy C. and Thomas Postlewait, eds., *Theatricality* (Cambridge: Cambridge University Press, 2004).

de Certeau, Michel, *Heterologies: Discourse on the Other* (Minneapolis: University of Minnesota Press, 1986).

The Practice of Everyday Life, trans. Steven Randall (Berkeley: University of California Press, 1984).

Dening, Greg, *Performances* (Chicago: University of Chicago Press, 1996).

Desmond, Jane C., *Staging Tourism: Bodies on Display from Waikiki to Sea World* (Chicago: University of Chicago Press, 1999).

Deutsche, Rosalyn, *Evictions: Art and Spatial Politics* (Cambridge, MA: MIT Press, 1996).

Diamond, Elin, *Performance and Cultural Politics* (London: Routledge, 1996).

Dibia, I Wayan and Rucina Ballinger, *Balinese Dance, Drama, and Music* (Singapore: Periplus Editions, 2004).

Dirks, Nicholas B., ed., *In Near Ruins: Cultural Theory at the End of the Century* (Minneapolis: University of Minnesota Press, 1998).

Dixon, Steve with Barry Smith, *Digital Performance: New Technologies in Theatre, Dance, Performance Art and Installation* (Cambridge, MA: MIT Press, 2006).

Doherty, *From Studio to Situation* (London: Black Dog Publishing, 2004).

Dolan, Jill, *Presence and Desire: Essays on Gender, Sexuality, and Performance* (Ann Arbor: University of Michigan Press, 1993).

Doniger, Wendy, *The Implied Spider: Politics and Theology in Myth* (New York: Columbia University Press, 1998).

Doyle, Jennifer, *Sex Objects: Art and the Dialectics of Desire* (Minneapolis: University of Minnesota Press, 2006).

Dwyer, Leslie and Degung Santikarma, "When the World Turned to Chaos: 1965 and its Aftermath in Bali, Indonesia," in Robert Gellately and Ben Kiernan, eds., *The Specter of Genocide: Mass Murder in Historical Perspective* (Cambridge and New York: Cambridge University Press, 2003).

Emigh, John, *Masked Performance: The Play of Self and Other in Ritual and Theatre* (Philadelphia: University of Pennsylvania Press, 1996).

Feldman, Allen, *Formations of Violence: The Narrative of the Body and Political Terror in Northern Ireland* (Chicago: University of Chicago Press, 1991).

Foley, Kathy and I Nyoman Sedana, "Balinese Dance from the Perspective of a Master Artist: I Ketut Kodi on Topeng," *Asian Theatre Journal*, 22.2 (Fall 2005), 199–213.

Foucault, Michel, *Discipline and Punish: The Birth of the Prison*, trans. Alan Sheridan (New York: Pantheon, 1977).

Fox, John, *Eyes on Stalks* (London: Methuen, 1990).

Fried, Michael, "Art and Objecthood," *Artforum* 5 (1967), 12–23. Rpt. in Gregory Battcock, ed., *Minimal Art: A Critical Anthology* (New York: E. P. Dutton, 1968), 116–47.

Frisch, Michael, *A Shared Authority: Essays on the Craft and Meaning of Oral and Public History* (Albany: State University of New York Press, 1990).

Fuchs, Elinor and Una Chaudhuri, eds., *Land/scape/theater* (Ann Arbor: University of Michigan Press, 2002).

Gallese, Vittorio and George Lakoff, "The Brain's Concepts: The Role of the Sensory-Motor System in Reason and Language," *Cognitive Neuropsychology* 22.3–4 (2005), 455–79.

Geertz, Clifford, *After the Fact: Two Countries, Four Decades, One Anthropologist* (Cambridge, MA: Harvard University Press, 1995).

The Interpretation of Cultures (New York: Basic Books, 1973).

Geertz, Hildred, "A Theatre of Cruelty: The Contexts of a Topeng Performance," in Geertz, ed., *State and Society in Bali: Historical, Textual, and Anthropological Approaches* (Leiden: KITLV Press, 1991), 165–97.

Giannachi, Gabriella and Nigel Stewart, eds., *Performing Nature: Explorations in Ecology and the Arts* (Bern: Peter Lang, 2005).

Gibson, James J., *The Ecological Approach to Perception* (Boston: Houghton Mifflin, 1979).

Goffman, Erving, *The Presentation of Self in Everyday Life* (Garden City, NY: Doubleday, 1959).

Goldberg, Roselee, *Performance Art: From Futurism to the Present*, 2nd edn (New York: Thames and Hudson, 2001).

Goldhill, Simon and Robin Osborne, eds., *Performance Culture and Athenian Democracy* (Cambridge: Cambridge University Press, 1999).

Goodall, Jane R., *Performance and Evolution in the Age of Darwin: Out of the Natural Order* (London: Routledge, 2002).

Gordon, Mel, *Dada Performance* (New York: PAJ Publications, 1987).

Goulish, Matthew, *39 Microlectures: In Proximity of Performance* (London: Routledge, 2000).

Haedicke, Susan C. and Tobin Nellhaus, eds., *Performing Democracy: International Perspectives on Urban Community-Based Performance* (Ann Arbor: University of Michigan Press, 2001).

Hemispheric Institute of Performance and Politics. http://hemisphericinstitute.org.

Jackson, Shannon, *Lines of Activity: Performance, Historiography, Hull-House Domesticity* (Ann Arbor: University of Michigan Press, 2000).

Professing Performance: Theatre in the Academy from Philology to Performativity (Cambridge: Cambridge University Press, 2004).

Jagose, Annamarie, *Queer Theory: An Introduction* (New York: New York University Press, 1996.

James, C. L. R., *Beyond a Boundary* (London: Hutchinson, 1966).

Johnson, E. Patrick, *Appropriating Blackness: Performance and the Politics of Authenticity* (Durham: Duke University Press, 2003).

Jones, Amelia, *Body Art/Performing the Subject* (Minneapolis: University of Minnesota Press, 1998).

ed. *Companion to Contemporary Art Since 1945* (Oxford: Blackwell Press, 2005).

Kaye, Nick, *Multi-Media: Video – Installation – Performance* (London: Routledge, 2007).

Site-Specific Art: Performance, Place and Documentation (Oxford: Blackwell, 1996).

Kershaw, Baz, *Politics of Performance: Radical Theatre as Cultural Intervention* (New York: Routledge, 1992).

The Radical in Performance: Between Brecht and Baudrillard (New York: Routledge, 1999).

Kester, Grant H., *Conversation Pieces: Community and Communication in Modern Art* (Berkeley: University of California Press, 2004).

Kirshenblatt-Gimblett, Barbara, *Destination Culture: Tourism, Museums, and Heritage* (Berkeley: University of California Press, 1998).

Kwon, Miwon, *One Place After Another: Site-Specific Art and Locational Identity* (Cambridge: MIT Press, 2002).

Licht, Ira, "Bodyworks," in *Bodyworks* (Chicago: Museum of Contemporary Art, 1975), n.p.

MacRae, Graeme, "Negara Ubud: The Theatre-State in Twenty-First Century Bali," *History and Anthropology* 16.4 (December, 2005), 393–413.

McConachie, Bruce and F. Elizabeth Hart, eds., *Performance and Cognition: Theatre Studies After the Cognitive Turn* (London: Routledge, 2007).

McKenzie, Jon, "Democracy's Performance," *TDR: The Drama Review* 47.2 (2003), 117–28.

Perform or Else: From Discipline to Performance (New York: Routledge, 2001).

Minh-ha, Trinh T., *Woman, Native, Other: Writing Postcoloniality and Feminism* (Bloomington: Indiana University Press, 1989).

Motherwell, Robert., ed., *The Dada Painters and Poets* 2nd edn (Cambridge, MA: Harvard University Press, 2005).

Mouffe, Chantal, *On the Political* (London and New York: Routledge, 2005).

Muñoz, José Estaban, *Disidentifications: Queers of Color and the Performance of Politics* (Minneapolis: University of Minnesota Press, 1999).

Murphy, Jacqueline Shea, *The People Have Never Stopped Dancing: Native American Modern Dance Histories* (Minneapolis: University of Minnesota Press, 2007).

Myerhoff, Barbara, *Number Our Days* (New York: Simon and Schuster, 1978).

Novack, Cynthia, *Sharing the Dance: Contact Improvisation and American Culture* (Madison: University of Wisconsin, 1990).

O'Dell, Kathy, *Contract with the Skin: Masochism, Performance Art and the 1970s* (Minneapolis: University of Minnesota Press, 1998).

Oliver, Kelly, *Witnessing: Beyond Recognition* (Minneapolis: University of Minnesota Press, 2001).

Ortner, Sherry B., *Anthropology and Social Theory: Culture, Power, and the Acting Subject* (Durham and London: Duke University Press, 2006).

ed., *The Fate of "Culture": Geertz and Beyond* (Berkeley: University of California Press, 1999).

Pearson, Mike, *"In Comes I": Performance, Memory and Landscape* (Exeter: Exeter University Press, 2006).

Pearson, Mike, and Michael Shanks, *Theatre/Archaeology: Disciplinary Dialogues* (London: Routledge, 2001).

Phelan, Peggy, *Unmarked: The Politics of Performance* (London and New York: Routledge, 1993).

Picard, Michel, *Bali: Cultural Tourism and Touristic Culture* (Singapore: Archipelago Press, 1996).

Pluchart, François, *L'art corporel* (Paris: Editions Rodolphe Stadler/Galerie Stadler, 1975).

Pollock, Della, ed., *Remembering: Oral History Performance* (New York: Palgrave Macmillan, 2005).

Pollock, Della, D. Soyini Madison, and Judith Hamera, eds., *The Sage Handbook of Performance Studies* (Thousand Oaks: Sage Publications, 2006).

Rayner, Alice, *Ghosts: Death's Double and the Phenomena of Theatre* (Minneapolis: University of Minnesota Press, 2004).

Roach, Joseph, *Cities of the Dead: Circum-Atlantic Performance* (New York: Columbia University Press, 1996).

Robinson, Geoffrey, *The Dark Side of Paradise: Political Violence in Bali* (Ithaca, NY: Cornell University Press, 1995).

Rojek, Chris and John Urry, eds., *Touring Cultures: Transformations of Travel and Theory* (London: Routledge, 1997).

Román, David, *Acts of Intervention: Performance, Gay Culture, and AIDS* (Bloomington: Indiana University Press, 1998).

Saltz, David Z., "The Art of Interaction: Interactivity, Performativity, and Computers," *The Journal of Aesthetics and Art Criticism* 55.2 (1997), 117–27.

Savigliano, Marta, *Tango and the Political Economy of Passion* (Boulder, CO: Westview Press, 1996).

Sayre, Henry, *The Object of Performance: The American Avant-Garde Since 1970* (Chicago: University of Chicago Press, 1989).

Schechner, Richard, *Between Theater and Anthropology* (Philadelphia: University of Pennsylvania Press, 1985).

By Means of Performance: Intercultural Studies of Theatre and Ritual (Cambridge: Cambridge University Press, 1990).

Performance Studies: An Introduction (2002), 2nd edn (London: Routledge, 2006).

Schimmel, Paul, ed., *Out of Actions: Between Performance and the Object 1949–1979* (Los Angeles: Museum of Contemporary Art, 1998).

Schneider, Rebecca, *The Explicit Body in Performance* (New York: Routledge, 1997).

Sedgwick, Eve Kosofsky, *Between Men: English Literature and Male Homosocial Desire* (New York: Columbia University Press, 1985).

Epistemology of the Closet (Berkeley: University of California Press, 1990).

Sharp, Willoughby, "Body Works," *Avalanche* 1 (Fall 1970), 14–17.

Shepherd, Simon and Mick Wallis, *Drama/Theatre/Performance* (London: Routledge, 2004).

Stucky, Nathan and Cynthia Wimmer, eds., *Teaching Performance Studies* (Carbondale, IL: Southern Illinois University Press, 2002).

Sullivan, Nikki, *A Critical Introduction to Queer Theory* (New York: New York University Press, 2003).

Szerszynski, Bronislaw, Wallace Heim, and Claire Waterton, eds., *Nature Performed: Environment, Culture and Performance* (Oxford: Blackwell, 2003).

Taylor, Diana, *The Archive and the Repertoire: Performing Cultural Memory in the Americas* (Durham: Duke University Press, 2003).

Tocqueville, Alexis de, *Democracy in America*, 2 vols. (1835, 1840), trans. Henry C. Mansfield and Delba Winthrop (Chicago: University of Chicago Press, 2000).

Turner, Victor, *The Anthropology of Performance* (New York: PAJ Publications, 1986).

From Ritual to Theatre: The Human Seriousness of Play (New York: PAJ Publications, 1982).

Van Erven, Eugene, *The Playful Revolution: Theatre and Liberation in Asia* (Bloomington: Indiana University Press, 1992).

Vergine, Lea, *Body Art and Performance: The Body as Language* (Milan: Skira, 2000).

Vickers, Adrian, ed., *Being Modern in Bali: Image and Change* (New Haven: Yale Southeast Asia Studies, Monograph 43, 1996).

"Views and Visions of the Intangible," *Museum International*, 21–222. http://portal.unesco.org/culture/en/ev.php-url_id=21739&url_do=do_topic& url_section=201.

Warner, Michael, *Publics and Counterpublics* (New York: Zone Books, 2005).

White, Hayden, "The Value of Narrativity in the Representation of Reality," *Critical Inquiry* 7.1 (1980), 5–27.

Willink, K., "Domesticating Difference: Performing Memories of School Desegregation," *Text and Performance Quarterly* 27.1 (2007), 20–40.

INDEX

Phelan, Peggy 160–1
Pollock, Jackson 156–9
practice as research, *see* performance as
    research
practice-led research, *see* performance as
    research
private and public spheres, *see* Sennett,
    Richard; tourism, gender and

queer studies
    class in 166, 169–71, 178
    feminism and 167–8
    genesis as academic field 166–78
    LGBT (lesbian, gay, bisexual, transsexual)
        politics and studies 166–71, 175–8
    queer and LGBT identities 5, 166,
        168–70
    methods
    methodology and theory 168–71
    self-reflexive 171–3, 178
    performance and 166–7, 174–8
    race in 166, 169–71, 174, 177–8
    Stonewall Riots 172–3
    subaltern practices 172, 174
    see also cultural studies

race relations, in performance art 156
    see also Mostar; oral history, Mr. Alder;
        queer studies, race in
radio 110
Rancière, Jacques 12, 19–20
Rauschenberg, Robert 157
Roach, Joseph 77, 98
robotics, *see* Kimira, Mari; liveness,
    computer mediation and
Román, David 177–8
Rosenberg, Harold 156–8

Schechner, Richard 6, 24–6, 64–6, 77–8,
    93–4, 121, 160, 164–5
Schneeman, Carolee (*Meat Joy*) 159
Schneider, Rebecca 161
Sehgal, Tino (*This Progress*) 19–20
Sennett, Richard 17–19
Sharp, Willoughby 160
Shawn, Wallace 108–9, 115
Sierra, Santiago 136–8, 144–9
    90 cm Bread Cube 147, 149
    Paid People 145
    250 cm Line Tattooed on Six Paid People
        145
Smith, Anna Deavere 130
Southbank Centre, *see* London's South Bank

spectatorship, *see* art, viewing and
    spectatorship; liveness, spectatorship;
    oral history, interviewer or audience;
    SS *Great Britain*, audience response;
    tourism, spectatorship; *Two
    Undiscovered Amerindians Visit...*,
    audience response
sports, and performance studies 15–17, 21,
    108, 109
    fitness and 48, 56–7
SS *Great Britain* (Bristol Docks) 3, 25–36,
    42
    audience response 31–5
StoryCorps (National Public Radio) 130–1
subjectivity 4
    see also art, intersubjectivity; art, socially
        engaged practice; oral history,
        intersubjectivity of listeners; oral
        history, subjectivity in; queer studies
Suharto 5, 63, 67, 70
Sukarno 65–7
Suppliant Women, The, *see* Target Margin
    Theater
Suteja, Anak Agung 65–6, 68

Target Margin Theater (*As Yet Thou Art
    Young and Rash*) 12–14, 21
Tectonic Theater Company 130
television 108–10, 115
theatre 3, 7, 11–12, 28, 121, 132, 161, 162,
    177
    scholarship of 161
    theatre and citizenship 13–15
    see also performance, democracy and
Theatre Piece #1, *see* Black Mountain
    College
theatricality, *see* Fried, Michael
This Progress, *see* Sehgal, Tino
Tiravanija, Rirkrit 138
Tisch School of the Arts (New York
    University) 160
Touchable Stories, *see* Flattery, Shannon
tourism
    economy and consumption 77–9, 82–4,
        86–7, 96
    gender and 78–80, 85–7
    Las Vegas 87
    performance and 5–6, 77–8, 85–7
    spectatorship 78–80, 83–7
    Tokyo (Odaiba) 87
    see also London's South Bank
trauma, *see* oral history, trauma
Turner, Victor 64, 160

Cambridge Companions to . . .

AUTHORS

Alexander Pope edited by Pat Rogers

Ezra Pound edited by Ira B. Nadel

Proust edited by Richard Bales

Pushkin edited by Andrew Kahn

Philip Roth edited by Timothy Parrish

Salman Rushdie edited by Abdulrazak Gurnah

Shakespeare edited by Margareta de Grazia and Stanley Wells

Shakespeare on Film edited by Russell Jackson (second edition)

Shakespearean Comedy edited by Alexander Leggatt

Shakespeare on Stage edited by Stanley Wells and Sarah Stanton

Shakespeare's History Plays edited by Michael Hattaway

Shakespearean Tragedy edited by Claire McEachern

Shakespeare's Poetry edited by Patrick Cheney

Shakespeare and Popular Culture edited by Robert Shaughnessy

George Bernard Shaw edited by Christopher Innes

Shelley edited by Timothy Morton

Mary Shelley edited by Esther Schor

Sam Shepard edited by Matthew C. Roudané

Spenser edited by Andrew Hadfield

Wallace Stevens edited by John N. Serio

Tom Stoppard edited by Katherine E. Kelly

Harriet Beecher Stowe edited by Cindy Weinstein

Jonathan Swift edited by Christopher Fox

Henry David Thoreau edited by Joel Myerson

Tolstoy edited by Donna Tussing Orwin

Mark Twain edited by Forrest G. Robinson

Virgil edited by Charles Martindale

Voltaire edited by Nicholas Cronk

Edith Wharton edited by Millicent Bell

Walt Whitman edited by Ezra Greenspan

Oscar Wilde edited by Peter Raby

Tennessee Williams edited by Matthew C. Roudané

August Wilson edited by Christopher Bigsby

Mary Wollstonecraft edited by Claudia L. Johnson

Virginia Woolf edited by Sue Roe and Susan Sellers

Wordsworth edited by Stephen Gill

W. B. Yeats edited by Marjorie Howes and John Kelly

Zola edited by Brian Nelson

TOPICS

The Actress edited by Maggie B. Gale and John Stokes

The African American Novel edited by Maryemma Graham

The African American Slave Narrative edited by Audrey A. Fisch

American Modernism edited by Walter Kalaidjian

American Realism and Naturalism edited by Donald Pizer

American Travel Writing edited by Alfred Bendixen and Judith Hamera

American Women Playwrights edited by Brenda Murphy

Australian Literature edited by Elizabeth Webby

British Romanticism edited by Stuart Curran

British Romantic Poetry edited by James Chandler and Maureen N. McLane

British Theatre, 1730–1830, edited by Jane Moody and Daniel O'Quinn

Canadian Literature edited by Eva-Marie Kröller

The Classic Russian Novel edited by Malcolm V. Jones and Robin Feuer Miller

Contemporary Irish Poetry edited by Matthew Campbell

Crime Fiction edited by Martin Priestman

The Eighteenth-Century Novel edited by John Richetti

Eighteenth-Century Poetry edited by John Sitter

English Literature, 1500–1600 edited by Arthur F. Kinney

English Literature, 1650–1740 edited by Steven N. Zwicker

English Literature, 1740–1830 edited by Thomas Keymer and Jon Mee

English Poetry, Donne to Marvell edited by Thomas N. Corns

English Renaissance Drama, second edition edited by A. R. Braunmuller and Michael Hattaway

English Restoration Theatre edited by Deborah C. Payne Fisk

Feminist Literary Theory edited by Ellen Rooney

Fiction in the Romantic Period edited by Richard Maxwell and Katie Trumpener

The Fin de Siècle edited by Gail Marshall

The French Novel: from 1800 to the Present edited by Timothy Unwin

Gothic Fiction edited by Jerrold E. Hogle

The Greek and Roman Novel edited by Tim Whitmarsh

Greek and Roman Theatre edited by Marianne McDonald and J. Michael Walton

Greek Tragedy edited by P. E. Easterling

The Harlem Renaissance edited by George Hutchinson

The Irish Novel edited by John Wilson Foster

The Italian Novel edited by Peter Bondanella and Andrea Ciccarelli

Jewish American Literature edited by Hana Wirth-Nesher and Michael P. Kramer

The Latin American Novel edited by Efraín Kristal

Literature of the First World War edited by Vincent Sherry

Literature on Screen edited by Deborah Cartmell and Imelda Whelehan

Medieval English Theatre edited by Richard Beadle and Alan J. Fletcher (second edition)

Medieval French Literature edited by Simon Gaunt and Sarah Kay

Medieval Romance edited by Roberta L. Krueger

Medieval Women's Writing edited by Carolyn Dinshaw and David Wallace

Modern American Culture edited by Christopher Bigsby

Modern British Women Playwrights edited by Elaine Aston and Janelle Reinelt

Modern French Culture edited by Nicholas Hewitt

Modern German Culture edited by Eva Kolinsky and Wilfried van der Will

The Modern German Novel edited by Graham Bartram

Modern Irish Culture edited by Joe Cleary and Claire Connolly

Modernism edited by Michael Levenson

The Modernist Novel edited by Morag Shiach

Modernist Poetry edited by Alex Davis and Lee M. Jenkins

Modern Italian Culture edited by Zygmunt G. Baranski and Rebecca J. West

Modern Latin American Culture edited by John King

Modern Russian Culture edited by Nicholas Rzhevsky

Modern Spanish Culture edited by David T. Gies

Narrative edited by David Herman

Native American Literature edited by Joy Porter and Kenneth M. Roemer

Nineteenth-Century American Women's Writing edited by Dale M. Bauer and Philip Gould

Old English Literature edited by Malcolm Godden and Michael Lapidge

Performance Studies edited by Tracy C. Davis

Postcolonial Literary Studies edited by Neil Lazarus

Postmodernism edited by Steven Connor

Renaissance Humanism edited by Jill Kraye

Roman Satire edited by Kirk Freudenburg

The Spanish Novel: from 1600 to the Present edited by Harriet Turner and Adelaida López de Martínez

Travel Writing edited by Peter Hulme and Tim Youngs

Twentieth-Century Irish Drama edited by Shaun Richards

Twentieth-Century English Poetry edited by Neil Corcoran

Victorian and Edwardian Theatre edited by Kerry Powell

The Victorian Novel edited by Deirdre David

Victorian Poetry edited by Joseph Bristow

Writing of the English Revolution edited by N. H. Keeble